SOFTWARE
METRICS

BEST PRACTICES
FOR SUCCESSFUL
IT MANAGEMENT

by Paul Goodman

ISBN #1-931332-26-6

Rothstein Associates Inc., Publisher

www.rothstein.com

Brookfield, Connecticut USA

ISBN #1-931332-26-6

PUBLISHER:

Philip Jan Rothstein, FBCI

Rothstein Associates Inc.

The Rothstein Catalog On Service Level Management

4 Arapaho Rd.

Brookfield, Connecticut 06804-3104 U.S.A.

203.740.7444+44

203.740.7401 fax

www.rothstein.com

www.ServiceLevelBooks.com

info@rothstein.com

ACKNOWLEDGMENTS

It is strange when looking at the second publication of a book, when you refer back to what you wrote in that earlier time and you realize how much time has moved on, not least because so many of the people I knew then have also moved on. Some things still ring true, however, and with these has come a lesson pleasantly learned. It is that I depend so much on the people I work with, both colleagues and clients, who contribute so much to my understanding of what makes this world of software engineering work. To try to name them all would be impossible because, of course; as I get older there are more and more of them, every one different but all always contributing. To them all goes my sincere thanks.

I also wish to thank my publisher, Phil Rothstein, for nurturing this tome through its second birth with patience and good ideas.

And finally, to my family. My thanks to Sharon, my wife, for her constant support that goes far beyond what many may realize and to Luke, my son, who brings me great joy and who makes me so very proud.

Paul Goodman

FOREWORD

by Andrew Hiles FBCI, MBCS

I have had the pleasure of working with Paul Goodman, on and off, for almost ten years. My first contact with Paul was with a client in the Netherlands, working together on what was then Europe's biggest ISO 9000 project for Information Technology. Paul was helping the client with Software Performance Metrics while I was developing Service Level Agreements (SLA) — and groping for effective performance metrics for a software development SLA. As a past developer myself, I had an idea but was not sure whether or not it would be viable. With Paul's input (and a particularly brave Applications Development Manager!) the result was highly successful.

It is this pragmatic approach, coupled with a huge depth of practical experience, that yields to Paul the commanding heights of the science of software performance measurement.

The topic is important enough. IT software projects are high risk activities.

For over ten years, the sad statistics on IT project failure have barely changed. Survey after survey shows that over half of all IT projects fail (especially large projects) and most projects are delivered over time, over budget. Accurate time and cost forecasting, based on sound performance measurement metrics, could reduce the number of project failures by helping to create more realistic cost / benefit cases. And better software quality would help, too.

Hugh W. Ryan, in an article for *Outlook Journal*, summarized research that showed:

> Only 8 percent of applications projects costing between $6 million and $10 million succeed.

> Among all IT development projects, only 16% are delivered to acceptable cost, time and quality.

> Cost overruns from 100% to 200 % are common in software projects.

> Cost overruns for IT projects have been estimated at $59 billion in the United States alone.

> Another study puts the figure at $100 billion.

> IT workers spend more than 34% of their time just fixing software bugs

The PMI Fact Book is even more pessimistic: it says the United States spends $2.3 trillion a year on projects and that much of that money is wasted because a majority of projects fail. Also:

Standish Group International found that only 28% of information technology projects are completed successfully.

Of 1,027 projects surveyed by the British Computer Society, the Association of Project Managers and the Institute of Management concluded that only 130 (12.7%) were successful.

Only 2% of the *successful* projects were development projects, yet over 50% of the projects reviewed were development projects.

A PriceWaterhouseCoopers survey found that, in the UK alone, over $1 billion a year was being wasted through poor software quality.

Cap Gemini Ernst & Young reports that 70% of Customer Relationship Management (CRM) strategies fail.

META Group reports 90% of enterprises cannot show a positive return on CRM.

Peppers & Rogers reports that nearly 80% of CRM projects fail to show a positive return.

Gartner research predicts that over 50% of CRM strategies will continue to fail.

Only around half of Enterprise Resource Planning systems are deemed successful.

According to the Cranfield School of Management, the more ambitious the return on investment for the project cited in the business case, the more lacking the project plan is likely to be.

Imagine the results if less than half of all passenger aircraft flying arrived at their destination!

Badly estimated software projects can waste serious money: money that could otherwise be invested in mission achievement, new product development and creating a competitive edge. Poor software quality can lead to poor quality — or even dangerous — products. It can cause public relations and marketing disasters, damage brand reputation and market share. While use of effective software metrics is not the total answer, it is certainly a crucial part of getting to grips with software development.

Paul Goodman's book makes a valuable contribution to IT Development Project success. It is comprehensive, lucid and packed with illustrations and practical examples. This makes it as accessible to the non-specialist as it is to the software guru. I commend it, not just to software developers, but also to:

CIOs

IT Project Accountants

IT Development Project Accountants

IT Development Project Managers

CFOs

Risk Managers

IT Service Delivery Managers and all those responsible for development, implementation and management of Service Level Agreements

Disaster Recovery, Business Continuity Managers

Business managers playing a role in the initiation, authorization and development of IT software projects.

Andrew Hiles, FBCI, MBCS

Director, Kingswell International

Oxford, United Kingdom

July, 2004

TABLE OF CONTENTS

ACKNOWLEDGMENTS iii

FOREWORD iv

INTRODUCTION 1

SECTION 1: INTRODUCING SOFTWARE METRICS 3

1   **Software Metrics: What and Why?** 5
    1.1   DEFINITION OF SOFTWARE METRICS 6
    1.2   AREAS OF APPLICATION 7
    1.3   PRINCIPLE NUMBER ONE — PRAGMATISM AND COMPROMISE 8
    1.4   PRINCIPLE NUMBER TWO — MEASURING PEOPLE — DON'T! 9
    1.5   PRINCIPLE NUMBER THREE — MODELING = SIMPLIFICATION 10
    1.6   PRINCIPLE NUMBER FOUR — ASK NOT FOR WHOM THE
           BELL TOLLS — ASK WHY? 10
           Figure 1.1   Test Defects Report 11
    1.7   PRINCIPLE NUMBER FIVE — "THE SUM OF THE WHOLE IS GREATER
           THAN THE CONSTITUENT PARTS" 12
           Figure 1.2   Field Defects Report 12
    1.8   PRINCIPLE NUMBER SIX — CULTURE SHOCK! 13
    1.9   SUMMARY 13

2   **An Overview of Function Point Analysis** 15
    2.1   SO, WHAT IS FUNCTION POINT ANALYSIS? 16
    2.2   USING FUNCTION POINT ANALYSIS 17
          2.2.1   Performing an FPA Exercise 17
          2.2.2   Defining the System Boundary 18
          Figure 2.1   FPA Example 20
    2.3   COMPLEXITY ASSESSMENT 21

2.4   SUMMARY 21

3   Software Metrics: Management Information 23
3.1   WHAT IS "MANAGEMENT INFORMATION?" 24
3.2   WHY DO WE NEED MANAGEMENT INFORMATION? 25
3.3   COLLECTING THE DATA 28
3.4   REQUIREMENTS FOR INFORMATION 29
3.5   SOME PORTABLE MODELS 32
3.6   WHAT ABOUT USABILITY? 33
3.7   FEEDBACK 34
3.8   SUMMARY 35

4   Cost Estimation 37
4.1   COST MODELS AND BEYOND 38
4.2   WHY DO WE ESTIMATE? 38
4.3   SOME BASIC PRINCIPLES 39
4.4   OLD DATA — LOOK IN THE BIN 43
4.5   MODELS AND TOOLS REVISITED 44
4.6   CALIBRATION 46
4.7   TECHNIQUES FOR ESTIMATION 48
4.8   A STRATEGIC TEMPLATE FOR COST ESTIMATION 49
4.9   MODIFIED DELPHI TECHNIQUE 52
4.10   BOZOKI'S RANKING TECHNIQUE AND PERT 53
4.11   "BOTTOM UP" ESTIMATING OR FUNCTIONAL DECOMPOSITION 55
4.12   ESTIMATION BY ANALOGY 56
        Figure 4.1   Estimation Template 57
        Figure 4.2   Role of the Support Group 58
        Figure 4.3   Typical Process Diagram 59
        Figure 4.4   Monitoring and Feedback (Actual vs. Estimates) 59
        Figure 4.5   Monitoring and Feedback (Estimate vs. Effort) 60
        Figure 4.6   Monitoring and Feedback (Variation Actual Against Initial Estimate) . . 61
4.13   WHAT ABOUT THE LEADING EDGE, BIG PROJECTS? 61
4.14   SUMMARY 62

5   Applied Design Metrics 63
5.1   WHAT IS COMPLEXITY? 64
5.2   McCABE METRICS 65
        Figure 5.1   McCabe Metrics Background Theory Example of Flowgraph (1) 66
        Figure 5.2   McCabe Metrics Background Theory Example of Flowgraph (2 67
        Figure 5.3   McCabe MetricsBackground Theory Example of Reduced Flowgraph (1) 68
        Figure 5.4   McCabe Metrics Background Theory — Example of Reduced Flowgraph (2)
        70

5.3	INFORMATION FLOW METRIC	73
	Figure 5.5 Aspects of Complexity	74
5.4	SUMMARY	78

6 Project Control 79
6.1	FEASIBILITY CHECKING	81
6.2	RISK MANAGEMENT	82
6.3	PROGRESS MONITORS	84
6.4	SUMMARY	86

SECTION 2: Building and Implementing a Software Metrics Program 87

7 A Lifecycle for Metrication 89
7.1	THE LIFECYCLE MODEL	90
	Figure 7.1 Software Metrics Initiative Context Diagram	91
	Figure 7.2 Level 1 Lifecycle Model	92

8 Stage 1 - Initiation 95
	Figure 8.1 Initiation Stage of a Software Metrics Program	96
8.1	THE INITIAL MANAGEMENT DECISION	97
8.2	ASSIGN MANAGEMENT RESPONSIBILITY	99
8.3	APPOINT FEASIBILITY STUDY TEAM	100
8.4	"WE NEED A PLAN!"	101
8.5	SUBJECT FAMILIARIZATION	101
8.6	INITIAL MARKET RESEARCH	102
8.7	PRESENTING THE RESULTS	104
8.8	MAKE IT A SUCCESS!	104
8.9	SUMMARY	105

9 Stage 2: Requirements Definition 107
9.1	THINGS TO REMEMBER	108
	Figure 9.1 Relationships Between a Standard Lifecycle, Software Metrics and Project Management	108
9.2	COMMONALITY	110
	Figure 9.2 Potential Phases of a Software Metrics Program	110
9.3	A COMMON FRAME OF REFERENCE	111
	Figure 9.3 Level 1 Engineering Process	112
	Figure 9.4 Functional Linkage	114
	Figure 9.5: Traditional Organization Hierarchy	115
	Figure 9.6 Work, Task and Linkages Within the Requirements Specification Stage	118
9.4	INITIAL PUBLICITY CAMPAIGN	118
9.5	CUSTOMER IDENTIFICATION	121

9.6   MARKET IDENTIFICATION 125

9.7   ESTABLISH USER INTERFACE 126

9.8   IDENTIFY POTENTIAL SUPER CHAMPIONS 129

9.9   CAPTURE INFORMATION REQUIREMENTS 129

9.10   ESTABLISH INITIAL DEFINITIONS 137

9.11   IDENTIFY AVAILABLE DATA SOURCES 139

9.12   IDENTIFY STORAGE, ANALYSIS AND FEEDBACK REQUIREMENTS 140

9.13   CONSOLIDATE REQUIREMENTS 140

9.14   SPECIFICATION REVIEW 142

9.15   SUMMARY 142

10   Stage 3: Component Design **143**

Figure 10.1   Tasks and Links Within Design Stage
(Showing Dependencies Between Streams) 145

10.1   PILOT PROJECTS 146

10.2   METRICS DEFINITION STREAM 147

10.3   MODEL DEFINITION OR GOALS, QUESTIONS, METRICS 147

10.4   IDENTIFY EXTERNAL PRODUCTS 156

10.5   ADMINISTRATION DESIGN STREAM 157

10.6   MAP BASE METRICS TO AVAILABLE DATA 158

10.7   ESTABLISH LINKS TO DATA ADMINISTRATORS 159

10.8   DEFINE DATA COLLECTION MECHANISMS 159

10.9   DESIGN STORAGE, ANALYSIS AND FEEDBACK MECHANISMS 160

10.10   MARKETING AND BUSINESS PLANNING STREAM 161

10.11   PREPARE A BUSINESS PLAN 162

10.12   PREPARE A MARKETING PLAN 166

10.13   INFRASTRUCTURE DESIGN STREAM 167

        10.13.1   Define the Infrastructure 167

        Figure 10.2   Example Organization of Staff Support Infrastructure 171

        10.13.2   Define Support Training 172

        10.13.3   Drawing the Streams Together, or Consolidation 173

10.14   MOVING THE DESIGN FORWARD 177

10.15   SUMMARY 178

11   Stage 4: Component Build **179**

Figure 11.1   Building the Components of a Software Metrics Program 180

11.1   LAYING THE FOUNDATIONS 181

        11.1.1   Select the Implementation Champion and Group Coordinators 181

        11.1.2   Launch Planning and Pre-launch Publicity 183

        Figure 11.2   Targets 185

        11.1.3   Build the Program Components 185

        11.1.4   Document Techniques 186

	11.1.5	Prepare Training Material	188
	11.1.6	Build the Metrics Database	189
	11.1.7	Build the Data Collection Mechanisms	190
11.2	REVIEW BUILT COMPONENTS		193
11.3	THE FINAL COUNTDOWN		193
11.4	SUMMARY		194

12   Stage 5: Implementation **195**

12.1	A PEOPLE-ORIENTED ISSUE	195
12.2	THE LAUNCH	198
12.3	IMPLEMENTATION	198
12.4	SUMMARY: CLOSING THE CIRCLE	199

13   Section 2: A Summary 201

	Figure 13.1	A Project-Based Approach	202
	Figure 13.2	Topic Scope	203
	Figure 13.3	Basic Strategy	204
13.1	INITIATION		204
	Figure 13.4	Initiation Stage	205
13.2	REQUIREMENTS SPECIFICATION		205
	Figure 13.5	Requirements Specification	206
13.3	COMPONENT DESIGN		206
	Figure 13.6	Component Design 1	206
	Figure 13.7	Component Design 2	207
	Figure 13.8	Component Design 3	208
13.4	COMPONENT BUILD		208
	Figure 13.9	Component Build	209
13.5	IMPLEMENTATION		209
	Figure 13.10	Implementation	209
	Figure 13.11	Implementation 2	209
13.6	A RECIPE FOR SUCCESS		210

14   Alternative Approaches to Metrication 211

14.1	PHASING OR SCOPE VARIATION	212
14.2	IN BY THE BACK DOOR	213
14.3	HITCHING A RIDE	214
14.4	HARD AND FAST	214

SECTION 3: GENERAL DISCUSSION 217

15   The Home Stretch 219

| 15.1 | SEI ASSESSMENT | 222 |

Figure 15.1   The CMM Process Maturity Framework 222
15.2   OTHER MEASUREMENT-BASED TECHNIQUES 226
Figure 15.2   Performance 227
15.3   SUMMARY 230

16   Closing Thoughts 231

Appendix A   Useful Organizations 233

References 234

INDEX 237

ABOUT THE AUTHOR 242

ABOUT THE PUBLISHER 243

OTHER BOOKS AND RESOURCES FROM ROTHSTEIN ASSOCIATES INC. 244

INTRODUCTION

More years ago than I care to remember, let us say twenty five to thirty, Software Metrics was a curiosity confined to a few university researchers and one or two industrial or commercial organizations. Now it is a well established discipline with a growing band of practitioners and adherents. Indeed there is now a whole train of theory and practice that is called "Software Metrics." But, I suggest, still the train moves too slowly. This book is an attempt to speed the train up by helping you to add momentum. Having said that, things have progressed enormously from that dim and distant past!

Today, it seems you cannot attend any software engineering conference or seminar without coming across at least one speaker who features the subject *Software Metrics*. We can find active user groups specializing in particular applications within the general domain of Software Metrics; there are research projects funded by the European Economic Community involving some of the largest industrial organizations in the world; and, there are specialist international conferences and workshops that attract large audiences on a regular basis.

However, despite the huge increase of interest in the use of Software Metrics within industry (and I include all types of commercial and engineering applications in the term "industry"), much of what we see is to do with the definition of particular techniques. One of the problems facing the IT industry today is the application of these techniques in a business environment. Little has been written about solving the very practical problems faced by organizations who wish to introduce the use of Software Metrics, and another aim of this book is to go some way towards correcting that.

The material in the book is based on many years of experience in implementing Software Metrics initiatives, four of them as a direct employee in two large organizations. This has been enhanced by experiences gained from acting in a consultancy role to a number of other organizations engaged in implementing similar programs over many more years. The suggestions and models presented in the text are the result of having to find pragmatic solutions to very real, business related problems.

I do *not* claim that this book is the last word that will ever need to be said about the topic of implementing Software Metrics initiatives; it is not. What it does contain are a set of approaches and techniques, presented as a coherent whole, that have worked in those real business situations together with discussions about specific aspects of Software Metrics based on those same experiences.

Nor can I claim that all of the components that make up this book are my own. I have been privileged to meet some very talented people in many organizations across the world who have been willing to share ideas and concepts freely so that everyone benefits. For this I thank them and I have provided references to their work, whenever I could, throughout the body of this book .

This has not just been a sharing of successes, but also of failures and frustrations. I am able to contribute very easily when it comes to failures! I believe that one of the things this work has to recommend it is that it is based, in part, on learning from those failures and the hope is that the reader can avoid the mistakes that I and others have made in the past.

Interestingly, I have found that there are great similarities in the mistakes we have made and also in the successes we have had. It is this that makes me feel that a book like this, which attempts to illustrate a generic approach to the implementation of Software Metrics programs, can work.

Turning from the background to the book itself, I hope that you find it to be readable. To help in this, the material has been separated into three sections.

The first defines exactly what I mean by the term "Software Metrics" and introduces the reader to the domain of Software Metrics by discussing the need for a measurement-based approach to the management of software engineering. This first section then, for reasons which will become obvious, looks at a particular measurement technique — Function Point Analysis — before discussing specific areas of application for Software Metrics.

The second section is really the core of the book. This section describes an approach to the development and implementation of Software Metrics initiatives. Essentially, the approach centers around a model that breaks the work into a number of stages. This division of labor into phases is, of course, nothing more than the way in which most successful projects are handled; it is what makes up those stages that I hope will be found beneficial.

The third section is a collection of chapters that belong in this book, but do not sit naturally in either of the other two sections. Here we visit the topics that seem to be generating discussion today and we will also look at some topics that may be key issues in the near future.

Appendices and references are also provided.

SECTION 1:

INTRODUCING SOFTWARE METRICS

In this section we will look at various aspects of measurement within software engineering that go together to form the body of knowledge and techniques we know as "Software Metrics."

1

Software Metrics:

What and Why?

Key Points

Software Metrics defined

Potential areas where measurement can be effectively applied

Some underlying principles to always keep in mind

In this chapter I would like to define what it is I mean by the term *Software Metrics*; to discuss in general terms the domain covered by that term according to my definition, and to discuss some of the reasons why an organization may consider the use of Software Metrics.

My introduction to Software Metrics came with a job move from a normal, commercial software engineering environment. The work had also involved some project management. The move required me to change location and I arrived for my first days work fully expecting to be put in charge of a development team only to be offered something completely different. The work they wanted me to get involved in seemed to be dealing with some rather ill defined problems and I also had to figure out how to stop a spreadsheet package beeping at me every few minutes as I made yet another mistake with this new tool.

The first problem we considered concerned the question of change requests that went to make up an enhancement project. Given that the scope of the release might have to be reduced, I had to identify those requests that could most easily be removed from the total package. My most abiding memory of those early days is of other people in the office walking up and asking what I was doing. My answer was invariably "I don't really know but it's good fun." And it was! I was making use of mathematical skills I thought had been consigned to the waste bin, I was meeting people and I had a good level of job satisfaction. What I did not have was a convenient handle by which I could describe my work.

However, we must have been doing something right because the team grew quite quickly from two, myself and my manager, to the grand size of five staff. As we grew we also started to hear of teams in other organizations who were involved in a new fad called *Software Metrics*. Well not that new nor, perhaps, that much of a fad. The ideas we were hearing about had been around for twenty years or more and some organizations had a significant investment in their use. Even more importantly, a few of these organizations seemed to be getting good returns on that investment. Yet it is true to say that the current widespread interest in Software Metrics only really started in about 1984. Since then, like Topsy, it has 'growed and growed!'

This scenario, of my initial involvement with Software Metrics starting from the organization's almost total naiveté regarding the subject to the point where the topic becomes recognized as being important to the business, is not uncommon. It typifies the way in which Software Metrics programs progress and it is worth remembering that a good way to learn about any subject is to start working in that area.

So, our team now had a name that we could associate with our work, "Software Metrics." But what are Software Metrics?

1.1   DEFINITION OF SOFTWARE METRICS

Software Metrics can be defined as:

> *"the continuous application of measurement-based techniques to the software development process and its products to supply meaningful and timely management information, together with the use of those techniques to improve that process and its products."*

As you will see, this definition covers quite a lot.

Software Metrics is all about measurement which in turn involves numbers; the use of numbers to make things better, to improve the process of developing software and to improve all aspects of the management of that process. Software Metrics are applicable to the whole development lifecycle from initiation, when costs must be estimated, to monitoring the reliability of the end product in the field and the way that product changes over time with enhancement. It covers engineers or programmers using techniques to spot error-prone components before they get as far as coding and controlling a project as it progresses so that the fact that it is going to be six months late is recognized as early as possible rather than the day before delivery is due. It even covers organizations determining which of its software products are the cash cows and which are the dogs.

1.2   AREAS OF APPLICATION

There are many different ways in which Software Metrics can be used, some of which are almost specialties in their own right. There are also many ways in which the domain of Software Metrics can be divided. The approach I prefer is to consider specific areas of application of Software Metrics.

The most established area of Software Metrics has to be cost and size estimation techniques. There are many proprietary packages on the market that will provide estimates of software system size, cost to develop a system and the duration of a development or enhancement project. These packages are based on estimation models, the best known of these being the COnstructive COst Model (COCOMO), developed by Barry Boehm, Boehm(1)and subsequently updated based on the experiences of many companies and individuals, Boehm et al (1). Various techniques, that do not require the use of tools are also available.

There has been a great deal of research carried out in this area and this research continues in the United States, Europe and elsewhere. The Department of Defense in the United States, various governments around the world and the European Economic Community sponsor much of it. One thing that does come across strongly from the results of this research work is that organizations cannot rely, solely, on the use of proprietary packages.

Controlling software development projects through measurement is an area that is generating a great deal of interest, both in Europe and the United States. This has become much more relevant with the increase in fixed price contracts and the use of penalty clauses by customers who deal with software developers, not to mention outsourcing, facilities management or "partnership" arrangements that are so prevalent today.

The prediction of quality levels for software, often in terms of reliability, is another area where Software Metrics has an important role to play. Again, there are proprietary models on the market that can assist with this but debate continues about the accuracy of these. The requirement is there, both from the customers point of view and that of the developer who needs to control testing and proving costs. Various techniques can be used now, and this area will become more and more important in the future.

The use of Software Metrics to provide quantitative checks on software designs is also a well established area. Much research has been carried out, and some organizations have used such techniques to very good effect. This area of Software Metrics is also being used to control software products that are in place and that are subject to enhancement.

Other applications of Software Metrics include research into the effect of soft or environmental factors on the effectiveness of the development process. Some years ago, this prompted one large organization to build a development complex specifically designed with the needs of engineers or programmers in mind, (McCue 1978). This option is not open to most organizations but there is usually a great deal that can be done to improve the development process by making changes to the environment that process operates in.

Measurement can be used to identify where change should be concentrated. Just starting to measure soft factors can often lead to useful insights regarding the way in which a process operates and this can lead to benefits to a business by improving performance in key areas such as lead time to market (Ahlgren 1992).

Using measured quantities to compare your own organization with others is an extremely popular area of Software Metrics, especially for senior managers. This is most commonly referred to as "Benchmarking" and indeed, it is often why a measurement program starts in the first place. Benchmarking does, however, involve effort on the part of the organization, so the benefits must be weighed against the costs. One result of using such an approach is that you can actually discover that you were as bad as you thought but that most other organizations are also as bad! This can be very useful information, but even more importantly such a service can help you identify who is "best in class." Once you have this information you can learn a great deal from it.

Finally, we come to the most common use of Software Metrics: the provision of management information. This includes information about productivity, quality and process effectiveness. It is important to realize that this should be seen as an on going activity. Snapshots of the current situation have their place, but the most valuable information comes when you can see trends in data. Is productivity or quality getting better or worse over time? If so, then why is this happening? What can management do to improve things? The provision of management information is as much an art as a science. Statistical analysis is part of it but the information must be presented in a way that managers can make use of, at the right time and for the right reasons.

All this shows that Software Metrics is a big field! Recognizing this fact is an important step in that it presents a choice. You can probably see many of the areas identified above as having relevance to your business. Do you try to implement Software Metrics in these many forms or do you adopt a "softly-softly" approach tackling one or perhaps two areas first? Both approaches have benefits and dangers associated with them. Resolving this issue within an organization brings us to the first principle of Software Metrics implementation: pragmatism and compromise.

At this point I would like to make a number of points regarding certain principles that, while I will attempt to justify them, I suggest are treated as axioms as far as this book is concerned. These are some of the concepts that form the foundation for the core of this book. I will also take the opportunity to discuss some of the dangers inherent if the approach taken to software engineering and its management excludes Software Metrics.

1.3   PRINCIPLE NUMBER ONE — PRAGMATISM AND COMPROMISE

The first principle of Software Metrics is that of pragmatism and compromise. Implementing Software Metrics in an organization of any size can be difficult. There are many problems that must be overcome and decisions which have to made, often with limited information to hand. One of the first decisions you will face concerns the scope of the work. There is a rule in software development that you do not try something new on a large or critical system and this translates, in the Software Metrics area, to "don't try to do too much." On the other hand, there is evidence that concentrating on too small an area can result in such a limited payback as to invalidate Software Metrics in an organization. As Darlene Brown, a long term metrics activist succinctly puts it: "don't bet your career on a single metric."

Metrics programs that work seem to be a pragmatic compromise between these two extremes. Identifying the key requirements of the organization and satisfying these, while avoiding truly esoteric areas such as predicting the portability of new systems (if this is not a key business requirement) is one approach that can be used to define the scope of a Software Metrics program. The work of Basili and Rombach, among others, has been instrumental in formalizing this strategy (Rombach, 1990). Organizations such as Hewlett Packard and Du Pont de Nemours who are recognized by many as having beneficial metrics programs can show a portfolio of applied measurement techniques that form a multifaceted program. Organizations that introduce one metric, for example the software system sizing technique known as Function Point Analysis (which will be discussed later), and nothing else, often end up without a Software Metrics program. This is truly unfortunate because Function Point Analysis can form the backbone of a successful program but alone it is not enough! So, help your program to succeed by linking areas of work within the program to specific business requirements in the organization.

This principle of pragmatism and compromise runs through successful Software Metrics program implementations.

1.4 PRINCIPLE NUMBER TWO — MEASURING PEOPLE — DON'T!

Measuring the performance of individuals is extremely dangerous. One organization I know of used individual productivity, in terms of functionality divided by effort, as a major determinant of salary increases. While this may appear attractive to some managers, the organization later stated that this was one of the worst mistakes it ever made. Using measurement in this way is counterproductive, divisive and simply ensures that engineers will rig the data they supply.

An associate of mine often says that management has one chance and one chance only. The first time that a manager uses data supplied by an individual against that individual is the last time that the manager will get accurate or true data from that person. The reasoning behind such a statement is simple — employees do not like upsetting the boss!

I do know of one organization that uses Software Metrics to measure individuals and who seem to do this effectively. A single measure is not used, but instead productivity is combined with the quality of the items produced and the environment of the individual is also considered. This information is used to benefit the individual by identifying training needs and ways that the environmental processes can be improved. Essentially, the information is used constructively rather than destructively.

Two points are worth noting about this second organization:

It has found that individuals with high productivity levels also tend to produce better quality products than individuals with lower productivity; and,

It is a Japanese organization.

My personal view is that most Western organizations are not mature enough to use the measurement of individuals constructively. Remember that, in the East, measurement is an integral part of life. In Japan, the kyu and dan grades are used to rank or measure many aspects of artistic life. I also believe that the culture in the West is such that any manager should be capable of assessing an individuals worth through knowledge of that individual. A good manager should not need measurement to know if an engineer is pulling his or her weight and it is dangerous to use measurement in this way.

1.5   PRINCIPLE NUMBER THREE — MODELING = SIMPLIFICATION

There is a great temptation in Software Metrics to look for the "silver bullet," the single measure that tells all about the software development process. Currently this does not exist.

Software Metrics depend upon the use of modeling and by definition this involves simplification. We may, for example, model reliability through *mean time to failure* or *defect density*, (these are discussed later), but nobody really believes that these measures truly tell the whole story about reliability. Yet they can still be used to assess this attribute of a software system. In this way, they are a pragmatic attempt to satisfy a real requirement for information.

Models that simplify reality have a large role to play in any Software Metrics program but recognizing and accepting the limitations of these models is another major step forward towards making practical use of Software Metrics.

1.6   PRINCIPLE NUMBER FOUR — ASK NOT FOR WHOM THE BELL TOLLS — ASK WHY?

If you attend conferences and seminars that address the topic of Software Metrics, the question often posed is: *"what do I do with all this data now that I've collected it?"*

One glib answer with a great deal of truth behind it is to give it to a statistician. There is a very good reason for this. Statisticians are trained to interpret data, which is an art in itself, but more importantly they realize that, for example, recognizing the presence of a trend is only the first step. The next thing to do is to find out why that trend is present. Why is something happening? Answer that question and you have useful information.

Of course, the answer to the question "why" may not be obvious from the data itself. Usually that data needs to be related back to the environment it came from. To illustrate this, imagine the trivial case where the number of defects found during testing suddenly rises from some norm. Let us also assume that the items being tested are essentially the same.

In *Figure 1.1*, each point could be an enhancement build on a generic software product where each build is of similar size and complexity.

Figure 1.1   Test Defects Report

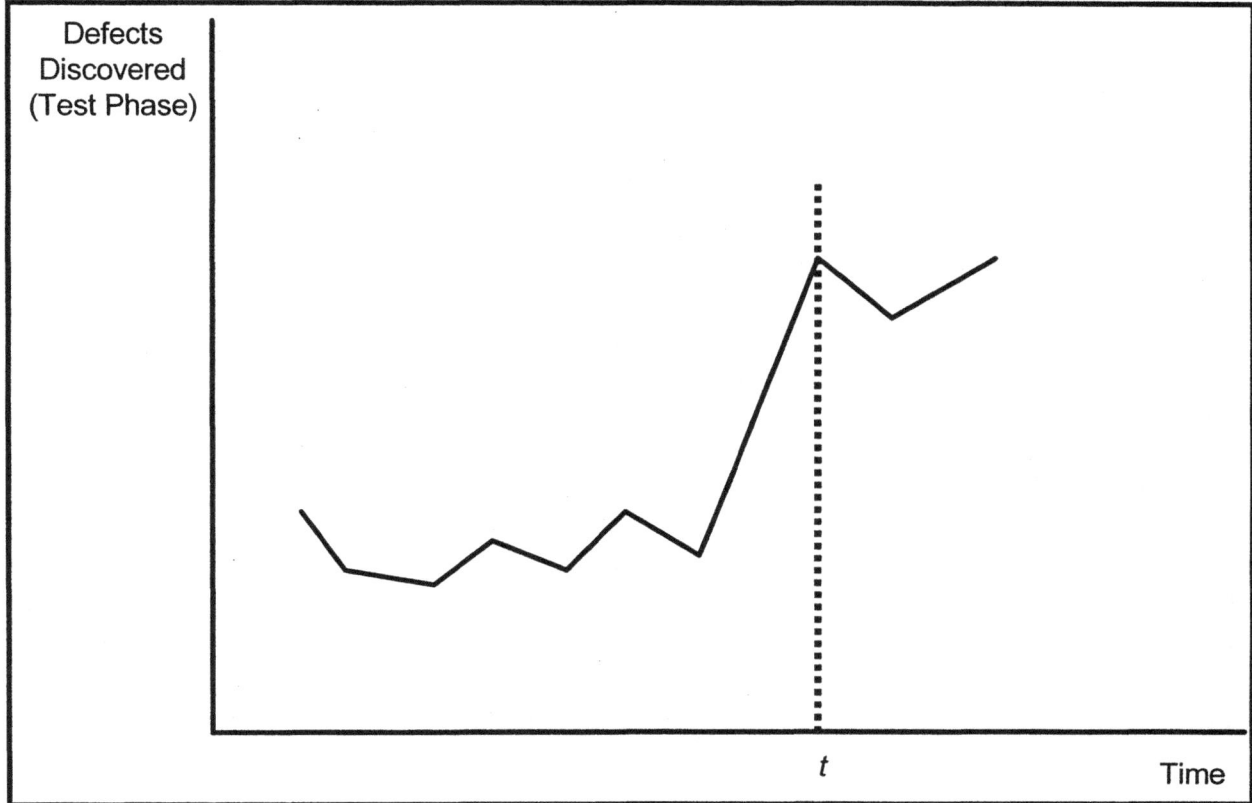

What does our data tell us? Unless we relate it back to the environment, very little. Looking at that testing environment, we may find that at time t we changed our test strategy, perhaps introducing a new tool that automatically generates test cases, thus freeing up effort so that more testing could be carried out. An initial knee jerk reaction that quality (in terms of the development deliverables to testing) had gone down would have been false.

Learning to ask "why" is yet another important step towards making practical use of Software Metrics.

1.7 PRINCIPLE NUMBER FIVE — "THE SUM OF THE WHOLE IS GREATER THAN THE CONSTITUENT PARTS"

This well-known axiom is often forgotten or ignored, yet it follows on from the previous principle. Consider again the situation outlined above. Also, imagine that you have the additional information to that in *Figure 1.1* showing field defects decreasing at time *t* as in **Figure 1.2.**

Figure 1.2 Field Defects Report

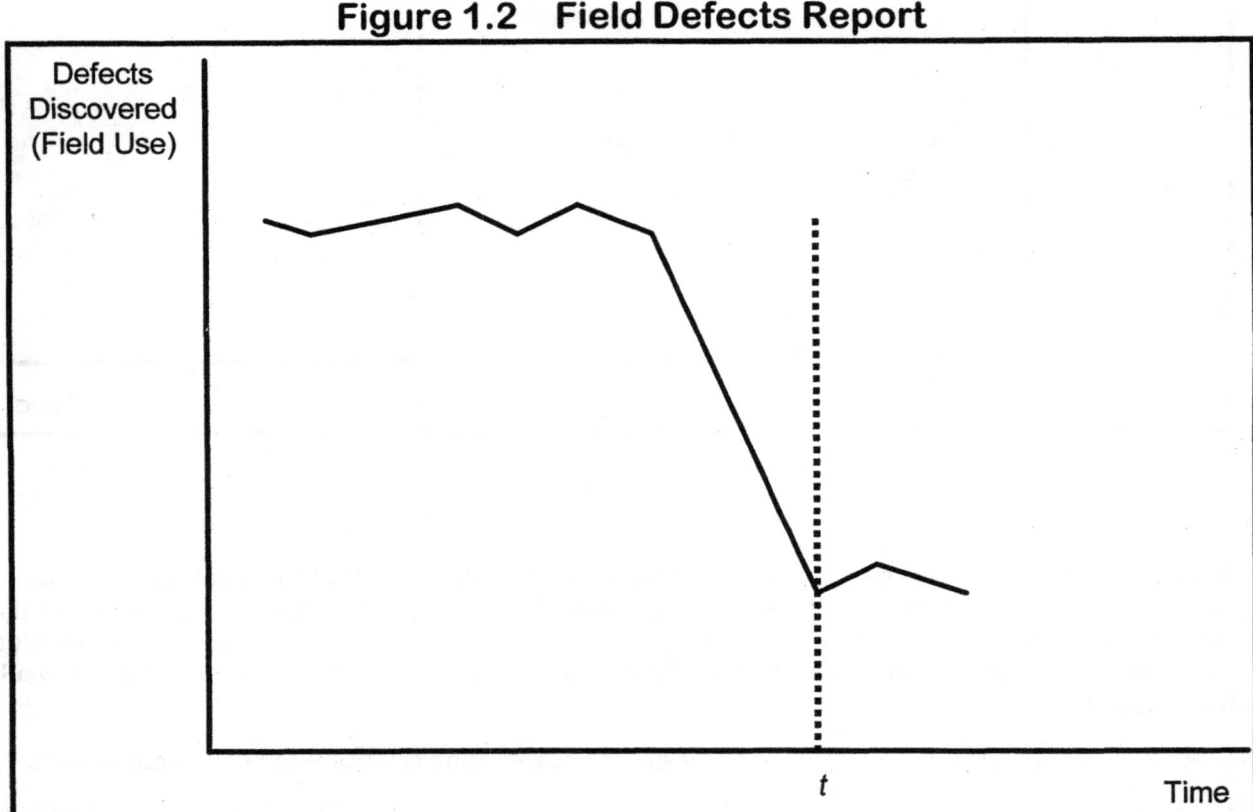

Putting the two pieces of information together may show that the new test strategy is discovering more bugs in testing before they are delivered to the customer. This information could be extremely useful, and may lead to the tool being made available to all test teams because of a demonstrable benefit.

Looking at the two items of information has given us much more than looking at each in isolation.

1.8   PRINCIPLE NUMBER SIX — CULTURE SHOCK!

This is more a fact of life than a principle. We must realize that implementing Software Metrics is about changing the way in which people work and think.

The software engineering industry is maturing. Customers are no longer willing to accept poor quality and late deliveries. Management is no longer willing to pour money into the black hole of IT, and more management control is now a key business requirement. Competition is growing. We, as IT professionals, have to change and mature as well, and this can be a painful experience as we find tenets of our beliefs being challenged and destroyed. Some simple statements that could be made by many in our industry together with my interpretation of current management trends will illustrate the point:

> *Software development is so complex it cannot be managed like other parts of the organization.* 'Forget it, it will be managed or the business will find developers and managers who will manage that development!'

> *I am only six months late with this project.* 'Fine, you are only out of a job!'

> *But you can't put reliability constraints in the contract.* 'Then you don't get the contract!'

The list is almost endless and the message is clear. We will grow up or we will cease to grow. Like any organism, no growth means no life.

Software Metrics cannot solve all our problems but they can enable managers to improve their processes, to improve productivity and quality, to improve the probability of survival. But this is not an easy option. Many metrics programs fail. One reason for this is that organizations and individuals who would never dream of introducing a new computer system without a structured approach ignore the problems of introducing change which is inherent in Software Metrics implementation. Only by treating the implementation of Software Metrics as a project or program in its own right with plans, budgets, resources and management commitment can such an implementation succeed.

Some organizations have already bitten the bullet and now have Software Metrics programs running successfully. From their experiences and my own, I have formed the opinion that the introduction of Software Metrics has a lifecycle not unlike that of other projects. It is that lifecycle model that we will investigate further in section 2 of this book. Before that we will look at some specific applications of Software Metrics in more detail.

1.9   SUMMARY

Software Metrics is simply the application of measurement-based techniques in a software environment. There are many, many ways in which such techniques can be applied and I like to simplify things by considering four main application areas:

Cost estimation

Project control

The use of metrics in the design process

Management information.

Some individuals still ask if the use of Software Metrics is justified. I would say to these people that not only is the use justified, but that it is actually inescapable. The reality today is that business managers are no longer willing to allow their IT departments or their software suppliers to operate without normal business controls. This is a new situation for the IT industry — the honeymoon is over! Either we will have such controls forced upon us, or we will grasp the nettle and start to put our house in order before the iron fist lands. Something of a mixed metaphor but it makes the point!

We used to hear it said that the role of Software Metrics was to enable software engineers to understand the process that they were involved in. I claim today that the role of Software Metrics is to enable engineers and managers to survive in today's business environment. Of course that means a greater understanding but it also means that the pressure is on to start to get it right now.

This chapter is intended to give some meaning to the term Software Metrics. We have looked briefly at various areas where the techniques we collectively call Software Metrics can be applied and we have looked at certain basic principles which, I would suggest, should underlie any measurement initiative. Finally, we have discussed some of the reasons why an organization may wish to invest in a Software Metrics program and in this respect the message is simple. *The use of Software Metrics does not ensure survival but it improves the probability of survival.*

2

An Overview of

Function Point Analysis

Key Points:

A brief introduction to Function Point Analysis

Why is this measure so pivotal?

While this section of the book deals with areas of application of Software Metrics I would like to spend some time discussing one particular measurement technique, **Function Point Analysis** (FPA) which is one class of a group, a small group, of measures known as *Functional Sizing Metrics*. I have two reasons for doing this:

Of all the metrics that can form part of a measurement program, Function Point Analysis is one of the most widely used, at least within the data processing sector of the industry. Now, with the new variant of FPA known as **COSMIC**, the real time sector is also starting to use this approach to software sizing. Indeed, the use of FPA seems to grow exponentially year on year. It is also true that FPA is one of the more contentious measures in use today, a point I would like to return to at the end of this chapter.

I wish to introduce this technique now as it is very difficult to discuss modern Software Metrics, as we will be doing throughout the book, without making reference to FPA. Without some introduction to the technique those references could be confusing.

If you are already a user of Function Point Analysis you may wish to skip this chapter, possibly returning to it later.

2.1   SO, WHAT IS FUNCTION POINT ANALYSIS?

Function Point Analysis is a technique that can be applied to system specifications or existing applications to derive a measure of the size of the information processing requirements of that system/application. A variation of the technique can be used to size changes to the information processing requirements of a system

The concept of FPA was first presented to a joint SHARE/GUIDE/IBM conference in 1979 by the developer of the technique, Allan Albrecht, (1). Albrecht had required a long term productivity measure for systems he was managing. The problem he faced was that his environment included different language types, and so he needed something that was technology independent, or at least independent of the programming language used. That was the start

Since then Function Point Analysis has moved from being a locally used metric within one organization (in fact in just one part of an organization), to the situation we see today which is that FPA is widely used in very many organizations in many parts of the world. Supporting this are a number of user groups, many consultancy organizations and many commercially available training courses. At times it seems as though there is a whole industry involved in promoting and supporting the use of FPA.

Given that Function Point Analysis has been so successful in terms of widespread adoption, at least within the data processing environment, it is sometimes surprising to realize that FPA provides a very basic item of data. FPA is simply a technique that can be used to derive a measure of the size of a software system.

The wide use of Function Point Analysis and the fact that it has been in the public domain has led to some problems. For example, there are many variants of FPA. Some of these have been developed to address perceived limitations in the original technique while others have been developed to extend the application domain of FPA beyond the data processing environment to the, real-time environment. For example, Charles Symons has developed a major variant of FPA, often called **Mark II Function Point Analysis** which has been adopted by the British civil service as a standard, (Symons, 1991). Being in the public domain has also meant that there has been numerous critical reviews of the technique, many of which have led the way to improvements in FPA or in its application.

Despite the wealth of information available on the subject, or perhaps because of it, many misconceptions exist about FPA. I would like to establish three basic ideas that should be appreciated by anyone before they start to use FPA. Before doing that I must stress that this chapter cannot fully explain or discuss Function Point Analysis. To do that would take a book of its own, and they do exist, so please view the rest of this chapter simply as an introduction to the technique and I would suggest that you contact either your national Sotware Metrics or Function Point User Group for further information. Having said that, we can now consider three of what I consider to be key points regarding FPA.

- Function Point Analysis is a technique, hence the use of the word 'analysis' in the expression "Function Point Analysis." It is *not* a simple count of specific characteristics nor is it a totally de-skilled activity. Organizations that are seen as the most effective users of FPA often bring together an FPA expert and a system expert when they wish to size an application. To use FPA effectively requires training, may require support and will involve an investment of effort.

- FPA produces a unit-less answer or score. This means that there is no such thing as a "Function Point." Appreciating this point can save much confusion later. If this appears odd then think of an FPA number as an index in the same form as the Dow Jones or Stock Market FTSE index. These are also unit-less measures and once you understand how the index behaves you can make use of the information it provides.

- The number produced by FPA is a measure of system size, actually a measure of the information processing requirements for the system, or the change to those information processing requirements. Of itself this has little value but it is a basic data element. I must stress that FPA is *not* an estimating technique nor is it a device for productivity measurement. What FPA does is enable such activity by providing the basic data, size. Once you have a size value this can feed into the estimation process for effort or cost. Size values are also used in basic productivity measures and, as you will see later, in many other measures that provide meaningful information.

Having set the scene regarding some of the basics of Function Point Analysis we can consider the technique itself. This will involve a fair degree of technical detail and if you wish to avoid the next section then simply go on to the summary at the end of this chapter.

2.2   USING FUNCTION POINT ANALYSIS

At this point I would like to give you a feel for what is involved in an FPA exercise. The variant used to describe an FPA exercise is the Mark II form of FPA, the design authority for which is the United Kingdom Software Metrics Association (UKSMA, www.uksma.co.uk). There is no claim in this book that the Mark II variant is "better" than any other form of the technique. It is, however my preferred approach and I claim "authors privilege."

2.2.1   Performing an FPA Exercise

People work in different ways. I would never try to force any individual to follow the description below sequentially. The important thing is to get the information you need and use it accordingly. We will approach this as if we were sizing the requirements for a new system or an existing application but will allude to other uses of the technique. Starting at the beginning, it would be nice to know what we are sizing. So...

2.2.2 Defining the System Boundary

The *System Boundary* is the conceptual interface between the application or system being sized and the world in which it exists.

Information moves into the application from users and from other applications across the System Boundary. Likewise, the application will produce information which is passed to users and to other applications. This information will move across the System Boundary. The processing that the application carries out is done within the System Boundary.

Defining the system boundary is the first step in FPA. The boundary is used to limit the scope of the sizing exercise and to help identify the other external parameters.

There are three views of the system boundary depending upon the type of FPA exercise that is being carried out. First we have the *application or product boundary*. This encompasses a full application and this type of count is often done at the end of a development project when handing over to the maintenance group or when an organization first starts to use FPA. This type of FPA count can also be derived from a live system.

Second is the *initial development project boundary*. This is a very similar kind of count to the previous one, the difference being that the count derives from requirements for which no system exists.

Finally we have the *enhancement project boundary*. This situation arises where a system exists and further releases are made of that system. The system boundary envisaged and used when applying FPA to an enhancement project may be partially that of the whole application The enhancement project FPA approach differs from the previous situation in that added, changed and deleted functionality is considered rather than the totality of the system. Do not fall into the trap of counting the total system before enhancement, then after and subtracting one total from the other. This is not a valid approach as you can see if you consider a project that adds a certain amount of functionality and deletes the same amount in another part of the system. Subtracting the size of the system before the project from the size after the project will give you a project size of zero!

This discussion of the system boundary may appear complicated but just remember that it is that conceptual line between the system and its world and most of the other stuff falls into place.

There is a subjective element in determining the system boundary and, obviously, changing the system boundary will change the FP score. While this may seem an unscientific approach, in practice the guideline that the analyst should consider is to look at what is managed as a discrete whole. This enables most system boundaries to be defined easily. From this point, FPA is a more mechanistic process but still demands skill unless you are operating a fully electronic design support system. Let's face it, most organizations are not!

Function Point Analysis is not difficult, in many senses, but can be vexing when there is little or no documentation — guess how often that happens!

Having defined the system boundary, break the system down into sub-systems and then into business operations. Keep going until you get to the lowest level business operation that, when completed either because the operation has been achieved or because the operation has bombed out because of an error condition, leaves the system in a consistent and predictable state. This lowest level of business operation is called a *Logical Transaction*.

Now, for each Logical Transactions you need to identify the number of unique data elements, such as a record key, entering the Logical Transaction. Next identify the unique data elements leaving the Logical Transaction as output. The final element is the number of Data Entities contained in the Logical Data Model of stored data for the system that are accessed during the course of the Logical Transaction. Note that this is the number of entities accessed, not the number of times that they are accessed.

So, for each Logical Transaction, you now have three simple counts:

> Input Data Element Types;

> Output Data Element Types; and,

> Data Entities Referenced.

Now these are weighted, using industry standard weights that look more precise than they probably are – but they work.

The weights are:

> For Input Data Element Types   0.58;

> Output Data Element Types   0.26; and,

> Data Entities Referenced   1.66.

Sum the weighted counts and then sum the counts for all of the Logical Transactions. Eh voila, we have our system size! I kid you not, it is that simple, at a conceptual level but, obviously there are details such as how dates are dealt with, what to do with post or zip codes, how to handle arrays, etc. To give you an idea, a training course typically takes two days to complete.

This diagram shows a simple example of Mark II FPA applied to a single Logical Transaction. In this case, a key (1 Input Data Element) is entered into the application which accesses two data entities to retrieve the

Figure 2.1   FPA Example

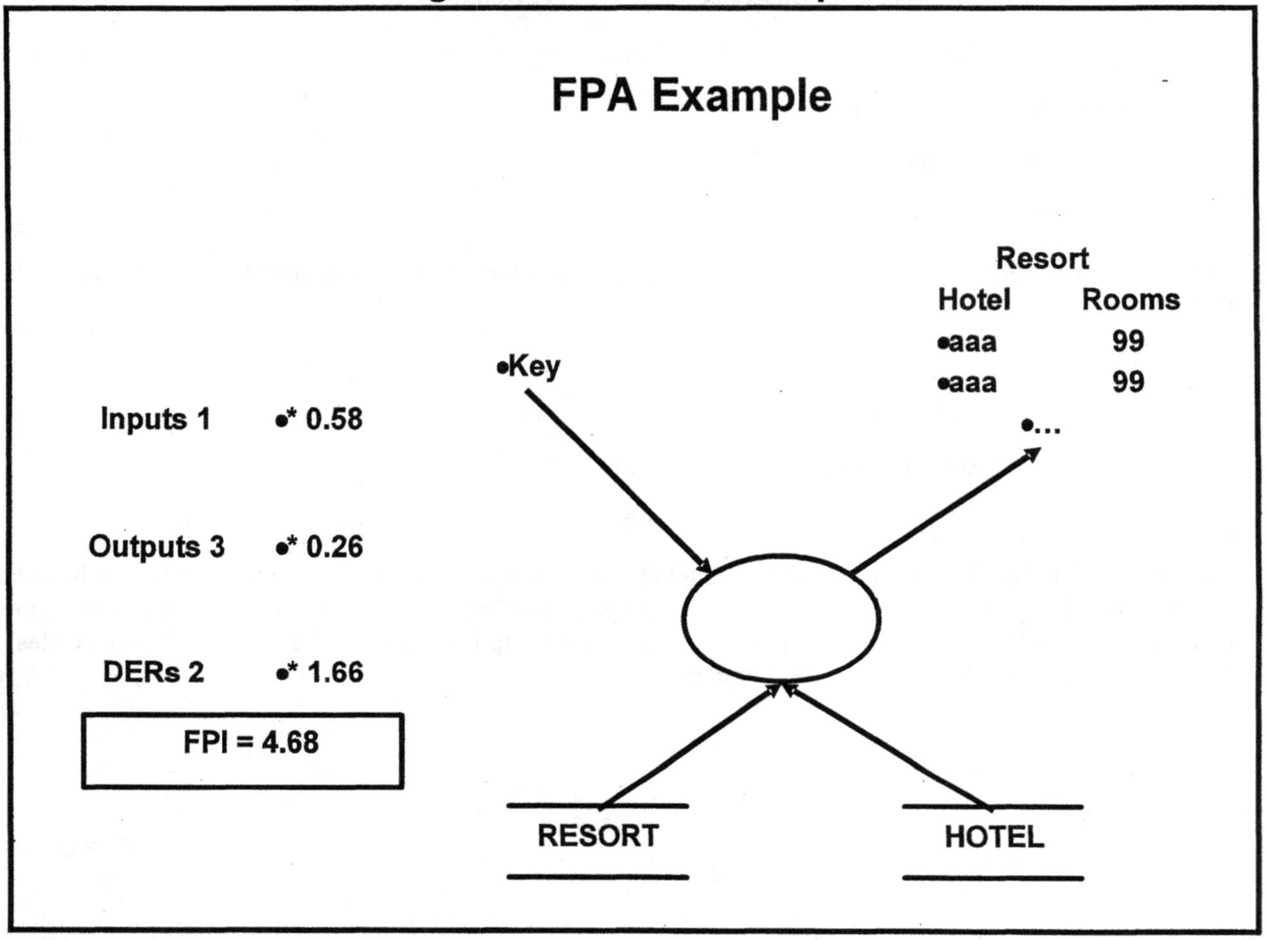

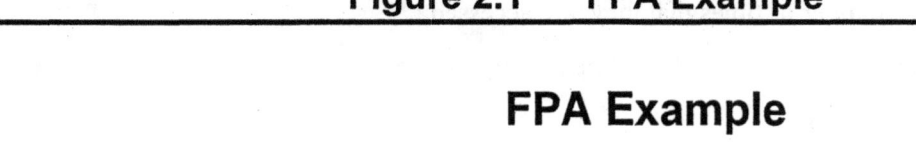

FPA Example

	Resort	
	Hotel	Rooms
	•aaa	99
	•aaa	99

•Key

Inputs 1   •* 0.58

Outputs 3   •* 0.26

DERs 2   •* 1.66

FPI = 4.68

RESORT   HOTEL

information to format and present a simple report. In this case, the report is simply a list of the hotels and the number of rooms in each for a particular resort. You score 1 Output Data Element for the resort name and one each for the list of hotel names and the corresponding list of room numbers (note that you do not count the number of entries in the list because you will not know this). Apply the appropriate weights to the basic counts and add the results up to get the overall score, or Function Point Index (FPI), for that Logical Transaction. The sum of the sores for all the Logical Transactions would give you the overall FPI for the full system.

This book is not an FPA training course but this hopefully gives you a feel for how the technique is applied. The principles behind the technique are both elegant and simple, borne of a managers need to control and report his work and that of his teams. It works; correlations of 0.7 and higher between size in terms of Function Points and development and enhancement effort are common in homogenous environments.

Remember also that you may come across a situation that is specific to your organization and that is not covered by advice in any set of counting guidelines. This simply reflects the fact that, as Albrecht has said at numerous venues, FPA is an evolutionary technique. In such cases it is up to you as the practitioner to make a decision or formulate a rule based on your experience and the experience of others with whom you have contact. The most important consideration is to document that rule and to apply it consistently. For the benefit of other practitioners it would be of great assistance if you were to advise the relevant governing bodies so that they can ensure a consistent and standardized application of FPA across the industry:

The International Function Point User Group (IFPUG; www.ifpug.org);

The United Kingdom Software Metrics Association (UKSMA, www.uksma.co.uk) .

2.3   COMPLEXITY ASSESSMENT

Both IFPUG and Mark II FPA have historically defined additional mechanisms for general system complexity assessment. It is now generally accepted that the approaches used are less than adequate, mainly because they are overly simplistic and often the factors used end up balancing each other out, so most practitioners do not use these unless they have to.

Finally, do not fall into the trap of looking upon FPA as the totality of a metrics initiative — it never is. FPA is a very widely used technique but all it provides is a measure of software system size. How you use that data to manage and improve your process is what really counts.

To finish off this chapter we should return to the point of contention around FPA. Put simply, some people express doubt as to the effectiveness of the measure, the validity of the underlying measurement model and, in some cases, the theoretical veracity of FPA. I do believe that we have to return to my first principle of Software Metrics: pragmatism and compromise. I do not wish to enter into an argument around the concerns held by some individuals but I will make the following point.

Size is a fundamental component of almost all Software Metrics initiatives. The only candidate size measures with any validity today are FPA or Lines of Code, which has many other issues associated with it. I am very happy to consider any viable alternative but I am not aware of any being used across a number of companies or organizations today. So the bottom line for me is, if you don't want to use FPA then you have to use Lines of Code or find something better.

2.4   SUMMARY

Function Point Analysis is a measurement technique that has been adopted by a large number of data processing organizations and some efforts have been made to apply FPA to real-time environments. The technique consists of various steps which together produce or derive a measure of system or project size.

The COSMIC approach is a newly emerging variant of Functional Sizing Metric that is providing initially very good results for both the data processing and real time communities.

Because of the widespread use of FPA and the fact that it has been in the public domain for some time there are many variants of FPA and numerous misconceptions. Used correctly FPA can be a valuable component of a measurement initiative but it should not be seen as the totality of such an initiative.

3

Software Metrics:

Management Information

Key Points

What is Management Information, in the context of Software Metrics?

The complexity and simplicity of Management Information - a paradox

Why do we need Management Information?

Avoiding the Data Hunter syndrome

Some detail within Management Information

If you ask anyone to explain what is meant by the term "Software Metrics," chances are that they will describe the provision of information through some form of statistical analysis applied to collected data; in other words, the furnishing of management information. Now, there is a mouthful! This aspect of the subject is probably the most traditional form of Software Metrics.

What I hope to do in this chapter is consider why such information is wanted by managers; how it should, and perhaps more importantly should not, be collected; and, how such information should be presented.

3.1   WHAT IS "MANAGEMENT INFORMATION?"

Before we look at these aspects of management information I would like to discuss some important background issues. Management Information and the systems developed to supply that information, whether they are being developed as part of a Software Metrics initiative or not, are often thought of as single entities that service the in-house needs of a relatively small group of individuals, i.e., the management. This can be a very dangerous viewpoint because MIS applications are often large and complex in two dimensions. First, they service, or should service, many different levels of customer from the managing director or CEO to the team leader. Second, they have to satisfy a large number of different requirements within each customer set but still recognize the similarities that cross the set boundaries if they are to avoid massive data redundancy. Just to make life interesting, they may also have to deal with ad-hoc requirements.

Now this may all sound as though it has little to do with a Software Metrics program but let me stress that such a program is a Management Information System. Whether it operates through fancy computer systems or good old pen and paper, it still has to deal with all of the complexities outlined above.

The first dimension tends to be a function of your own organizational structure and it will be for you and your own management group to determine the levels at which your information system should operate. The second dimension has to do with the different requirements placed on that system by its users or customers. This implies that the use to which the information will be put is considered. There are many different, specific requirements that will be placed on the system but they will all have something in common, namely they should satisfy a need for information. Consequently, the aspect of a Software Metrics program that we are talking about has to do with the provision of information. Output from the system should be related to a requirement for information and should not be generated in any random way. Consider that requirements for information generally, if not always, should relate to an attribute of either a product or a process.

To make this clear we can consider a couple of examples. A manager of a number of product teams may wish to know how those teams are performing and how that performance is changing over time. This is a basic information requirement if the teams are to be managed effectively. This requirement relates directly to the process attribute we call productivity. In other words, what do I get out for what I put in?

On the other hand, a product manager may wish to know how reliable his or her software system is during the first three months of live use across a number of releases.

This information can be used as a direct quality measure of the product or as an indirect quality measure of the process that produces the product but however it is used, it relates to the product attribute of reliability.

To manage an attribute means realizing that there are two information requirements associated with each of them.

For any attribute, a requirement exists that the attribute be monitored. For example, if a manager feels that group productivity is important to him then it needs to be measured and periodic reports fed back to the manager so that the information can be used. This is, traditionally, the type of requirement that Management Information Systems seek to satisfy.

A second requirement for any attribute is that it be predicted. This can be much more difficult. For example, given a new product group within a division, how can we be confident that we can predict the productivity level for that group? But unless we can do this we may find our business in danger, especially if we are operating in a fixed price environment.

Another example can be drawn from the area of quality. One of the biggest changes in the software industry over the last few years has been the rapid growth in maturity of our end users. They are much less willing now to accept loose specifications of quality and, to be honest, it is not only the fixed price contractors who are having to cope with the need to predict values for various attributes. For example, one of the largest organizations in the UK, an organization with a massive IT procurement budget, appear to be moving towards contractual specifications of reliability for software systems.

This means that we, as software developers have to be much more capable than we have been in the past when it comes to being able to predict value levels for attributes.

How we do this needs to be given a great deal of thought. Should we attempt to use theoretical models of, say, reliability growth? The problem is that while various reliability growth models may work for certain environments it does not seem to be possible to identify the environment attributes that would enable a match to be made to a specific model with any degree of certainty. In my opinion, the only alternative is to use empirical models developed from data collected in-house. This would imply that our Management Information System should collect the data that would enable the derivation of such a model. Obviously, it is difficult to specify the requirements for data collection if you do not have the model defined which will use the data. However, a pragmatic and educated guess as to what will be required is often a valid starting point.

From these two examples you may appreciate some of the problems that arise when you move into the area of predicting process or product attributes and it would seem that the provision of management information is not quite as simple as we may first think. To summarize, requirements for information can be many, varied and complex. Attributes of both the process and the products of the process would seem to be fundamental to this aspect of Software Metrics. Attributes, once identified and defined, generate requirements of two types, the need to monitor and the need to predict values for the attribute.

Before continuing and having mentioned reliability, I would like to digress slightly. As far as attribute definitions are concerned, you might like to watch out for some of the definitions of reliability that are still floating around.

These generally start by defining reliability as "the probability that a software system will..." This is not a definition of reliability because anything that is expressed in terms of a probability is in fact a prediction. The probability that a ten year old male child will grow to a height of six feet does not define the attribute height. This may seem a trivial point but things like this do show the need for rigor in Software Metrics, as such a definition can cost you time and money. Imagine going to senior management with a reliability measurement proposal only to have it kicked out because the basic definition of reliability was seen to be flawed. If you think such a thing could never happen then let me assure you that I have seen it happen.

3.2 WHY DO WE NEED MANAGEMENT INFORMATION?

Having discussed some of the background issues relating to Management Information let us take a step back and consider something even more fundamental: why are we bothering, anyway?

One of the most widely used, valid and succinct justifications for the collection of management information comes from Tom DeMarco and says simply that if you don't measure it, you can't control it. I would also like to paraphrase a statement from Dieter Rombach, at the time working with the Software Engineering Laboratory in the United States. He said, at the Eurometrics '91 conference in Paris (was it so long ago, yet still it rings true), that we no longer seem to be asking if we *should* measure, the question today is *how* do we measure? This is certainly true for some organizations and individuals but it is still true to say that many still need to be convinced or even exposed to the idea of measurement within a software development or support environment.

The next few paragraphs are included for those people who have the job of convincing such organizations or groups that management information is necessary.

The verb *to manage* is defined in my dictionary as "to control the movement or behavior of," which implies some form of control mechanism or loop. Control loops operate on a very simple principle. Measurements are taken of the process output, either by sampling or some other means, and these are fed into a comparator to relate attribute levels of the output to target or ideals. The difference between actual and optimum is then used to instigate corrective action if necessary. Such a control loop is easy to understand if you are a hi-fi buff or if you think in mechanistic terms, but what about other processes? Well, I suggest that the same control loop model can be applied to any process.

For instance, consider the situation where you have to move from point A to point B, twenty miles apart across open moorland or heath. You have with you a compass and you know that B is due west of A. Assuming that you walk at four miles an hour would you walk from A for five hours without checking your compass and expect to be at B?

What you would probably do is use your compass and bearings to periodically check your course and to make corrections to it. In other words, you are sampling the process and, through measurement, initiating corrective action. This type of process control is epitomized by long distance sailors who use celestial navigation, by means of compass, timepiece, sextant and chart to get from one coast to another.

It is worth noting that all of these examples include the concept of instrumentation and this idea has been extended to the control of software development and support through the dashboard analogy put forward by Howard Rubin, Rubin(1), and others.

This simply says that managers within the software industry need instrumentation if they are going to be able to control the processes they manage and that part of Software Metrics is the discipline of supplying that instrumentation.

Another analogy that I use likens management in the software industry to the job of flying a plane. In the past it was very similar to flying one of the old biplanes. It was new, exciting and there were few rules. Instrumentation was rudimentary; if you wanted to know how high you were you looked over the side of the cockpit; if you got lost you just followed a convenient road or railway track. Even a disaster like running out of fuel wasn't too bad: if you were lucky, you just set down in a convenient field.

Nowadays, things are different. Software development has increased in complexity and in importance to the core business of most organizations. We can think of management within the software industry of today as akin to flying a jumbo jet. We have to get there on time, we have to give "good" service and we have to be reliable because many others depend on us. And yet, for most organizations their managers are flying that jumbo with the same instrumentation that they were using when they flew the old bi-planes. Is it any wonder that we have so many disasters within the software industry? Do you still wonder why we need that instrumentation?

Having said all of that, let nobody think that putting in the right instruments guarantees success or removes the need for good management. Instruments in a jumbo jet do not remove the need for a pilot nor will Software Metrics ever replace good managers. What Software Metrics can do is improve the probability that a good manager will succeed!

So, one reason for installing a management information system is to do with controlling the processes for which managers are responsible.

If controlling the process you are responsible for does not interest you then perhaps you might like to think about protection.

Protection and fear are two very emotive words but they are starting to have real meaning within the IT industry. Amazing things are happening; much of what is going on around you today was science fiction ten years ago, our culture has changed almost beyond recognition in the space of one generation, the policemen really do look young and the management are thinking about shutting down the IT function!

What was that last one again? Well, you may think that it is unbelievable but, unless IT is your core business, you may be shocked to learn that this is a very real option open to managers. If you need convincing I suggest you consider the following: A few of years ago the whole team on a large UK Government project was disbanded and the work was handed over to a private contractor. Again in the UK, some Government departments have been converted into "agencies," basically private companies owned by the Government but managed under normal market forces. Almost invariably this has reduced job security. Finally, you need look no further than the growth in the facilities management sector of our industry.

Think about facilities management for a moment. An organization is going to come in, take over your IT function and, for let's say, the same amount of cash that you pay out now, will provide you with the same IT support. Why do they do this? Quite simply, they know that, for most organizations, the IT function is performing so badly that the facilities management company can make a significant profit just by improving working practices and, it must be said, by either redeploying some of the staff onto other work or by shedding some of those staff. Of course it could never happen to you, or could it?

The one way to protect yourself from these kinds of threats is to be able to demonstrate that your IT function runs as a tight, lean machine and that nobody could do IT better! Of course you cannot do this without effective, quantitative management information.

The other side of this coin is how do you manage the situation when you do outsource, or "off-shore" aspects or even most of your IT operations and projects? Effective measurement becomes even more vital from the point when the contract is first being drafted, and the relevant measures are being defined, through to…

Hold on. Over recent years I have come across numerous situations where outsourcing contracts have been set up and agreed to by both supplier and client only for them to find that the measurement clauses, often labeled as the Benchmarking Clause, is indecipherable and/or unworkable. What follows is often acrimonious, time consuming and counterproductive, even in otherwise well-founded relationships. I cannot stress strongly enough that great care needs to be taken when establishing the measurement aspects of any outsourcing arrangement. If the situation arises whereby the measurement clause is either nonexistent or unworkable, both parties must recognize this and work together to rectify a situation that is harmful to both.

Software Metrics work within outsourcing arrangements just as with any other management scenario. In fact, it is often easier to get the measurement momentum going in these situations. Apply the principles embodied in this book and I suggest you will not go far wrong but above all else, keep it simple! The other key thing to remember is that a deal that only benefits one party may make you feel great, for an hour or two, but it is ultimately a sucker deal!

Fear can be a powerful motivator. Management through control is appealing. However, by far the most attractive reason for collecting and using management information has to be the concept of optimizing the process, actually using information about the process and its products, in our case the software development process and the systems that result, to improve the process.

This fundamental concept underlies the Crosby, [Crosby (1)] and Deming, [Deming (1)], quality models and Deming in particular points out that the concept cannot be applied without having the necessary information provided as part of the process itself. In fact, Deming uses various experiments to illustrate that tweaking the process, whatever it is, can actually make the results worse if this tweaking is done in a random and haphazard way. In other words, if you try to fix the process on gut feel rather than on the basis of quantitative information you will probably make the process and the results worse! I would suggest that there is an exception to this: if you are so intimately involved with the process as to be a complete and integral part of it then you probably can fix things on gut reaction and make it better. Equally, if you are that close to the process you probably do not have the power to change it. This is why engineers and IT staff are very good people to ask if you think there are problems. They know many of the answers but cannot do much about it. They are constrained by the very organization they seek to serve. That is quite an indictment of our society. Management information enables management by *fact* rather than management by *opinion*.

Let us now assume that I have browbeaten you into accepting that there is a need for management information. We now need to consider the typical requirements for management information, the problems of data collection and how we present results. I am going to do this in a slightly different order, looking at data collection first. The reason is that this is still the way many organizations approach the provision of management information and measurement in general. I hope to show that this is not the way to do things!

3.3   COLLECTING THE DATA

"Yes!" shouts the MD or SEO, thus giving you the management commitment you may believe you need, "we want information." What do you do next? Unfortunately many groups and organizations who have started an initiative to provide management information have gone out "data hunting." The average dedicated data hunter is nothing if not thorough. He or she has two guiding principles: if it does not move then measure it; and if it does move, pin it down *then* measure it!

The average data hunter is also something of a fanatic who wants to involve everyone else in their abiding interest. The data hunter will lay traps with forms and procedures seeking to include everyone in their passion. Only when everyone is spending great chunks of time and effort supplying information to the data hunter will they be truly happy.

And what is the result of all this happy hunting? Well, the first thing that people realize is that it tends to be costly. You see, one thing about the average data hunter, they are impatient. Not only do they want lots of information, they want it *now*. This means that they often get teams of people to sift through old data or even possible sources of old data. Joy to a data hunter is a 50,000-line COBOL listing (OK, I am showing my age but there is also a confession coming). There are so many ways the data can be cut! Sorting through any form of old documentation, except code which is at least available electronically so that the hunter can get lots of data quickly, takes time and effort. Lots of it. This costs money.

Now having got the data, what do you do with it? Obviously you analyze it! Do you know how much raw data you can get from a 50,000-line COBOL listing? Let me put it this way, do you have a spare room? And all of this data needs to be analyzed when, despite the advances in electronic data analysis support, working with more than about ten variables (ten being the number of subjects the preconscious brain can handle), is pushing your luck. So you need huge amounts of effort to carry out the analysis of all this data which increases the cost again. In fact, some organizations have rooms full of data that they have neither the time nor, to be honest, the inclination to analyze. Such organizations fell into the hands of data hunters.

Even if you do manage the data analysis the results may cause you even more heartache. You see, if you have lots of data and lots of variables, something is almost bound to relate to something else just by chance. And by the way, do not fall into the trap of believing that the laws of probability apply in anything but their fullest sense. This means, to paraphrase Murphy's law, "if event E has a probability P of occurring on a specific day this means that event E will occur when it can do the most damage or on the first day after counting begins, whichever has the greater disaster potential." In other words, the probability of two data items relating to one another through chance may be mathematically small but this means you will probably go into your senior managers meeting and state that programmers who keep hamsters make good testers, because that's what the data shows! Chance got you again.

The final problem of the data hunting approach I can vouch for from painful experience. As someone who did once dabble with data hunting and someone who also believes that data, somehow, must be of some use if only I had the time to... (I told you there was a confession coming) As I was saying, the final problem is that you will always miss the most important variable. Murphy's law strikes again!

More seriously, organizations who do operate under a data hunting regimen tend to have very disgruntled employees because all they see is bureaucracy and yet more bureaucracy.

But if data hunting is not the answer, then what is? One of the key points that I hope this book can get across is that measurements should only be made to satisfy specific requirements for information which in turn should be linked to business objectives. Management information is no exception to this rule: you collect data because your modeling process indicates that the collection of that data will satisfy an information requirement.

3.4   REQUIREMENTS FOR INFORMATION

Before I go any further I do need to talk about models and measures. We are going to be discussing requirements during the next few paragraphs and it is very possible that some "solutions" to those requirements may creep into the text. Now some people will immediately get annoyed about this claiming that "off-the-shelf solutions" never work. Let me make my case very clearly. I suggest that business objectives across organizations are very similar. At their most basic these objectives reduce to the objective, i.e., to maximize output while minimizing cost and waste. I suggest that the problems faced by organizations (especially in the IT industry), are also effectively the same. Consider cost estimation and project control, for example.

The question is, *are the solutions to these problems also the same, or at least similar across organizations?*

Solutions tend to be detailed and are often specific to specific organizations.

I believe however that what are truly portable in many cases are solution models. Metrics or measures, as will be discussed in more detail in *Section 2, Building and Implementing a Software Metrics Program* are derived from models and will probably be different between different organizations. If I offer a solution to any requirement talked about in this chapter it is a model. If you decide to use any of these you still have some work to do to in order to turn the model into a metric. An approach to this is also described in section 2, when I describe the Goal/Question/Metric paradigm of Basili and Rombach, [Rombach (1)].

To illustrate a requirements-based approach to management information let us look at some of the typical requirements managers have for information. One of the most common requirements for management information is to have productivity figures available. Productivity measures are seen, in many industries other than IT, as performance indicators. You often see export performance expressed in terms of sales over units of time, the implication being that the cost over time is constant. The car industry uses cars produced per work day or month as a measure of factory performance.

Productivity can be defined as the work product divided by the cost to produce that product and in the IT industry productivity is usually expressed in terms of Lines of Code or Function Points produced, divided by effort, in terms of engineering days, months or hours (big hint: person hours is by far the best to use).

These types of measures do not tell us everything we wish to know about performance but they do give us a high level indicator of performance provided you remember one very important fact. Absolute productivity values, in any terms, do not provide much in the way of useful information. To get any real value out of productivity measures you need to consider the trend over time and what you want to see, of course, is an improvement over time.

The other thing to remember is that productivity should not be considered in terms of good or bad, only higher or lower values. For example, I would expect a small, in-house development team who work within very loose documentation constraints to achieve much higher productivity values than a team developing safety critical applications in, say, the defense sector of the industry where documentation control is extremely stringent. This does not mean that the small, in-house team is performing better or that the defense application team is performing worse. What I would want to see, over time, is both teams improving their productivity rates.

This does mean that you need to be very careful when you compare productivity across teams or organizations. Not only can the simple productivity measures lead to erroneous comparisons but you also need to be very aware of differences in terms of the definitions used for the base data elements. There are, for instance, many perfectly justifiable ways of defining a Line of Code. There are also many variants of Function Point Analysis around. As if this wasn't bad enough it is often instructive to ask how the cost element of the productivity function is defined. My idea of an engineering day can be very different than yours. Now, it may be that someday we will have recognized standards in these areas but they do not exist today. This means that such comparisons can give totally false impressions. This is why it is much better to use person hours rather than days.

Having said this, such comparisons can be useful if used sensibly, with great care and always in the presence of a large salt cellar from which to take the occasional pinch.

Finally, never measure productivity at the personnel level. This has been said before but I make no excuse for repeating myself. I know that it can be tempting to do this but individual differences and circumstances will probably swamp any meaningful interpretation of the results.

For example, I once knew a programmer analyst who was superb at her job. Her productivity rate over anything other than a carefully selected short period of time was abysmal for the simple fact that she was used to train and assist the less able team members. This was actually an excellent use of this lady as a resource because she was not only excellent at her official job, she was also an excellent teacher. Now you may feel that you would always be sure to take that kind of circumstance into account but can you be sure that everyone else would all of the time? Anyway, measuring at the individual level, and even worse using that data as part of assessment activities, could lead to demotivated staff, lousy team spirit and an abdication of responsibility by management. A decent team leader should never need that kind of individual measure to assess performance.

Productivity measures have their place. Use them wisely and you can get hold of a great deal of useful information that enables you to assess process performance, provided you avoid the traps!

Certain other requirements, like productivity, seem to crop up time and again. Getting a handle on the effectiveness of cost estimation within the organization is an example of such a requirement. This is a relatively simple requirement to satisfy in that you really only need to compare the accuracy of estimates to the actual results. Few things in Software Metrics are that simple, and this is no exception. Very often such a request hides the real requirement which is for the implementation of a cost estimation strategy — but more about that later.

Another basic requirement for management information is in the area of quality assessment. This can really be fun!

If you ever want to waste half an hour or so, get a group of IT professionals together and ask them to define what is meant by "quality." With all of our experience, this still causes difficulty. In the "old days" we used to have the role of Quality Managers in many organizations. Asking them to define quality really was fun. It wasted lots of time but it was fun. If you try this, after the half hour is over you will still not have a definition of "quality" but you will have seen the whole range of human emotion expressed by normally reasonable men and women. I leave you to draw your own conclusions!

Of course, the problem is not with the *definition* of quality, it is with the *application* of that definition in any sensible way.

I am quite happy to accept the common definition that quality is *the satisfaction of user or customer requirements*. I fully accept that a small hatchback can be a quality car and that this accolade is not reserved for the best of the super cars. I agree that a quality service is one that meets, or exceeds, where cost effective, customer expectations. Does this help me measure quality? Well, it is a start, but that is all. I believe that one must go further than this and that the concept of "quality" must be further subdivided into a number of quality attributes.

Identified quality attributes apply to specific applications and to specific deliverables from the development process such as designs, to a greater or lesser extent. This is well worth remembering as you will see.

Typical quality attributes for IT products include, and I apologize in advance for the number of words that end in "-ity" but that seems to be the nature of the beast: reliability, maintainability, testability, usability, portability, etc. The list can go on and on and on and on...

Defining product or process attributes and then relating these to the quality requirements for the process or product is a very effective start when you need to measure "quality."

Again there are certain points that should be borne in mind. Not all attributes apply to all applications. For an embedded application required for a single mission, such as a space satellite, portability may not be a concern. The level of quality required by specific applications may vary according to the attribute being considered and the application type. For instance, the reliability required in a piece of games software is likely to be lower than that for a life support system. Interestingly, modern games software is extremely reliable.

Defining quality in terms of specific attributes may seem a difficult task but you would be pleasantly surprised at how clear most managers are in their requirements when asked to talk about the kinds of information that they would find beneficial. If you would like a good starting point I would suggest that you look at a document, item *IS9126* in the reference list, that is available from the International Standards Organization, ISO (www.iso.ch). ISO and the International Electrotechnical Commission, the IEC (www.iec.ch), have been working on standards for quality attributes for some time now and this document is the result of their work. Their definitions of the various quality attributes that they have deemed to be important are certainly a valid starting point although you may have to do some tailoring to suit your own organizations needs.

My only major disagreement with the ISO attribute definitions is in the area of Maintainability. Within the IT industry there is a great tendency to use maintenance, and hence maintainability, as a catchall for corrective, adaptive and perfective maintenance as defined by Swanson (1) many years ago.

While this made sense at the time when applications were somewhat simpler it does seem to cause us problems now. Based on research carried out by the Inland Revenue in the United Kingdom and supported by discussions with many IT managers, most IT functions seem to devote about 60% to 70% of their overall effort to maintenance according to this definition but most of this effort is expended on enhancing existing systems in line with new or additional user requirements. This is a direct result of the IT industry adopting, almost universally, a strategy of sequential builds or releases against a generic product or system. The production of these new builds or releases involves all the stages of most of the standard lifecycle models used for development of new systems with, of course, the added complication of integrating new and changed functionality with the core system.

This being the case it would seem to make sense to treat enhancements to a system separately from "bug fixing" or corrective maintenance and I feel that maintainability and enhanceability should both be considered as top-level quality attributes in terms of management information requirements. Of course maintainability is now defined in terms of corrective maintenance. Perfective maintenance should be included under enhanceability as it is generally carried out as part of a release development project rather than being part of any patching work.

3.5   SOME PORTABLE MODELS

I now intend to provide a small number of models that I believe can be used as the basis of a set of management information measures within an organization. These are my own personal choice and have resulted from applying the metrics derivation procedures described later in section 2. I have used them successfully in a number of organizations but let me stress, they are models, not measures, and they will need additional work before you can use them as metrics for your organization. Also, I do not guarantee universal applicability — all I can say is that they have worked for me, so far, in a number of environments.

For measuring reliability, or at a higher level the quality of a software product, I suggest a simple defect density measure, i.e., defects reported from the field or customer divided by the size of the product. If you need to compare applications that are used at different rates, say in terms of the number of site installations, then I suggest you build in a usage metric to the denominator, multiplying not adding. I prefer defect density to the common *Mean Time Between Failure* (MTBF) measure for two reasons. First, I am always wary of using means within software data sets which tend to be skewed so that the mean is not a suitable level indicator and, second, I have never found it easy to collect failure data for the environments I have worked in. One other minor point is that failures are the really visible defects, the showstoppers. Many users get very fed up with the less critical defects that do not cause the system to fail but which are, nonetheless, defects or faults.

It is also possible to classify defects according to their severity but one should beware of introducing sophistication before the basics are in place. Incidentally, defect, error or fault reports used in this measure should be reduced to include only validated and non-duplicated reports. That means that only defects that are found to be the result of genuine faults should be included in the reliability measure and that if a defect is reported by more than one source, i.e., user, it should be treated as a single defect from the point of view of this measure.

3.6 WHAT ABOUT USABILITY?

As a starting point you could do worse than looking at the number of user complaints, defect, fault or error reports, from the field where the root cause is not related to the reliability of the software. Here I intend that you should consider all such reports and not reduce the set by considering only validated non-duplicates. The reason for this is that you are looking for the "pain" level felt by the customer as a result of your not providing sufficiently good documentation, training or support to that customer. This is an incredibly simplistic approach to usability measurement and I would accept that it ignores the ergonomic aspect of systems. In defense of this measure I would say again that it is a "pain" measure and that pain is really the inverse of usability.

Maintainability, as I consider it as corrective maintenance, results in the most complex of the suggested models. I find that there are three parameters that affect managers and users view of the system maintainability. These are:

> The number of defects fixed

> The time it takes to fix a defect

> The number of defects outstanding, i.e., not fixed.

Combining these, I suggest that a maintainability metric can be derived from the following model:

- For a given time period, say one calendar month, consider the average time taken to fix a defect multiplied by the sum of the defects fixed and the defects outstanding.

- In this model, if any parameter worsens, the overall result also worsens and the source data, the three parameters can be investigated to identify the cause. Simply recording the parameters separately can cause you to miss a developing problem, especially when the three parameters all start to get slightly worse at the same time. You do not see a problem but the user does.

- Finally, for enhanceability, the ease by which requested changes can be made to a system, you can consider the number of components affected by a change divided by the total number of components in the system. The reasoning behind this model is that systems do degrade as more and more enhancements are made and the system level cohesion and coupling properties worsen. In other words, the mix of functionality within a given system component tends to increase and the number of links between components increases. This tends to reduce enhanceability. This model reflects those effects and enables corrective action such as strategic rewrites, namely work that adds no functionality to the system but which is intended to improve enhanceability, to be carried out.

Again, these models are presented as suggestions or starting points. I do not claim that they are perfect models, or even the best available, simply that they have worked for me. What you use in your organization is up to you.

3.7   FEEDBACK

Of course, having the models, defining the measures, collecting the data and even analyzing that data is not the end of the story. You now have to present or feedback the information to managers. This is an art in itself and there are some classic examples around of how it should not be done which I am sure everyone with any management experience has come across.

Now this is an area where a trained statistician can be worth his or her weight in gold and much of what follows is the result of assistance given to me by such individuals over the years.

The first thing to remember is what is required from such feedback, what does your customer, a manager, want? Well, what is not required is an example of how clever you have been collecting all this data and collating it into nice tables pages long! Managers are, by definition, simple folk; otherwise they would still be programmers or technical designers. They are also busy, or believe they are, which amounts to the same thing, and as a result of this have only a limited amount of time available. Do not expect them to analyze data sets or to develop relationships between results. That, as the presenter of this information, is your job.

Remember also that different people relate to different styles of presentation, and as you may not know everybody who will see your feedback of information you will not know whether or not they relate to pictures or words. For this reason I advocate the use of pictures, in the form of graphs (which I will talk about later), together with text. Use the text to briefly summarize what the graphs are saying but also use a separate section or paragraph to emphasize any points and relationships you feel are important. Simply presenting the summarized data is seldom adequate.

I favor a management summary at the front of any report that summarizes the summaries in both words and pictures and I try to use this to point out potential problems. Do *not* be afraid of doing this. Provided you maintain a reasonable tone to the presentation and do not insist that your interpretation is the only one, most managers quite like to be told what is happening. It makes a change for them to get usable information, and they like to be told things.

There are some important points to note about management information that relate to feedback or presentation. Some people lay great store by the idea of *Statistical Process Control*. This is an extremely useful concept and approach but it does depend upon a process or product attribute being statistically stable. By this I mean that most variation is predictable. For example, assuming I was any good at archery, the process of firing an arrow at a target would probably be statistically stable in that my arrows would normally be clustered within a certain circumference away from the gold. If I then shot an arrow and it hit the target rim it would be exceptional, in statistical terms an outlier, and I should ask why it happened. I may investigate and find that the arrow was warped so I could improve the process of firing by not using that arrow again. Unfortunately, I have problems hitting the target, let alone getting a predictable cluster. Think about it — in those circumstances, statistical process control may not be appropriate.

For a software system I may also observe statistical stability when, say, reliability values in terms of defect density for a system enhanced and released quarterly, remain within a certain range for a given space of time. Once I have this stability I can set two bounds around the norm. If I am using defect density as a reliability measure, then if the value increases it is bad. Buut remember that, if statistically stable, just because the current value is worse than the previous value it is not a cause for concern (provided the current value is within the expected range). I should set a control bound at some value greater than the highest expected and acceptable value. You will find references to three or two sigma, usually defined as standard deviation from the mean, for this control bound but I believe that common sense and your own business constraints are a much better guide. This is especially true when dealing with software systems. If a value exceeds the control bound then it should trigger investigation and, potentially, corrective action.

The other bound I can set is a target for the attribute value. Using our reliability example I would set a target at some value lower than the least expected value. I assume that the target is reached when the values for reliability over some period of time, not just for one data point, or the associated trend values are lower than the target value.

Of course, norms and control bounds should be periodically reassessed. Target levels should be changed once the target has been met, but do make sure that everyone concerned knows the target has been reached and make sure that they all get a pat on the back.

3.8   SUMMARY

Management information is a major topic in most Software Metrics programs. It is to do with the collection of information which can be combined through measurement models so that meaningful information can be conveyed to managers. It is also to do with the presentation of that data and, ultimately, its use to improve the process that supplied the data in the first place. Do not fall into the trap of believing that simply supplying information will bring about change — the metrics program also has to enable change.

Which brings us to the end of this discussion of management information as part of a Software Metrics Program. Much of this chapter is simply an expression of common sense and good practice but then metrics, like most enabling disciplines, is just that.

4

Cost Estimation

```
Key Points

Using metrics to enable cost and duration estimation

Basic principles of estimation

Using historical data that you may not even know you have

Estimating models and how they work
```

While many people see traditional Software Metrics as the provision of management information, it is the area of estimating, and especially estimating the cost of software development or enhancement projects, that has received the most attention over the years. Given the amount of work that has been done in this area and a history of over twenty years for commercial IT, it is somewhat surprising that the industry has such a terrible, and often well-deserved, reputation for poor cost estimation. Basically, we still cannot get it right! Even if a project is delivered "on time" the amount of functionality that is delivered on that date is often a drastic reduction over what was "contracted" to be delivered.

4.1 COST MODELS AND BEYOND

Why are we still getting it wrong? Part of the answer lies in the type of work that has been done. For many years, cost estimation has been seen in the context of parametric or mathematical models derived from sets of collected data. Examples of such models include COCOMO II, Boehm et al (1), and SLIM, Putnam (1). The premise has been that such models can be applied to different organizations and project types without any loss of accuracy, provided you calibrate, of course. Unfortunately, the term "calibration" is often misunderstood or the process of calibration is misapplied. I will discuss calibration in more detail later.

Another problem with the various cost models is that they have, mainly, been driven by a size estimate in terms of Lines of Code. Now more than one project manager has said to me that they find it as difficult to estimate the Lines of Code to drive a cost model as it is to estimate the effort directly. Despite this, cost models are widely used and many find them beneficial.

Within the industry we are starting to realize that cost estimation is a process in its own right and that optimizing that process depends on more than simply adopting a model or cost estimating tool.

Of course the attraction of the model-based approach is obvious. To derive a cost estimate from a mathematical model is inherently satisfying as it smacks of a scientific approach. Such models are also mechanistic in use and their application is repeatable. These are two of the criterion for the automation of a process, so many people quickly realized that such models could be packaged within software and an industry has grown up around this idea.

I am loath to list a set of cost estimation packages as it may be seen as a recommendation when in truth I only have experience of some half dozen such tools. It is also true to say that there is little to choose between the various tools in terms of accuracy. Also, any such listing would be out of date before this material is published, so frequently do new packages arrive in the market place.

The underlying theme of this chapter is to take a different viewpoint. I claim that cost estimation is a discipline and a process in its own right and I hope to give a coherent view of that process. I firmly believe that the commercially available cost estimation tools have a place within that process and I also hope to show where that place is.

4.2 WHY DO WE ESTIMATE?

I wish to start by stating what, for some people, will be the obvious. I am going to discuss why we in the IT industry need a cost estimation process within our installations and why, from a business viewpoint, that process can be vital to our success and, in some cases, to our survival.

Software development and enhancement centers around a project view of work. That is, around components of work that are managed as discrete elements with a defined end point and, if we are lucky, also a defined start point. The management of these elements is documented in the project plan in the sense that it is this plan that guides management activity. For example, if we are failing to meet the milestones described within the project plan we would hopefully instigate some form of corrective action to identify and deal with, or at least to contain, the problem that was causing the slip.

The foundation of the project plan is the estimate of cost or duration for the work items within the plan. The plan, in another form, may also be used to "bid" for the work in the first place. Based upon an initial statement of requirement from a potential customer, information is prepared that tells the customer what the cost of that work and its duration is likely to be and this can form the basis of a contractual agreement between the customer and the supplier.

So we can already see a process beginning to evolve around the "estimates." An estimate can form the basis of a bid for work and it can also feed into the more detailed planning process, including plans for risk management, when the work is won.

I remember attending a project planning course some years ago that most certainly did not live up to the expectations of some of the audience. Although the course was presented in an exceptionally clear and professional manner it concentrated on the techniques of project planning such as critical path analysis and earned value reporting. As such it did not address the problems that some of the audience wanted resolving which was ways of answering two questions; "What will this work cost me?" and "How long will it take?"

Project planning, as presented, seemed to consist of a applying very clear techniques to a very basic item of data, the estimate. What the individuals who felt somewhat cheated required was, obviously, a course that taught them how to estimate — or was it? As you will see, my belief is that estimation and project planning are so closely related that you cannot totally separate the two and make either work.

Of course, once you use an estimate and a planning process to produce cost and duration figures you are effectively making a promise. "This work will be done for this cost and it will be delivered to you, the customer, at this point in time." If your organization, be it the organization as a whole or an internal IT function, intends to operate a policy of "quality service" then you should, by definition, meet those promises.

This implies that your estimation processes, and I now include planning in that process, had better produce figures that you can meet. You cannot deliver a quality service if your projects arrive late and cost more than originally stated.

This should always be seen as a success factor for any business but it becomes a truly critical success factor if you operate in a fixed-price environment! Such an environment has no mercy on the poor software supplier. If the project you have bid on and won costs more than you thought, then you have no contractual right to cover those costs. Get those estimates wrong and you will suffer the consequences – totally!

4.3 SOME BASIC PRINCIPLES

Given that cost estimation is important from a business viewpoint then we need to consider how effective cost estimation can be obtained. To do this we need to consider, as a first step or starting point, some basic rules or principles of estimation. Most of these are common sense but I make no apology for stating them here as they are so often forgotten or ignored. Most of these principles are also generally accepted within the world of cost estimation. That is to say that if you attend a conference on cost estimation or one of the user groups that exist you will hear the same points made there as I will make here. Notice the use of the word "most" two sentences back. I have taken the liberty of sliding one or two of my own "principles," based on experience, in with the others. Those of you who have been to cost estimation conferences can have fun spotting the interlopers.

The first point I would like to make is more a statement of fact than a principle. It is simply to point out that life is a harsh but fair task mistress. If you give nothing you should expect nothing. So why is it that many of us expect to be able to use some magic approach that enables accurate cost estimation at the very start of the initiation stage when we have practically no information or understanding of the work to be done?

Imagine a similar situation in another environment. "Good morning sir," says the friendly travel agent, "and what can I do for you?"

At this point you should imagine a John Cleese or Peter Sellers character. "Oh hello. I would like to know how much it would cost for a two week, foreign holiday please."

"Of course sir, let me just check the price chart, yes that would be three hundred and twenty two pounds."

"Guaranteed price?" which is simply the equivalent of fixed price.

"Of course sir."

Away goes our customer wondering how this agent can manage to send him to Hong Kong, Thailand, Bali and Australia all for three hundred pounds!

Now we all know that this situation is ludicrous but it happens every day in the IT world. In fact you can almost guarantee that, as you read this, someone, somewhere is making a promise to deliver on a system requirement that they know very little about.

Of course, there is an easy answer to this problem. Organizations that initially commit only to a requirements definition activity, often at fixed price, and who, as the final part of this work, carry out an estimation process that leads to a formal quotation for doing the actual implementation often find that they operate more effectively. It is easy to understand why. Requirements definition can be managed effectively on a fixed price basis because it can be constrained within a set of identified viewpoints. The implementation estimate is then only performed when the requirement is well understood. Is it strange that this leads to more accurate estimates?

There are two points to bear in mind about this approach. First, it does not guarantee success or accuracy. Requirements can change, things can go wrong on the project or you may simply come up with the wrong estimate. The chances of getting it wrong, however, are reduced.

Second, you can find a great deal of resistance to this approach. Interestingly this resistance tends to come from the IT professionals rather than the customers. Customers quite like the idea of getting things when you said they would!

Of course, this approach is not ideal for every environment. In a fixed price, competitive scenario you may have to bid for the whole job. If you are close to the prospective customer though, you could ask them why they were doing it in this way. You may get an interesting reply like, "because that's the way we've always done it, but now you come to mention it..."

The next point concerns the presentation of estimates and again impinges upon the maturity of our industry. An estimate is an estimate, not an actual. Obviously this is true but what does it imply? The implication is that an estimate will contain a degree of error. As such, estimates should not be presented as absolute figures. Now, we all know that when a project manager presents a cost estimate as, for example, twelve engineering months, what is actually being said is that the most likely estimate for this work is twelve engineering months give or take x percent. It is the x that causes the problems.

The project manager may be thinking in terms of give or take three engineering months but the more senior manager, or worse the customer, may be thinking in terms of give or take one month, or no give!

A cornerstone of our industry is communication. We should take our own medicine and start to communicate estimates clearly as bounded intervals. We should also realize that such intervals can be severely skewed. For instance an estimate that is presented as, "this work will cost at least six engineering months effort but the most likely estimate is eight, mind you we can definitely do within fourteen."

"Note that because of various risks associated with this project, consideration of the worst-case scenario produces an estimate of fourteen engineering months" should be perfectly acceptable. I was amazed to find that this kind of bid estimate is even being adopted in one fixed price arena. The idea is that the customer and the supplier communicate more honestly and share benefits if the project is delivered early, while sharing risk and cost if the project is delivered late, up to some predetermined limit. Much as I would like to, I cannot name the organizations involved because the supplier sees this as a major competitive advantage. I wonder why?

Again, you may find resistance to this idea of presenting estimates as bounded intervals but, yet again, it is only a recognition and application of common sense.

The next point concerns what should be estimated. Size and cost are valid candidates for estimation. Duration, which is often estimated, should, in fact, be planned. Size is driven by the functional requirement and cost is driven by the functional requirement, possibly expressed in terms of size, and the development environment including the productivity rate that applies within that environment. Duration is very heavily influenced by the organizational environment. Duration depends on so many factors that are outside of the functional requirement that it can rarely be estimated effectively. This is one of the most common complaints from estimators. Even teams that are very good at estimating cost or size find it difficult to estimate duration — which in many ways makes sense.

If I size a decorating job up as having to paint four walls and I know that I can paint two walls in three hours, effectively an evenings work, am I right to say that the duration of that job will be six hours or two evenings? This is true only if I use the term "duration" to mean cost, as many planners do. To my mind, duration is more to do with calendar time than with cost. For this decorating job, I may plan to do two walls on Monday evening but then I am away from home Tuesday, I am out on Wednesday and there is a film I want to see on Thursday. If I plan to finish the job on Friday then the duration of the decorating project will be five days. This is because I have planned it that way, not because of an estimate. This is certainly how my wife sees it when she, as the customer in this case, finds that she cannot use that room for five days!

The same is true of a software development or enhancement project. I may estimate that it will take nine engineering months, with bounds of course, but the duration it will take depends upon its priority, how I ramp up staff, who I put onto the project and many other factors.

This may be one reason why cost estimation tools tend to produce acceptable cost estimates, after calibration, but tend to perform less effectively for duration estimates.

Next I would like to consider our view of the estimates themselves. How often have you come across a project that is missing milestones or about which there are serious concerns, only to find that they are still working with the very first set of estimates that were made? Estimates should be seen as dynamic entities and they should be reassessed whenever a significant milestone is completed, in other words when we have gained significantly more information or when the requirements we are seeking to satisfy change.

Yet again this is simply the application of common sense. For most projects the estimates that the project team are working to should be reassessed at the end of the design and implementation or coding stages as a minimum. This assumes that you used the approach of estimating development *after you did the requirements definition*. For short term projects of up to six months duration it is probably more practical to assess the estimates at the end of each month because of the degree of phase overlap common on smaller projects, re-estimating as necessary.

Long term projects of more than two years duration, (from initiation to first delivery), will probably have a greater number of milestones identified. Typically these will include the end of requirements specification, high level, intermediate and low level design together with delivery to the test group of major functional items or subsystems. Estimates should be reassessed at each of these points.

These are simply ideas about suitable points in the development lifecycle at which re-estimation makes sense. The main point to understand is that re-estimation is not only acceptable but it should be seen as desirable because you will know a great deal more about the project and the work involved at the end of the design stage than you did at the project's initiation. When you re-estimate will depend upon your own environment and development methodology, but you should ensure that you have clearly defined points within the project plan at which re-estimation will occur.

The other trigger that should cause you to re-estimate is when the requirements change significantly. How big a change is "significant" is a moot point but most project managers know when this type of volatility is going to cause them problems.

If you are using a sizing technique like Function Point Analysis or even estimated Lines of Code then I would suggest, as a rule of thumb, that a ten percent change in the size of the project as a result of requirements change should trigger the re-estimation process.

Incidentally, have you noticed how requirements changes always make the project grow rather than shrink? Remember, one of the aims of re-estimation is to ensure that probable delays are identified and discussed with the customer early so that they do not come as a total shock. At the very least, the project manager should be aware of these potential problems and not have to report a six month delay, one week prior to delivery.

Now what about the estimators themselves? How do they fit in to the estimation process? I will have more to say about this later but, for now, I would like to make two points. First, the techniques that are made available to estimators, such as cost models, are there to assist the estimator. They do not remove the responsibility for the estimates from the estimator.

Second, estimators should use the techniques in a sensible way. If two or more techniques are applicable at a given point in the development lifecycle then two or more techniques should be used. There is a very simple reason for this. Estimation is always going to be something of an art and, at the end of the day, it relies upon the judgment of one or more individuals. To assist in this judgmental activity the maximum amount of information should be made available. As each technique could provide more information (or at least a different view of the same information), it makes sense to use as many techniques as is practical. At the very least, an estimator should not rely upon one technique to produce an estimate.

You should also be aware of an interesting phenomena in the area we are discussing. When it comes to making an estimate people tend to produce optimistic predictions. I am tempted to say that people always underestimate but there is one case where this is not true, namely when estimating productivity. Of course, this does not apply only to software projects.

My wife has the endearing habit of always expecting me to finish a DIY job in half the time I estimate it will take, and I always underestimate anyway, at least as far as DIY is concerned!

You also come across this when you ask people how long it will take to get from one place to another. An ex-colleague of mine, when asked how long it would take him to get from his house to an airport, quoted a time that would require a mean speed of one hundred and fifty five miles an hour. But as he said, he was not going to be traveling during the rush hour! Another ex- colleague arranged to meet me at the end of a meeting that "...would take no more than two hours so I will see you at 2pm." At four thirty I was still waiting for him to finish that meeting. And I think he put his finger on it when he did finally emerge, "yes I remember now," he said, "we only ever actually finished at two o'clock on one occasion."

People tend to remember good times or successes and try to ignore memories of failures or problems. This is why, when you ask someone to estimate, say, the cost of a job they will give you an answer based on the best case scenario. The organization that asks four project managers for an estimate then doubles or triples the average result would probably be most likely to survive in a fixed price environment! It is worth remembering that this phenomena exists next time you have to accept or produce an estimate.

4.4   OLD DATA — LOOK IN THE BIN

Now if all of this is good advice and you take it on board should you expect to see an improvement in estimation effectiveness? Could you prove it?

You may remember earlier that I said there is at least a twenty-year-plus history of software development in some organizations. You would expect to be able to get hold of some data from these organizations. Think how likely it would be to find a similar project to the one you have to estimate today if you had twenty years worth of data to fall back on. You will be lucky if that data is available. Well, okay, ten years worth would be good enough; in fact five years worth would probably be better as it is probably closer to what we do today.

You may like to go into a project team and ask them if they have data, even just estimation data, from their last project. If the answer is yes then you are in luck! Many teams do not even keep the past estimates for their current projects.

Keeping data about itself and its work is not something the IT industry does well, which is ironic when you consider what "IT" stands for. If you wish to do something practical then you should insist that your projects start to keep some basic data about themselves. It does not have to be a sophisticated or complete system of measurement. Raw data such as size of project, estimated cost, planned duration and the updates to these figures together with the actuals can be a good starting point. Get really clever by asking the project manager to summarize his or her feelings about the project. What made this one different from other projects that the manager had been involved in? Keep this summary short, no more than one page, and you have a very useful source of information even if it is somewhat subjective.

To summarize, there are certain basic principles that appear to apply to the estimation process no matter what environment you consider. These principles are:

The first estimate is likely to be an underestimate. Act accordingly.

Estimates are estimates, so use bounds and not absolutes.

Cost is estimated, duration is planned.

Estimates are dynamic; re-estimate when milestones are completed and additional information becomes available or when the requirements change.

The best estimation technique is to use an expert, if you can find one.

The estimate is the responsibility of the estimator, not the tools or techniques.

Keep previous estimates.

4.5 MODELS AND TOOLS REVISITED

To apply a set of principles, which operate at the conceptual level, you have to develop an operational process model and that should be founded upon an logical view of the process. This is a fancy way of saying that we start with a set of ideas, the principles; we use these to put together an approach; and, we build a set of mechanisms that we can use on a day-to-day basis within that approach.

There are basically two strategies for cost estimation that are generally seen as competitive. Fortunately, more and more people are realizing that the two strategies can work harmoniously within a cost estimation process. The two strategies can be termed *Model Based* and *Technique Based*.

Looking first at the model based approach we find a profusion of models to choose from and we may be forgiven for asking "where did they all come from?" or perhaps, "why are there so many?"

Models are really a scientific answer to the problem of cost estimation and they appeal to many individuals within the IT industry. The size of the potential market is one reason why there are so many models, basically everyone would like a chunk of what is going. It is also true that most, if not all, of the models are really nothing more than a variation on a theme. So how does a model come about? There are two approaches that you can adopt, both well recognized and accepted within the world of mathematical modeling which is what we are really talking about.

The first approach goes something like this: First go and collect a lot of data about a lot of projects. Next, investigate the relationships between input and output variables, for example size and complexity as inputs, cost and duration as outputs, and use these relationships to construct a model. Finally, validate your model on a different set of data by comparing actuals to the model predictions.

The second approach is only slightly different: First produce a hypothesis that you believe models the reality. This will usually be in the form of an input/output model. Next apply your model to a data set to test the hypothesis it contains. Modify the model in the light of these experimental results. Finally, validate your revised model on a different set of data, again comparing actuals to predictions. That final validation step is often missed out which is one reason why these models need such careful calibration.

What you do when you have your model then depends upon your own personality and preferences. Some people take the very admirable step of placing their models in the public domain. The best known of these are Barry Boehm, (COCOMO II), Boehm et al (1) and Larry Putnam, (SLIM), Putnam (1). Of course, once a model is in the public domain then it becomes fair game for everyone to adopt, package or shoot down in flames.

Another approach is to package the model yourself and to then present it as a black box solution to the cost estimation problem. I would say the best known individual in this category is Capers Jones, (CHECKPOINT, US or CHECKMARK, UK). Now this really irritates some people but I must admit that I can see the commercial sense of this approach. After all, the individuals who do go public come in for a great deal of criticism — sometimes unjustified, sometimes justified.

Which leads me to an interesting point. Within Software Metrics there are a number of gurus, some of whom are best known for their work in the cost modeling area, and I have heard most of them speak at some time. One thing has impressed me. They are fanatical only about improving processes that they see as needing improvement. They are not fanatical about their own particular ideas, ideas that they have very often moved on from anyway. Howard Rubin, Barry Boehm, Putnam and Jones and the others in their league all recognize that they have only provided partial solutions and they actively welcome constructive criticism that can be used to enhance their own original ideas. It is in this direction that we should be focusing our activities and energy rather than the rather pointless arguments about whose model is best, arguments that the developers of the models studiously refrain from.

Having made my plea for sanity I think we should get back to the topic and think about the basic construction of these models.

Essentially the models apply mathematical operations such as multiplication by a constant, to an estimated size, usually in terms of Lines of Code although some models derived from and driven by size in terms of Function Point scores are available. Note that many of the packages that claim to be driven by Function Point scores are in fact only converting those scores to Lines of Code values using in built tables.

I would like to talk a little bit more about the COCOMO cost estimation model as I find this to be one of the most widely used. In my opinion, COCOMO is also a very typical cost estimation model but in some aspects is also one of the more sophisticated.

In the original model, there were three levels but I would like to consider the basic model. This takes the form of a formula:

$$Effort = a * Size \wedge b$$

where Size takes the form of *thousands of delivered source instructions* or KDSI with *a* and *b* as constants. COCOMO being quite sophisticated recognizes three types of development environments and provides different variations of the basic model for each environment. The *Organic Environment* is essentially that of a small scale, non-bureaucratic project and for this environment the model takes the form:

$$Effort = 2.4 * Size \wedge 1.05$$

The *Embedded Environment* is the opposite of the Organic in that it relates to a very bureaucratic, tightly controlled and formal organization. For this environment the model takes the form:

$$Effort = 3.6 * Size \wedge 1.2$$

The so called *Semi-Detached Environment* is one that falls between the two extremes and for this the model takes the form:

$$Effort = 3.0 * Size \wedge 1.12$$

Various other elements of the model can then be used to modify the basic result. These elements are often termed "cost drivers." For further information the reader is referred to Boehm et al (1).

I make no apology for referring back to what is, by today's standards, an old model, defined some years ago by Boehm, Boehm (1) and further developed since then. Why do I not apologize? Simply, do you or your organization have better today? For most readers the answer will be "no."

There is a great deal of debate currently about the validity and usefulness of the cost drivers used to modify the basic formulae, which can range from things like the experience of the project team to the layout of the office. There are two easily identified camps that can be identified with respect to cost drivers. One feels that the basic set of cost drivers that come with most models are insufficient; the other believes that there are too many cost drivers being considered. Personally I feel more affinity for the second view and this seems to be borne out by research that has been done as part of the ESPRIT MERMAID project, Kitchenham (1). The results of this research which is based upon a statistical analysis of both newly collected data from a number of sources and the data sets originally used by the developers of some of the better known cost models indicates that the drivers are not orthogonal. In simple terms, the same thing is being addressed by more than one driver. When you use the drivers to adjust the base estimate you are effectively double-counting or perhaps canceling out effects depending upon how you answer specific questions.

It is also interesting to note that locally developed cost models, that is models developed from data within a single environment or installation, tend to have no more than five or six adjusting drivers, and these are often different to the drivers provided by the publicly or commercially available models, which I will call "generalized cost models."

This may indicate why there is a group that seems to be looking for more drivers. My feeling is that there is a level of dissatisfaction with the drivers already identified within the generalized models. This dissatisfaction exists because users feel that other drivers are needed for their sites or application environments. It is not so much that more drivers are needed it is that different drivers are needed.

4.6   CALIBRATION

If there is debate about the number of cost drivers that are required within a cost model there is one thing that just about everyone agrees about as far as generalized cost models are concerned. They need to be "calibrated."

Checking my dictionary again I find that to calibrate means, *"to fix or correct the scale."* How is this done for a cost model? Well, calibration is more than simply redefining the questions that a package implementation of a cost model asks you so that the questions have meaning to your site. This is necessary because, while people tend to underestimate, they do tend to present worst-case scenarios when asked certain types of question. Ask a team leader how complex his or her application is and I guarantee that the answer will be "very complex," even if it is the most simple of batch processes.

So what is meant, in the practical sense, by this term "calibration?" I think that I can best illustrate the answer by example. Part of the work that I do includes assisting with the evaluation, and often the introduction, of generalized cost models. The evaluation goes something like this: For a number of projects that have been completed, data is put through the cost model and the predicted effort, and often the predicted duration, is recorded. The actuals are also obtained from historical data held by the installation. Obviously, if the organization does not record effort data or the start and end dates of projects then I have a problem with this approach, but such an organization may not be ready to use generalized cost models as they cannot calibrate them. An alternative that is sometimes viable within an enhancement environment is to use one project, across perhaps a six month period as the calibration vehicle.

The next step is to compare the predicted values with the actuals, at which point you usually find glaring discrepancies. It is at this point that people fling their hands up in horror and prepare to throw in the towel, but why? Do you really expect a model that was derived from a specific set of data in specific installation to be immediately applicable to your installation? Of course not.

Some tools salesmen will also throw their hands up in horror and then patiently explain that it is your "actuals" that are inaccurate, not the predictions. All I can say to this is that, time and time again, I have found locally collected cost data to be perfectly acceptable — not accurate to decimal places, but accurate enough. In fact, one piece of research that I was involved in, albeit to a limited extent, found that cost data extracted from a particular time recording mechanism on a specific site was very inaccurate, but it was consistently inaccurate. Think about that.

Because, of course, that is the key thing to look for when you compare predictions to actuals. You should expect to see inaccuracy but you should hope for consistent inaccuracy. For instance, one such evaluation found that two of the commonly used cost models were consistently underestimating effort by 40%, give or take a percent or two either way. Interestingly enough, I found that one of the models, when used within a different organization, was overestimating effort by about 80%, consistently. That certainly illustrates the need for calibration!

But what do you do if you find that there is not even consistent inaccuracy? Faced with that situation on one occasion I very nearly did throw in the towel until a consultant with one of the companies that sold the tool we were evaluating suggested that we look at the hot buttons, the drivers that really affected the results significantly. Which at least shows that there is good in some of these people!

Well, we went further than that, we reduced the parameters supplied to the tool to size together with the type of work being done in terms of it being new development or enhancement. The one other parameter we included was the type of system in terms of it being commercial, telecommunications, systems software, etc. What did we find? The inaccuracy was still there but now it was consistent inaccuracy, which again may illustrate that cost drivers should be treated with extreme caution.

There are three further points to make about these calibration exercises. First, I have found that calibrating for effort or cost predictions takes a lot less data than calibrating for duration. This is one reason why I feel that duration should be planned rather than estimated.

Second, while most if not all cost estimation tools will break the overall estimate down into the cost associated with specific phases of the project, I am still wary about using this. Again, you need a significant amount of data to calibrate these to your environment and I believe that few organizations are able to do any more than treat these as more than ballpark figures. Anyway, most organizations would be quite happy if they could get accurate project estimates let alone, for example, accurate design phase estimates!

Third, these types of calibration exercise do tend to use actual size figures as the input to the models. If you do have estimates available you could try running the models with that data but you may find problems in variability of size estimate accuracy. If you were to simply introduce the tools or models and expect that to solve your estimation problems then you may be in for a shock. I hope to show that there is a place for these types of tools but only as part of an overall estimating strategy or process. That strategy must address the question of estimating project size which is then used as input to the models.

A final point about calibration. If you are operating within an environment that develops products over a long period of time, and by that I mean about five years from initiation to first delivery, then you will have a problem with calibration. For all sorts of reasons, you will probably not have historical data available and you, obviously, cannot calibrate in real-time the way, say, a group producing new builds every three months can. The best you can probably hope for from generalized cost models is to use them as a stimulus for practical and sensible discussion. The great value of cost drivers, and one case where "the more, the merrier" principle applies, is that they are excellent vehicles for getting project managers to think about the things that can effect the cost and duration of their projects.

4.7 TECHNIQUES FOR ESTIMATION

Having discussed the model-based approach to cost estimation we should now consider a different and, I believe, complementary approach. I call this approach *Technique Based* and think of it as "People-Oriented." You will see, when I discuss specific techniques in the context of the estimation process, that some elements of the model based approach also creeps in. The difference is that here we are really considering estimation as a people driven activity, if you want as a slightly technical art, rather than as a formal, repeatable, scientifically based activity.

The points to note about the people-oriented approach is that they take more time than simply cranking parameters through a model and that the techniques used often appear to be very simplistic, almost trivial. The most important point to note is that they also work.

The people-oriented approach and the techniques it encompasses have two main aims. First, they make estimators think about what they are doing and introduce some degree of discipline to the estimation activity. Second, they encourage communication by encouraging estimators to seek assistance from other people rather than leaving them to estimate in isolation.

Which is all I have to say about this approach to estimation just now. As you will see, it is this approach that forms the backbone of the estimation process template which is where all this talk is leading us.

Now many pundits claim that it can take ten, fifteen or twenty years for an organization to develop such models because it takes that long to get sufficient data. Experience within a few organizations suggests that this is not so. One retail organization, JC Penney, IFPUG(1), in the US took three years to develop a cost estimation model, to validate that model and to go public with the statement, supported by statistical data, that it gave them as accurate a set of predictions as those claimed by the leading generalized cost models.

Another organization, again in the US, claimed in passing at another IFPUG conference that their local cost estimation model which included factors for requirements growth, gave them an accuracy of plus or minus five percent, that's +/- 5%, against actuals for predictions made at the end of requirements specification. It only took them five years to get this good!

Now what was common to those models? They were local, they both used Function Point Analysis as the size parameter and they both had a limited set of cost drivers. The other thing that they share is that they worked! Oh, they also took a lot less than ten years to develop! The other thing that these two local models shared is that they both fitted into an estimation strategy that went beyond the models.

4.8   A STRATEGIC TEMPLATE FOR COST ESTIMATION

Estimation is a process. To control estimation, to improve its effectiveness within our own organization we must stop treating it as a black box activity and remove the air of formula-driven magic so often promoted by IT staff. Do this and the process can be defined, managed, modified and optimized.

I will now present a template definition of that process which I hope can be tailored to your organization. This will give you the process definition and you can then get on with managing that process.

We start with an overview of the estimation process. If you imagine the development process as a V model with requirements definition, high- and low-level design as the components of the left leg of that V, coding or implementation as the apex and the various testing activities, unit, sub-system or link and system testing forming the right hand leg you may ask where the estimation activities fit. I suggest that you think of a second V model paralleling the development V. The components of the second V includes work consolidation to form the basic project, estimation at different stages of development, project control and project, rather than technical, reviews. This chapter concentrates upon the estimation activities.

You can think of the various techniques used to help estimators as "bricks" out of which we build the estimating process. You can select from those presented here and from the various commercial tools to form your own organizational estimating strategy. All of the techniques mentioned here are described in other technical books that deal with the subject. If you can still find a copy, one of the best collections of such descriptions can be found in the appendices of the "Software Reliability Handbook," Rook (1). This is possibly one of the best contributions to our understanding of metrics, albeit that the author is sadly no longer with us.

In fact, so much has been written about estimating techniques that I do not intend to repeat the very detailed technical discussions here, if you are interested then I suggest you use the sources quoted in the bibliography and form your own opinion. Here you will only find a brief discussion of technical aspects.

The estimation process must interact with its environment and you may wonder if this template can apply to both enhancement projects and to new development work. I will state quite categorically that the template does apply to both environments. Corrective maintenance, that is fixing bugs in the current release of the a system, is better considered as support. This type of work needs to be managed and that management depends upon the collection of relevant management statistics that will allow you to estimate the likely support costs for a given release for your own environment. However, it is not feasible to produce estimates from some formal mechanism when you have a red priority defect that has to be fixed ASAP!

The most important impact that the environment has is that things tend to be easier in a maintenance environment where more than one release is made during a financial year. The reason is simply that you have data available to you on a regular basis and this data can be used to manage and assess your estimation process.

Given that estimation is a process that involves people, then we should consider the different roles that those people can play. This brings us to an interesting point: there is considerable debate as to whether estimation should be the responsibility of individual project managers or of a centralized estimating group. The arguments go something like this:

- If my IT group is regularly required to produce estimates then I am tying up valuable project resources by diverting them onto this type of work, which would seem to suggest that we could improve effectiveness by establishing a centralized function that took on the responsibility for estimate production. Furthermore, a group of individuals whose main role was to make estimates should quickly develop expertise in that work. Essentially, this approach would produce an experience center.

- The counter argument is that people do not react well to imposed estimates whether they come from management or from an estimating group. In fact, presenting a project manager with an estimate and then expecting him or her to deliver against that estimate is almost certainly going to lead to projects that do not deliver on time and in budget! Of course, if every project manager is going to be expected to take responsibility for estimation, then this does increase the scale and complexity of the job if you try to improve your own organizational estimation process.

So, what is the answer if, as it appears, both approaches have positive and negative aspects? A wise man once said that, when placed on the twin horns of a dilemma, you should seek the third horn. In other words, there are more than two ways to skin a cat!

I believe that ownership of the estimates by the project manager is vital and I suggest that the primary estimator be the project manager. The primary estimator is the person who has the final say over which estimate is submitted to the estimate recipient. Assuming that the estimate is accepted, the project manager cannot then claim that the estimate was imposed on him. One thing that your own organization will have to do is define the level of project or projects for which there will be a primary estimator.

The primary estimator should not be expected to do the work in isolation. Your organization should define the role of assistant estimator. Assistant estimators help the primary estimator by providing additional views of the project, by providing different levels and types of experience and by providing sounding boards against which the primary estimator can bounce ideas of cost and duration.

Additionally you should, in my opinion, establish an estimation support group. This group can develop into the center of experience mentioned earlier, the main difference is that they act in a consultative role rather than in a prescriptive role and that their position in respect of the primary estimator is clearly defined. They also have another role. In most organizations the estimation process can be classified as "ad hoc." This is a polite way of saying chaotic! Changing this situation so that the organization boasts a defined, managed and optimizing estimation process will not happen overnight and somebody must facilitate this evolution. The estimation support group can provide training, can cross check estimates from managers to assess their feasibility and can monitor the process to identify improvements and areas that need improving.

While such a group represents an additional overhead it must be realized that change does not happen automatically or without cost. To rephrase a common quotation from the Quality guru Crosby, Quality is free – eventually!

The final role that needs to be defined is that of the estimate recipient. This can be a real customer, especially in a bid situation, a planner, marketing or a manager. I often remember a tale told to me by a technical director of his project manager days. He went in with an estimate which was then cut by his boss. Needless to say, the project managers estimate proved to be much more accurate even though, he assured me, he tried to do the job as quickly as possible.

I often wondered how he treated his project managers now that the shoe was on the other foot. Which raises an important question, what happens when the estimate recipient questions that estimate?

In reality this situation will be constantly present and the estimation process must identify and facilitate a sub-process of negotiation and reconciliation. Obviously personalities will have an impact on this activity but I feel that it is safe to assume that most individuals involved in project management, and hence in the estimation process, are actively committed to making sure that a project succeeds. There should be a formal, minuted meeting between the primary estimator and the estimate recipient which is structured around the concept of the project management triangle.

This model simply states that there are three, high level parameters that affect projects; duration, cost and content. Only two of these parameters can be fixed. For example, if I have to decorate a house then the content may appear to be fixed. I can only do the work faster if I load resources onto the job increasing cost, in other words if I fix content then duration and cost trade off. But of course the content, even in this job is not necessarily fixed. I may reduce content by specifying one coat of paint instead of two and in this way I may work to a fixed duration by trading off content and cost.

Such a discussion assumes that my estimates of cost, content and duration are true and in software engineering projects it is impossible to be sure of this. What I can do is increase my confidence in those estimates by recording past performance and, most importantly, by recording the assumptions that lie behind my estimates. It is much easier to discuss, or argue, about assumptions than about estimates because my ownership of the assumptions is less solid.

Of course, if a manager insists that my estimate be reduced then he should expect to have to justify that reduction by recording and stating the underlying assumptions that apply. This acceptance of responsibility should form part of your estimating procedures or strategy and should be accepted and endorsed by your organization. Implementing such a strategy is not easy and this is one area where the estimation support group can help because they should be responsible for auditing the process and its application. The manager who insists that an estimate be reduced records the reasons why and the support group ensures that this is done.

The worst-case scenario where a project manager has to accept estimates imposed from above that are lower than those he or she believes apply needs careful management. What has happened is that a risk has been associated with the project and two things should occur. The project manager should be allowed to record the fact that the estimates are imposed and the resulting project should receive management attention to a greater extent than normal during the whole of its life or until the risk is resolved through re-estimation.

If your organization has a central project control office then this risk management action should be their responsibility. But you may be in for a pleasant surprise. It does seem that when estimation processes are defined along the lines described so far, the perception of imposition concerning estimates reduces because the project manager will be more involved in the estimation process than may otherwise happen. Why is this? It may be that the fact that everyone is now working within a defined procedure that, in part at least, de-mystifies the estimation process and that sets out clear responsibilities with lines of communication. This results in clearer understanding and a depersonalization of that process and, hence, a reduction in conflict. After all, none of us want a project to fail but sometimes we don't talk about the problems.

Which is fine in theory but what about the estimation template? Let us start with some of the possible building bricks that we can use, the estimating techniques I have mentioned. What follows is a description of those techniques as I have helped implement them in more than one organization.

I will start with something called the *Modified Delphi Technique*. This is based on the Wideband Delphi Technique that is fully described in "Software Engineering Economics" by Barry Boehm and it is nothing more that a slightly formalized approach to using expert opinion.

4.9   MODIFIED DELPHI TECHNIQUE

The Modified Delphi technique is a way of eliciting and reconciling the opinions of a group of individuals. It can be used, as can all of these techniques except the use of models, to derive cost or size estimates. Because it relies on opinion it can be used at any time during the development lifecycle, but I feel it is best used from initiation to the end of high level design.

The first thing the primary estimator should do is form an estimating group consisting of themselves and at least two other assistant estimators. One individual should be nominated as the Coordinator. In reality, these groups usually exist permanently within product groups and are activated as necessary. In this way they act as good training grounds for estimators. The group should not exceed seven individuals even for large projects as larger groups often become unmanageable.

Next, each group member is given access to any material about the new project, typically this will be a customer request document or a requirements specification.

They should be given sufficient time to study this material bearing in mind their other work and, typically, we are talking about a week of elapsed time. They should also be notified of a date when a reconciliation meeting will be held.

Each group member makes their estimate and submits these to the Coordinator at least two days before the reconciliation meeting. The Coordinator calculates the median or mid-point of the estimates received and returns this value to the estimator together with his or her own estimate. Optionally, the estimator can submit a revised estimate to the Coordinator.

The reconciliation meeting is held and starts with each estimator being made aware of the latest median value. The purpose of this meeting is to reach a consensus regarding the estimate value. The ownership of particular estimates should remain confidential during the meeting unless someone owns up but other than using this confidentiality to avoid embarrassing particular individuals, open discussion should be encouraged. If the Coordinator feels that new estimates should be made because an important point has been agreed, for example everyone is now convinced that it is a more complex system than they originally thought, then this is perfectly acceptable.

A consensus level should be pre-specified, for example you could state that consensus has been reached when the extreme estimates are no more than thirty percent either side of the median if this was a session at the initiation stage of a fairly large project.

The value of the Delphi approach is that it involves more than one individual and it encourages discussion. It also tends to produce more accurate estimates than most organizations enjoy today.

4.10   BOZOKI'S RANKING TECHNIQUE AND PERT

The next technique has been formed by taking elements of Bozoki's ranking technique and concepts from Putnam's Program Estimating and Reporting Tool, PERT. It can be combined with a Delphi session or can be done by individual estimators. It applies once functional entities of the system have been identified so it should be used during high-level and intermediate design stages. You should also have data from earlier projects relating to at least two similar functional entities that are similar in size and development environment. Do not use more than seven of these reference points or it becomes confusing.

The first thing to do is rank the *functional entities*, FE's, that is discrete and identified system components such as programs, for the new project in respect of those of the known or *reference entities*, RE. For example, my first FE may be smaller than one of the RE's but larger than the second. My second FE may fall into the same category but be larger than the first FE.

What I am doing through this technique is reducing the scope of the problem. Rather than having to think about where an entity fits in terms of the whole project or system I am now relating it to the known reference points and to where I have placed my other FE's.

Now expert opinion is used to assign three estimates to each of my functional entities. These estimates are a smallest, a most likely and a largest estimate. Note that these are seldom distributed evenly about the most likely estimate. For instance, I may say that for one of the entities, if all goes really well and we face no problems, the minimum cost is going to be three engineering months. However, I know what things are like on most projects and, being honest, it will probably take us four engineering months. But, if things really hit the fan and that sneaking suspicion I have about the message switching function turns out to be right, then this component could take us eight engineering months. Hang on, if I am right then the only person who has experience of that is Jane and she is on leave for a month when we will need her so make that nine engineering months because she will need time to get back into it! Notice the skew — when things go wrong, they *really* go wrong.

Once you have your three estimates you draw them together by multiplying the most likely by four, adding the smallest and largest and then dividing the total by six. To get the total cost or size for the whole system you add the results for each of the individual entities.

Let us work through a very simplistic example of this technique. Let us assume that I have an extremely simple development project that consists of two functional entities, F1 and F2. Further, assume that I have data from a previous project of a similar type relating to two functional entities that have been delivered, R1 and R2. The data for these is given below:

ENTITY	COST
R1	50 person days
R2	100 person days

I now consider the work I have to do in terms of the reference entities. Let us say that in my opinion, F2 is a bigger component than R2 and that F1 is bigger than R1 but smaller than R2. So ranking gives me:

```
R1

F1

R2

F2
```

In this case the ranking exercise is trivial as we are dealing with so few components but in real life projects of many units it is a worthwhile exercise.

The next step is to produce estimates for the two components that have to be developed. To do this I may use Delphi or analogy or simply expert opinion. The key is to provide the three types of estimates already mentioned, a Minimum, Most Likely and Maximum estimate.

So:

	Min	ML	Max
F1	40	60	90
F2	100	140	200

Notice that the ML estimate does not necessarily fall half way between the Min and Max estimates.

To calculate the estimates for F1 and F2, I apply the formula:

$$Estimate(Fn) = (Min(Fn) + ML(Fn)*4 + Max(Fn))/6$$

So:

$$Estimate(F1) = (40 + 60*4 + 90)/6 = 62$$

$$Estimate(F2) = (100 + 140*4 + 200)/6 = 143$$

$$Estimate(Total\ Cost) = 62 + 143 = 205$$

One word of warning: you should watch out for the accumulation of rounding errors on projects of many functional entities. I suggest you work to four decimal places and then round your final answer to whole days, or months for very large projects.

There are other statistical techniques that you can apply but most practitioners are wary of this as the basis for the whole thing is still subjective opinion and you can convince yourself of "certainties" that, in reality, are built on very weak foundations.

The next technique I suggest is one of my favorites because it is less dependent on personnel opinion and it can be applied and improved very quickly. It depends on historical data but one project gives you enough to start with. It is also very conceptually simple. This is always a good point.

4.11 "BOTTOM UP" ESTIMATING OR FUNCTIONAL DECOMPOSITION

Often known as "bottom up" estimating or functional decomposition, it is applied during intermediate and low level design. This is quite late in the development lifecycle but given the high cost of testing, estimation is still necessary at these points.

You start with low level components identified Looking to historical data you determine the average effort or size associated with these components, note average indicates mean, median or mode whichever is most suitable for the distribution, and all you do is multiply total project components by the average. To illustrate this with a simple example, if we have a new development that is adding 50 new low-level components and we know that it takes on average 10 person days to develop a "typical" component then our estimate would be 10 * 50 = 500 person-days. So simple as to be trivial — but there is power in simplicity.

Looking at your historical data you can also use standard deviations or percentiles to associate risk, in other words bounds, to your estimates.

As you get more historical data you can get more sophisticated by classifying components by size or even by functional type, for example by looking at average costs for input, output and processing functions. You could get really smart by looking for an association between high level designs and the number of low level components but it must be said that, to date, this has rarely been done.

This would involve analysis of historical data to determine what elements of a high level design were related to the number of low level components finally produced as the implementation of that high level design.

4.12   ESTIMATION BY ANALOGY

The last two techniques I want to identify as potential candidates for a cost estimation strategy can be applied at any time during the development lifecycle. The first is estimation by analogy.

If you ask a group of software developers how they estimate, this will be the technique most will claim to use, except the honest ones who usually answer by sticking a wet finger in the air. Estimation by analogy is a simple approach that asks you to look at your project in terms of what it is expected to deliver, what is the function of the product, and how you expect to achieve that, not in design terms but in terms of the development environment. Then you simply find a project that has already been done that is similar to yours and you use data from the completed project to help you estimate for yours.

For most organizations it is reasonably easy to find a project that was similar in terms of functionality. It is also very easy to forget about the soft factors or the development environment. It is no good finding a perfect functional match where the completed project was done using a top flight team using tried and tested techniques and then expecting to deliver in the same time and at the same cost using a team consisting of mainly new graduates using tools never employed before.

Now while these concepts are simple there is one major sticking point as far as estimation by analogy is concerned. The technique depends upon having an accessible history file of projects. But, most organizations, as I have said earlier, fail to keep much data on current projects, let alone past work. Given this situation you should concentrate on establishing that history file. It does not need to be complex. Record data such as size, actual effort, actual duration, type of project through a simple classification scheme, team size and composition. You can add other elements to your records such as effort per phase, but remember, it is better to get something simple going than to have a detailed procedure that is never used.

Also remember that you will seldom find a perfect match for your new project so again expert opinion is needed to guide judgment. In a maintenance environment where new releases occur regularly, building up a usable history file does not take long.

The final component I wish to discuss are the generalized cost models and the associated tools that were discussed earlier. The tools can be used at any time during the development lifecycle provided that you have a size estimate with which to drive them. This estimate can come from any of the other techniques described so far and, in this way, the tools can provide a good confidence check provided that they have been correctly calibrated.

The other great benefit that can come from using these types of tool is that they can get project managers thinking about the different factors that can affect projects. One organization, a large UK clearing bank, has integrated an estimation tool with Delphi sessions using the tool to stimulate discussion with interesting and beneficial results.

Figure 4.1 shows how the various techniques fit against a typical development lifecycle. There is overlap and it is quite deliberate as you will realize from our earlier discussions regarding the basic principles of estimation.

So, we have a variety of bricks but we really need to put them firmly within a template by considering the channels of communication between bricks and the development lifecycle and the management of that lifecycle. *Figure 4.1* presents one such view and is offered as an estimation template that could be tailored to your organization.

Figure 4.1   Estimation Template

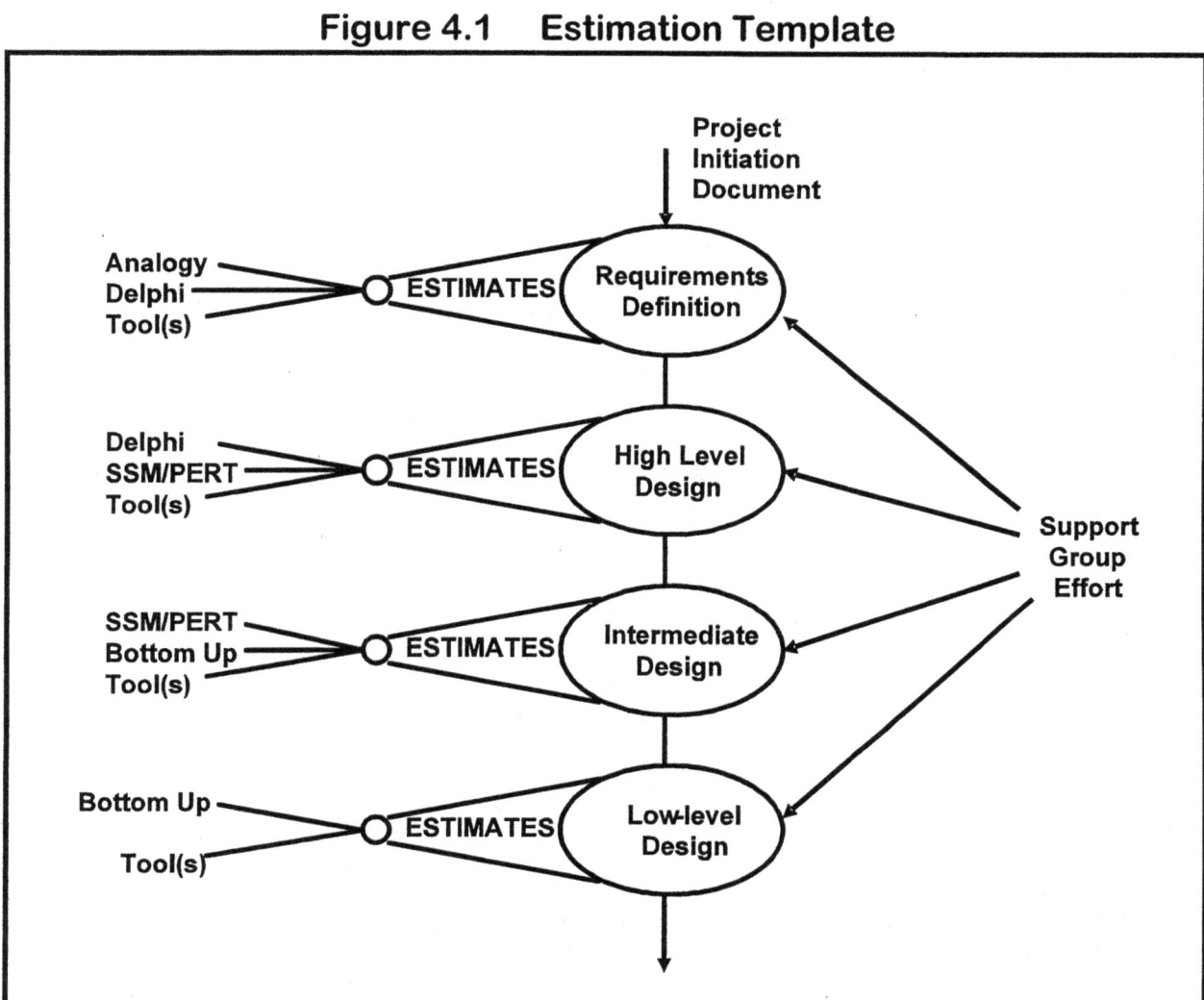

This diagram shows a set of bricks or estimating techniques associated with certain lifecycle phases, for just the "development" arm of the V but not for testing, together with a link from the project manager to the estimation support group. Notice in the expansion of the estimation support group's role in *Figure 4.2*, there is a commitment to training, checking and to the development of local models. This model is presented as a strategy for a typical software engineering organization of today, and will apply, I suspect, for some years. It is not presented as the final solution. We will only have fully solved the estimation process when organizations tie effective estimation to the project management process. This will take effort and time but will provide rich dividends in terms of customer satisfaction.

Figure 4.2   Role of the Support Group

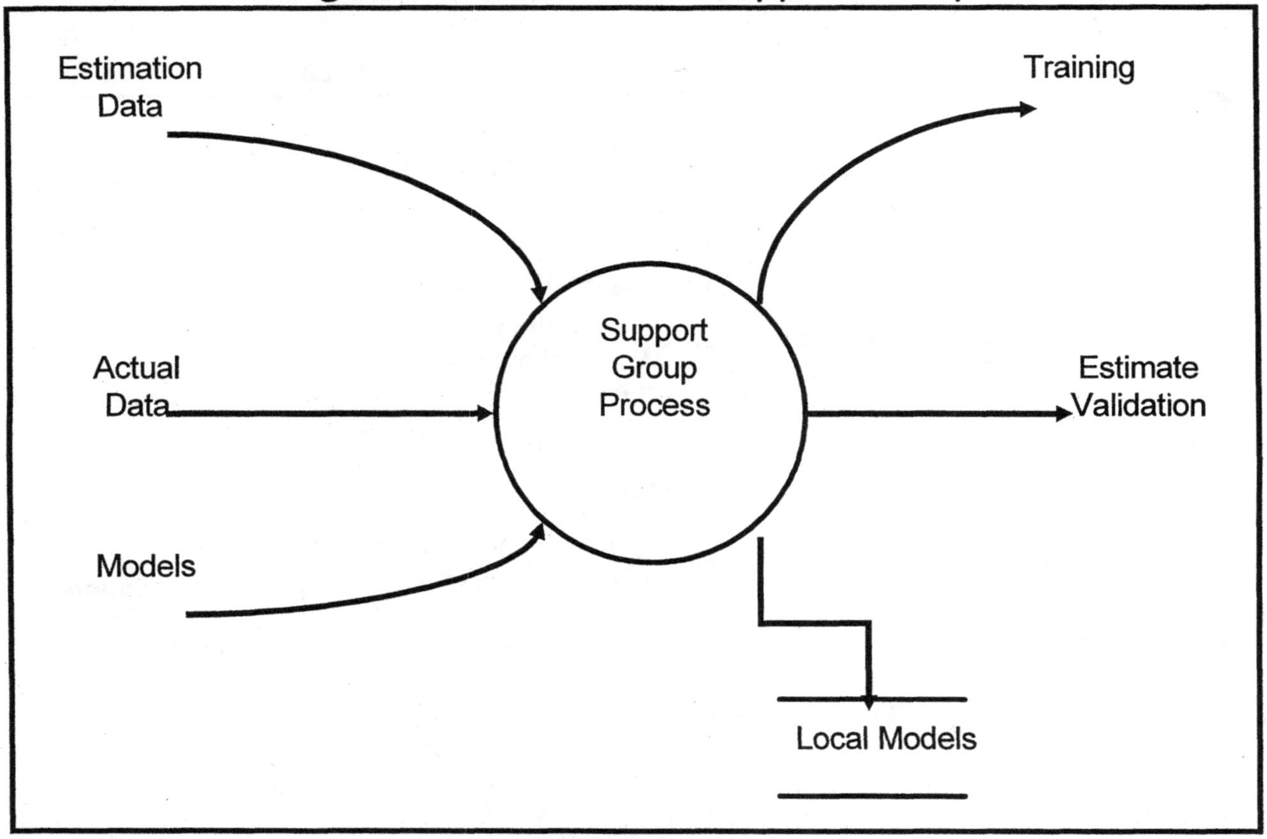

Figure 4.3 shows a typical process diagram of a first-stage estimation process as implemented in a number of organizations. Notice the use of Function Point Analysis to size individual work requests and the final project. This two-stage sizing is used because economies of scale can sometimes be realized at the project level. FPA is also used to drive the negotiation with the customer, sometimes in conjunction with cost estimates against individual work requests.

Finally, there is one element of estimation that has not been discussed: how do we monitor the effectiveness of the process? In essence this is simply a comparison of estimates made at specific lifecycle points to actual results within projects. In practice this data needs to be collected, analyzed and presented to management to demonstrate an improvement over time. Again, this will not happen automatically and this responsibility should fall to the estimation support group from the very start.

Figure 4.3   Typical Process Diagram

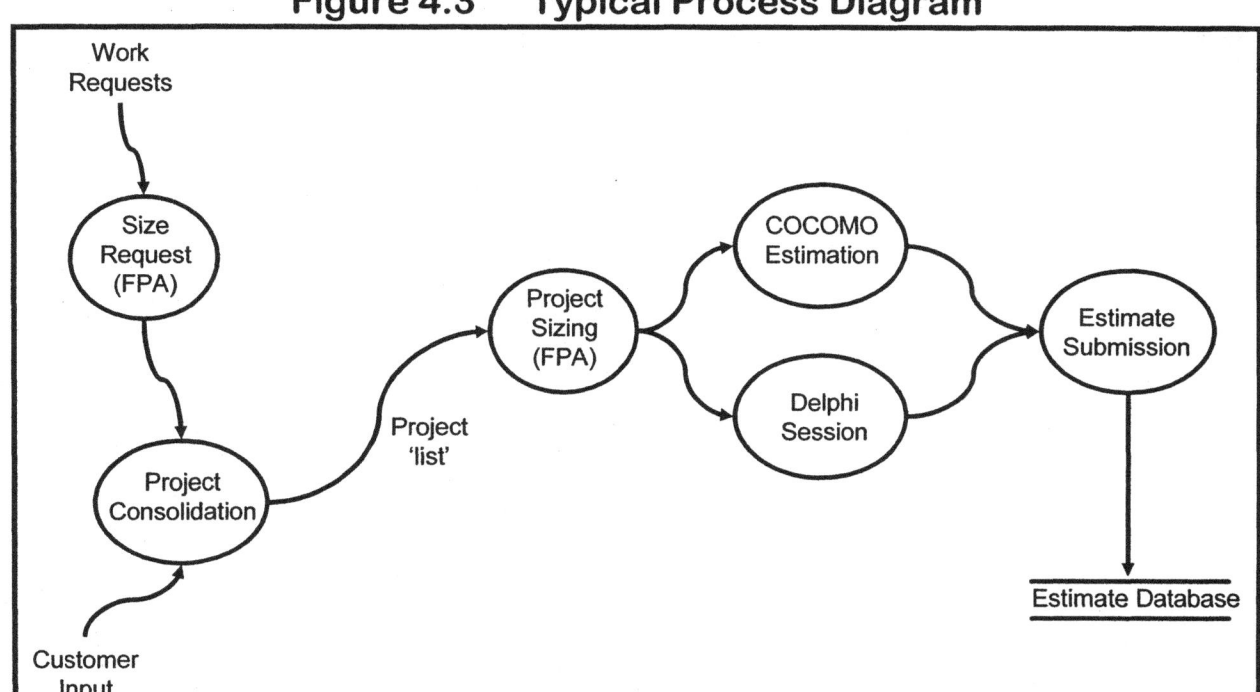

Figure 4.4   Monitoring and Feedback
(Actual vs. Estimates)

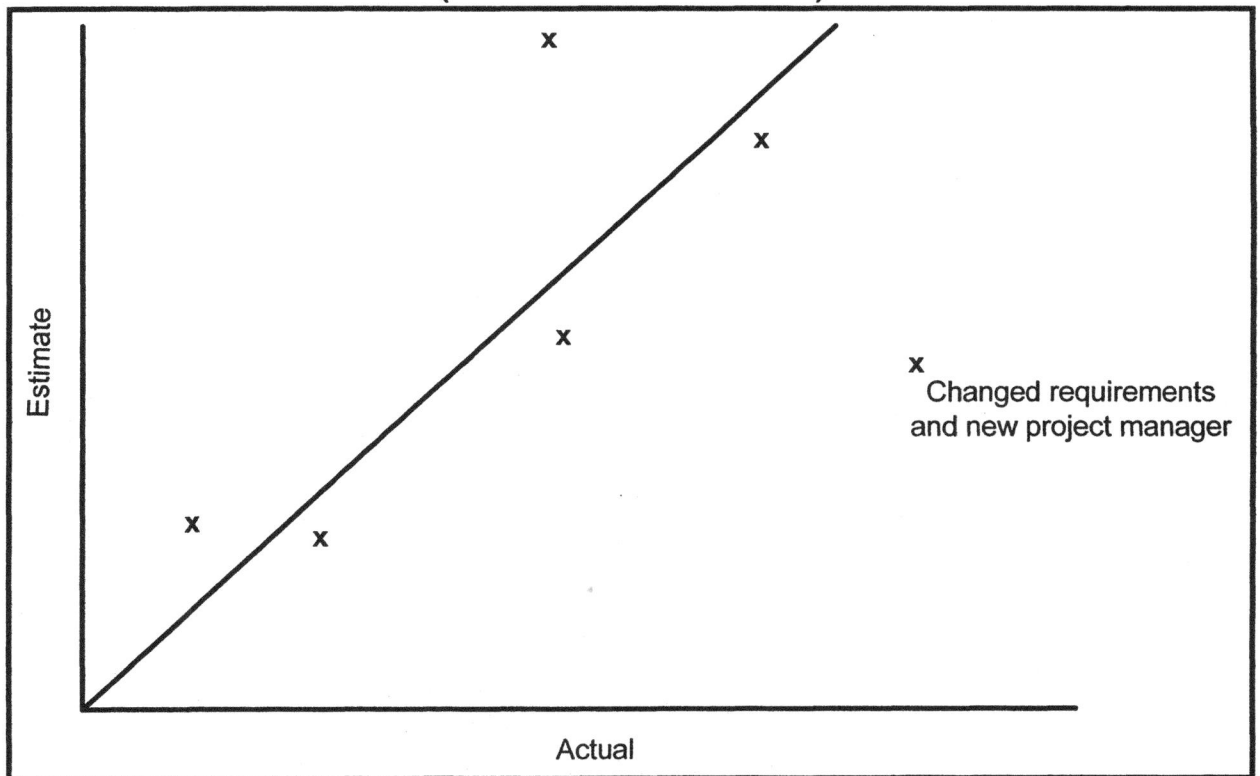

I have included three suggestions that may help get you started as far as presenting this type of effectiveness measure is concerned. All three charts are simply based on collection of actuals versus estimates. The first, *Figure 4.4*, plots the estimate against the actual so that the distance from the 45-degree line indicates the level of estimate accuracy. A plot on the line means that the estimator got it spot on!

Figure 4.5 shows four estimates taken during the course of two separate development projects. An actual line is included and the variance against the actual is the apparent. As this is based on real data, notice the way the estimation process has become more sensible by the time we are working on the third project. This should be compared against the wild variances experienced on the first project.

Figure 4.5 Monitoring and Feedback (Estimate vs. Effort)

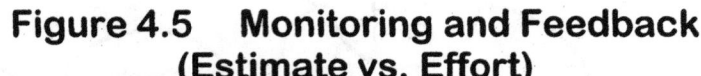

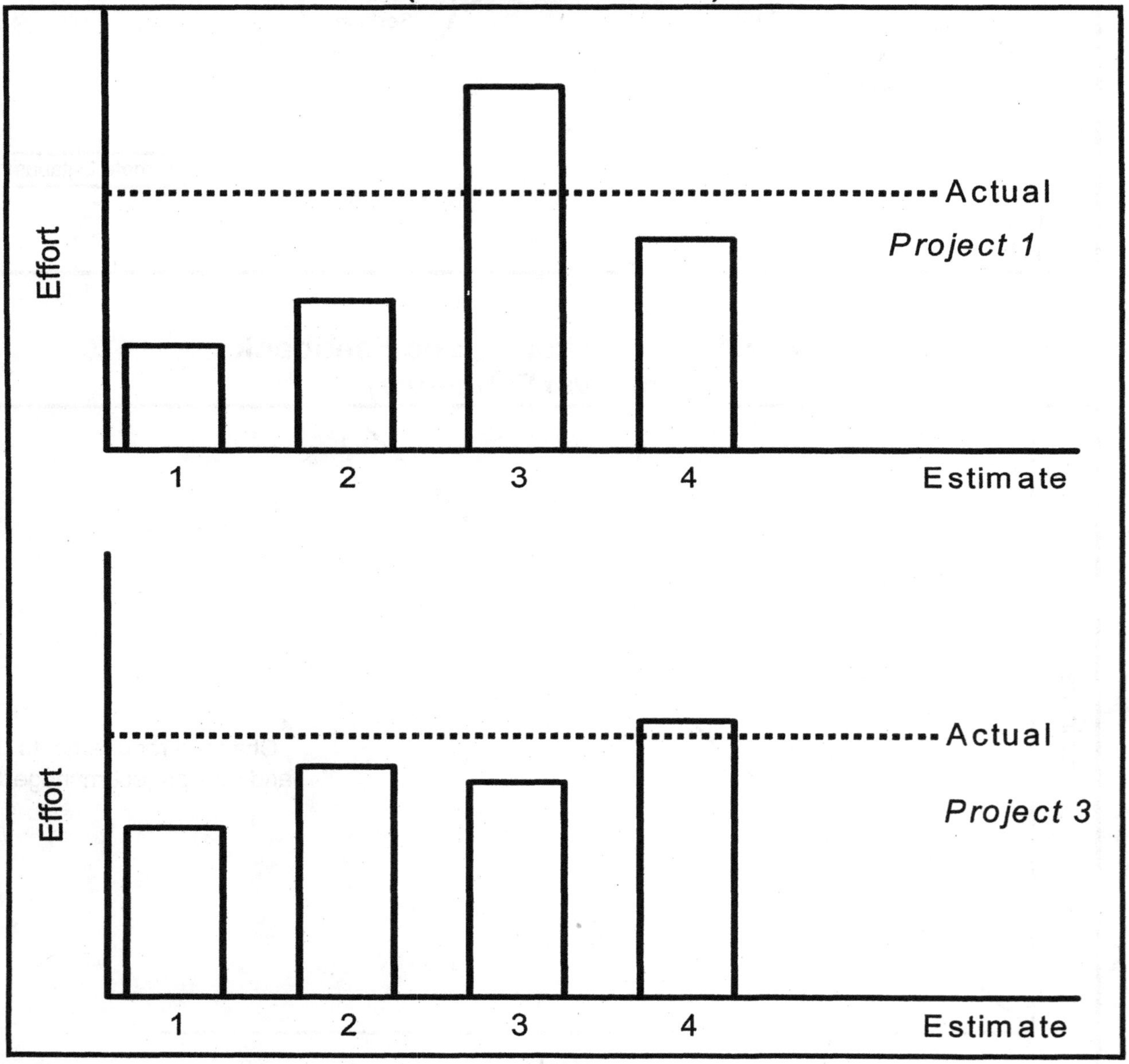

Figure 4.6 takes the absolute variance, that is ignoring the fact that it may be an over or underestimate, between the estimate and the actual and plots this for a number of projects. In this case we are using the initial estimates and we have data from four projects that have used an estimation strategy. This type of diagram enables the benefits of such an approach to be represented to managers and to customers.

Figure 4.6 Monitoring and Feedback
(Variation Actual Against Initial Estimate)

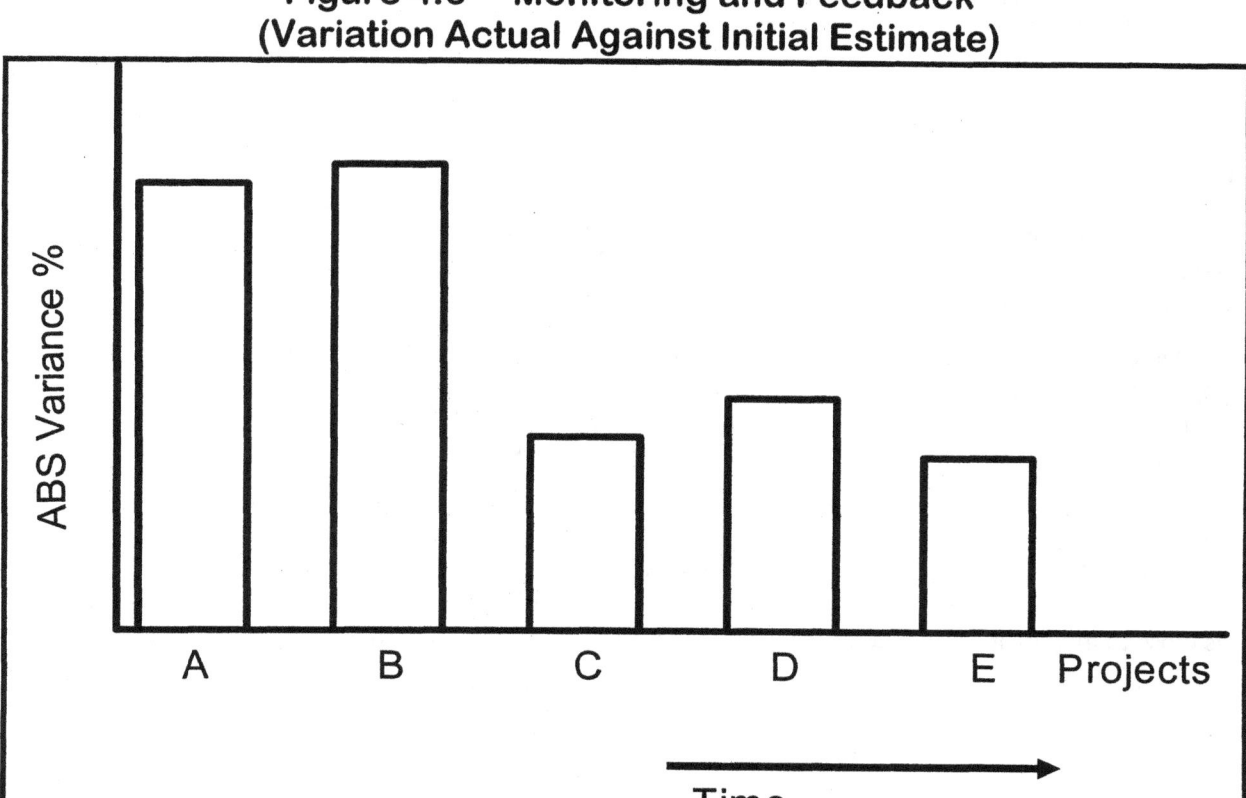

4.13 WHAT ABOUT THE LEADING EDGE, BIG PROJECTS?

One final point: I am often asked what can be done to help with the cost estimation problem in very large projects, possibly developing for ten years before the first delivery of software is made, and where the systems being developed are at the leading edge. This is a very difficult question to answer as proving the effectiveness of the answer takes so long. The best suggestions I can give are:

> ensure sufficient contingency to cover the many risks associated with this project;

> base your initial estimates on the Delphi method: and,

> apply rigorous project management to control the project.

The reality, of course, is that if you are at the leading edge of technology and you are dealing with big projects then you are unlikely to have much chance to develop the historical data upon which so many estimation techniques depend.

4.14 SUMMARY

This chapter has discussed estimation within the software engineering environment. We have looked at the need for effective estimation and the effect that poor estimates can have on a business. For most organizations, effective estimation is a critical factor for success and for customer satisfaction. Remember also that you may appear to be delivering on time but if you are only achieving this through significant reductions in the amount of functionality that is delivered compared to what was agreed for delivery, your customers will not be very happy.

We have considered estimation as a process and we have looked at various techniques that can be used to populate that process. We have also discussed the use of tools within a cost estimation process or strategy. Remember, cost estimation is not simply about tools or fancy techniques — they alone will not solve your problems. You need to have a strategy or process for cost estimation.

If the estimation principles in this chapter strike you as nothing more than common sense and if you are singularly unimpressed with the complexity of the estimation techniques presented here then I make no apologies! Estimation, like most areas of Software Metrics, relies heavily on common sense and simple solutions often work best, especially when the starting point is an ad hoc, undefined process that many view as close to magic, or blind chance. Managers and customers tend to dislike magic.

5

Applied Design Metrics

Key Points:

Using the poor relation of Software Metrics to radically improve quality

Managing complexity in software systems

McCabe Metrics

Information Flow Metrics

Now we come to an area that always strikes me as the poor relation in the area of metrics use. This is a great shame because the techniques are easy to apply, they cost very little in terms of additional effort, they are used by engineers or programmers and it is one form of Software Metric that can have a very real impact on the quality of the product delivered to the customer.

So what is this new wonder cure? Well, firstly they are not new, in fact the concepts are as old as systems theory itself and secondly, as with all Software Metrics, they are not a panacea. Put simply, I am referring to a set of techniques, firmly based upon measurement, that are applied to designs at different levels to assess the complexity of those designs. Hence the name that I choose to describe the collection of such techniques, "Applied Design Metrics." The basic premise behind such metrics is as follows; *designs that exhibit higher levels of complexity will also exhibit poorer reliability and maintainability characteristics.*

You can see by the wording of that last statement that I view the results of using these techniques as indicators of quality. I will not claim that a design with a high complexity rating will always produce a system that is unreliable and unmaintainable, but I do claim that such a system is potentially more likely to exhibit those characteristics. Applied Design Metrics provide indicators or pointers to likely trouble spots within systems and, at the highest level, to potentially troublesome systems. Having said that these metrics are indicators there is one example that I will discuss for which absolute figures are suggested as a boundary beyond which it is not safe to travel.

5.1   WHAT IS COMPLEXITY?

Of course, it is easy to talk in terms of complexity but it is not always so easy to pin down such a term. Towards the end of this chapter I will discuss aspects of complexity in more detail but, for now, I present a working definition:

> *"**Complexity** is the degree of entanglement*
>
> *within a system or its components"*

Before we look at specific examples of Applied Design Metrics I would like to stress one other point. These techniques are not "management metrics" in the sense that they are used to assess performance at any level. They are in no way related to the normal productivity and quality metrics we looked at when discussing management statistics. These metrics are used by engineers or programmers on a daily basis. They should form part of the basic training and then the toolkit of every competent engineer working on software development or maintenance because more and more evidence is being presented that shows their use directly affecting delivered quality.

As with many aspects of Software Metrics there are many variations on the theme of Applied Design Metrics, one common classification being that of the inter and intra measures. *Inter measures* are concerned with the way in which modules or components connect while the *intra measures* are more concerned with assessing what goes on within an module. While this classification can be useful I believe that it is important to consider the application of any measurement-based technique in terms of its business benefit. For this reason I would like to concentrate on what are possibly the two most widely used and accepted design metrics and I wish to discuss them in terms of their business application. In fairness, I should add that these techniques are not universally accepted by the software engineering community and are often the subject of discussion. However, my belief is that they offer a clear route to rapid payback of the investment necessary to implement them in a business environment.

5.2   McCABE METRICS

The first of the techniques I would like to discuss is the use of *McCabe Metrics*. McCabe measures are among the more established Software Metrics in use today and they do seem to be going through a revival after a somewhat troublesome time when numerous individuals criticized their effectiveness. I was also among the doubters until I had the good fortune, some years ago, to hear their originator, Tom McCabe, present a paper at a conference. This taught me two lessons. One, any Software Metric will be criticized, not least because so many people are looking for the silver bullet, the one metric to solve all our problems and, frankly, this will not be seen during our lifetime. Many of the criticisms of McCabe metrics stemmed from them being put to uses for which they were never intended. Two, if you want to learn about something then, if possible, go to the source.

That presentation coupled with the opportunity to talk to some individuals who were making use of McCabe metrics in the way that was intended induced me to try them. I can honestly report that the results I have had with their application convinces me that they are a very powerful tool.

So, what are McCabe metrics? There are two principle measures commonly known as McCabe Metrics, *Cyclomatic Complexity* and *Essential Complexity*, both founded upon graph theory. I am going to concentrate on describing Cyclomatic Complexity because Essential Complexity, as you will see, is very similar in its application.

Now this is going to get a bit, well, complex, but bear with me because the basic concepts are very simple to use. McCabe metrics are applied against "flowgraphs" which are simplified flowcharts, all "boxes" being represented as simple, unmarked nodes. Now I am tempted to leave it there but for a recent salutary experience when a young engineer told me that he had never been taught how to use flowcharts, "after all, they went out with the ark!" So for those young enough never to have had the pleasure of flowcharting, and anyone who has forgotten the basic principles let me try to explain what a flowgraph is in more technical terms.

If you look at *Figure 5.1* you will see a fragment of code that contains an example of sequence, selection and iteration. By representing each statement as a simple bubble or node and each control flow between statements as a connecting line or edge we can present that code fragment as a flowgraph, simply a collection of nodes and edges. For the code fragment in *Figure 5.1* an associated flowgraph is shown.

Now a flowgraph can be constructed for any code fragment that can be seen to have a single entry and exit point. Generally speaking, McCabe metrics are applied to low level system components such as COBOL paragraphs, or sections, C functions etc.

Flowgraphs can also be derived from most psuedo-English design notations so that you do not have to wait for code before using these techniques. Even so, McCabe metrics do come into play relatively late in the development lifecycle but consider, how late is too late? Even if I was at the point of producing code, it is still cheaper for me to make changes rather than produce and deliver system components that are prone to defects and maintenance problems. Equally important, by using McCabe metrics I can identify potential hot spots in my system and advise the test people that these should be even more rigorously tested than the rest of the system surely will be.

Having got the flowgraph, count the number of edges, *e*, and the number of nodes, *n*, then simply apply the formula below to calculate the *McCabe Cyclomatic Complexity value, v*:

$$v = e - n + 2$$

A simple example is provided in *Figure 5.2* to illustrate the use of this formula.

Figure 5.1   McCabe Metrics Background Theory
Example of Flowgraph (1)

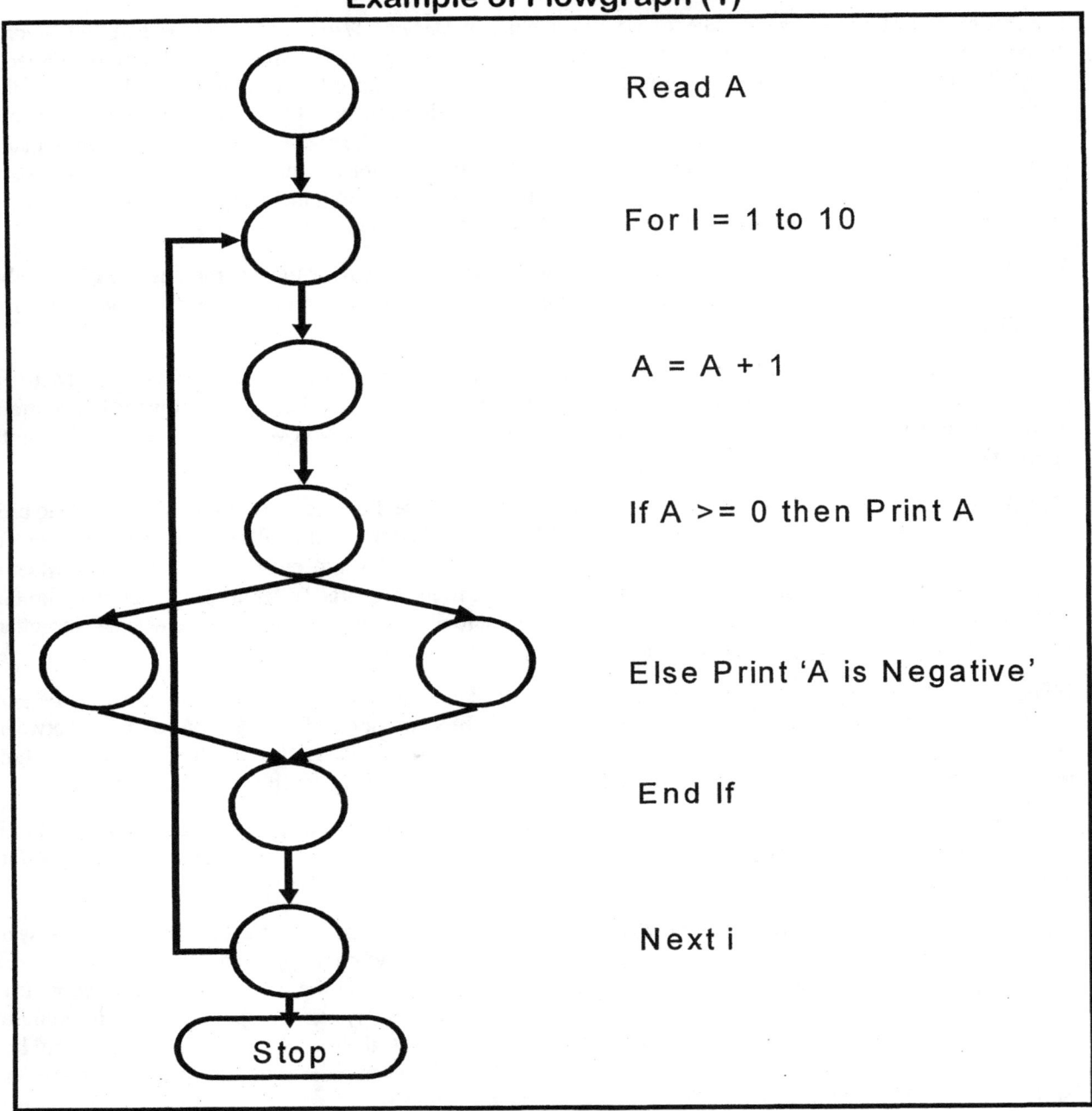

Figure 5.2   McCabe Metrics Background Theory
Example of Flowgraph (2)

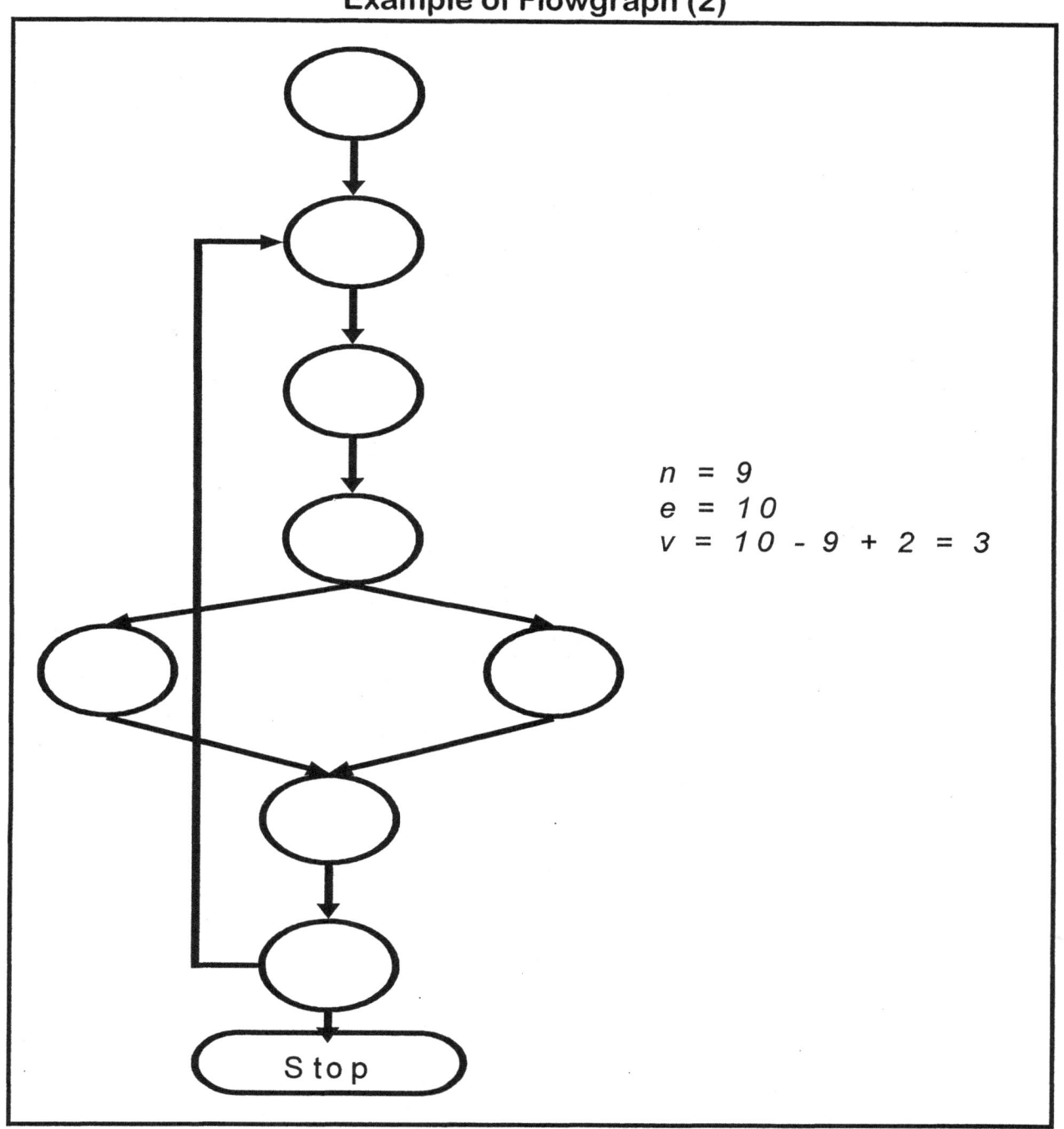

$n = 9$
$e = 10$
$v = 10 - 9 + 2 = 3$

There are other ways to calculate the value *v*. Perhaps the most useful is, given code or a good psuedo-English approximation, to count the number of IF statements and add 1, remembering to treat compound conditions as multiple IFs. This basic algorithm can be used to produce a very simple automated tool that will calculate the value *v* once it has code to work on.

McCabe's Cyclomatic metric is a measure of how complex a specific realization of a design is. Basically, if my code or low-level design is seen as a black box that exists to do something, how complex have I made the innards of that black box?

Essential Complexity is a much more simple concept to explain in that it is a measure of "structuredness." If you look at a piece of code, or the low level pseudo-English that is one step away from code, you will find standard constructs within it. These are sequence, selection and iteration constructs. If you look at the flowgraph representation you will find that you can reduce it to the essential flowgraph by replacing these constructs by single nodes.

When you cannot do this because the basic rules of sequencing, selection and iteration have been broken the degree of structuredness is reduced.

Figures 5.3 and *5.4* show the reduction for a flowgraph that is well structured and for one that contains illegal constructs.

Calculating Essential Complexity is simply a case of applying the same formula to that used for Cyclomatic Complexity but with counts taken from the reduced flowgraph, thus:

$$vr = er - nr + 2$$

where *vr* is Essential Complexity and *er* and *nr* are the edge and node counts from the reduced flowgraph.

But, of course, all we have so far are some numbers. What do they mean and how do we use them?

Let me start to answer that question by putting forward some very concrete guidelines and I will then discuss a slightly less pedantic approach.

Figure 5.3   McCabe MetricsBackground Theory
Example of Reduced Flowgraph (1)

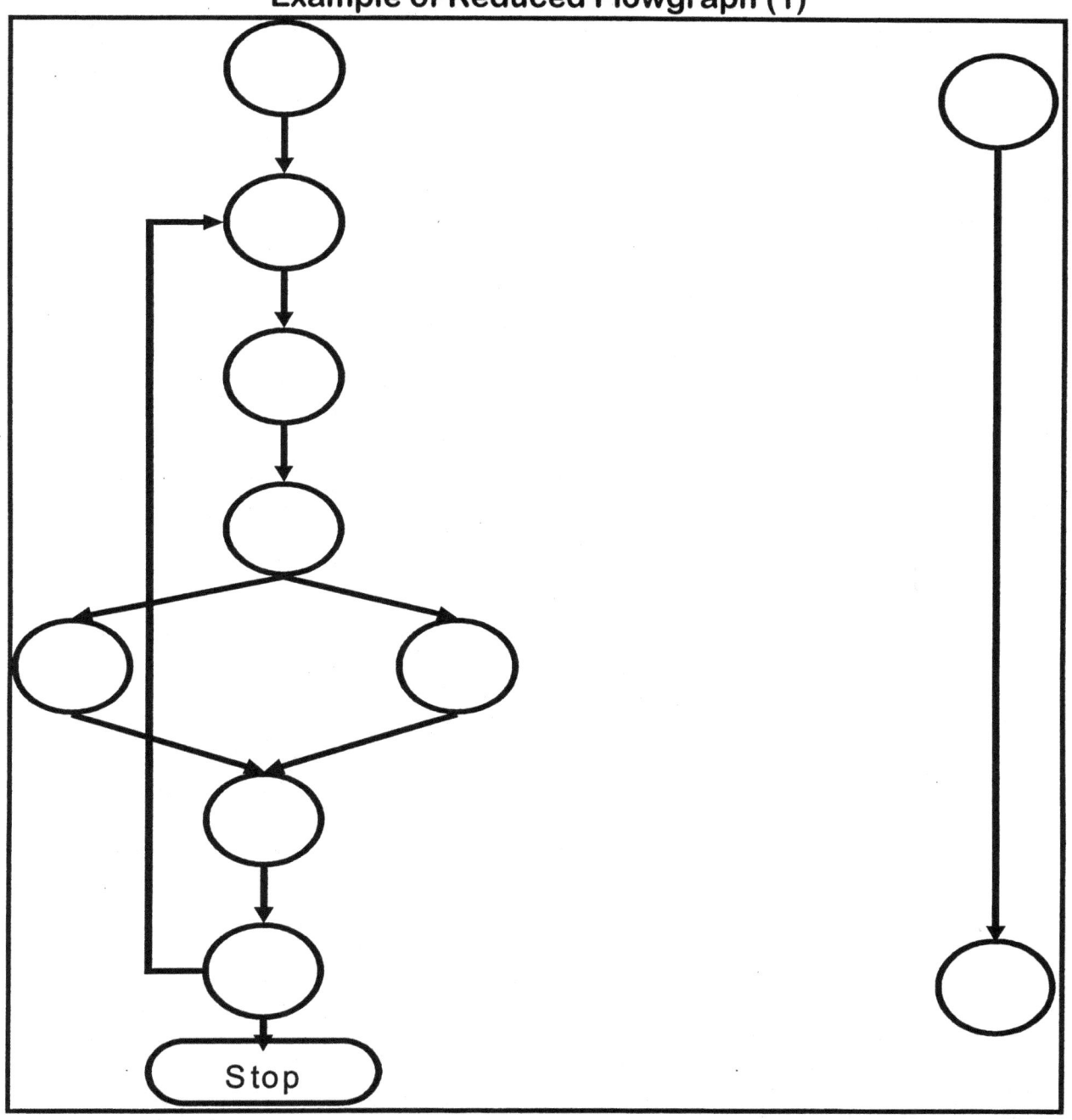

Figure 5.4　McCabe Metrics
Background Theory — Example of Reduced Flowgraph (2)

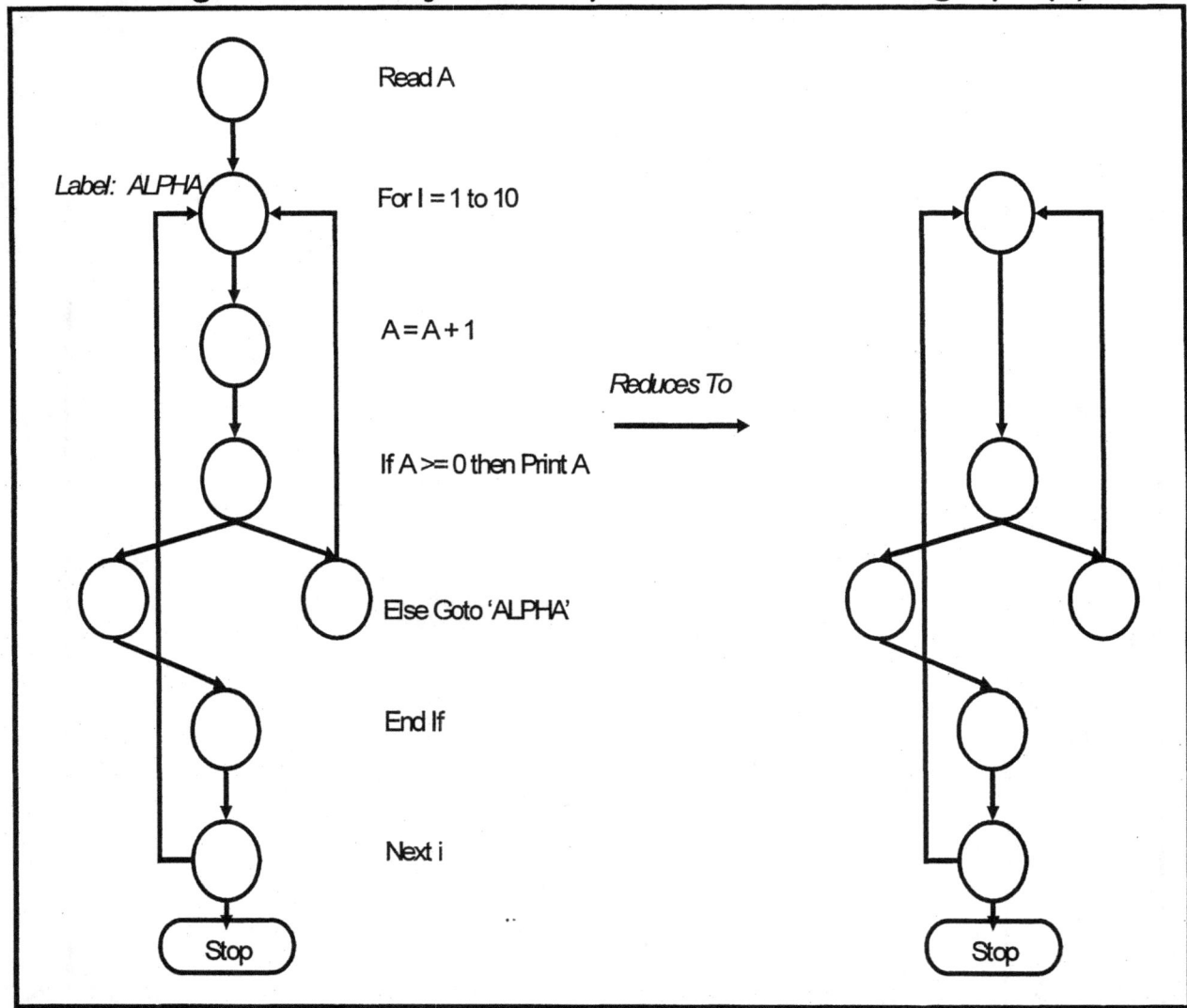

The rules are quite straightforward. If you are working on a new development or an enhancement project that is adding functionality then, for any single low level component, the value for v, Cyclomatic Complexity, should not exceed 10 and the value for vr, Essential Complexity, should not exceed 2.

One project I know of in the United States that applied these rules did achieve zero defects for at least twelve months after delivery. Think about that. The system was being used as well!

Now let us talk about the reality. Most of us do not have the pleasure of working on new developments, and any additional functionality that we get to add to systems as part of an enhancement project tends to be swamped by straight changes to existing stuff. Also, if we are managing a system we may feel it to be slightly over the top to suddenly insist that everyone start bringing things in line with the ten/two rule (i.e,. that Cyclomatic Complexity, should not exceed 10 and the value for vr, Essential Complexity, should not exceed 2).

In a maintenance environment a good guideline is to do a McCabe analysis before you do a change and to then do another one after you have designed the changes. If the values for v and vr are the same or a little bit better than you found them, then implement the change. If they are worse, then go back and do it over — because otherwise you are storing up trouble for the future.

If you are in the situation of developing new systems or adding low-level components then, in all honesty, you could do a lot worse than to apply the ten/two rule. In a maintenance environment this may be a bit much for your people if they have not come across these ideas before. In this situation you could do an analysis of the system you are responsible for, either by analyzing the whole system through a tool that uses code as its source or by sampling components from the system. You may be surprised, or even shocked, to find components with Cyclomatic values of five hundred plus, yes I know the guideline was ten but that is not a mistype, I really do mean 500+! I regularly see components with values like this. I have even been told about one component with a value of 2,800! Believe it and weep.

Now we do have to take a deep breath here for two reasons, one being the fact that there are modules around like that, and we wonder why we have problems in this industry! Second, what you must realize is that there is one very easy way to bump up the Cyclomatic Complexity value of a component without destroying its reliability or maintainability. How? Use a CASE statement or its equivalent that implements a multiple "if" construct. Which is where I have a fundamental difference with some individuals in our industry. CASE statements are fine and have a role to play in designs and coding, however, there is a limit that, when reached, makes a CASE-heavy component as unmaintainable as a module that does the same thing through multiple IFs.

It may upset the fundamentalist structured programmer but if I am presented with a design that goes over a Cyclomatic value of 50, and the excuse given is that a CASE statement has been used, somebody had better find cover very quickly! Complex CASE statements are difficult to understand. I make this statement as an ex-maintenance programmer who regularly had to attempt to decipher CASE statements that went to twenty or thirty lines and that were not easy to comprehend.

Enough of the problems, what can be done about them?

If you wish to introduce the use of McCabe metrics you could use a sampling exercise like that I have outlined to set short-term targets. For example, looking at our current system the average McCabe values are 25 and 5 for Cyclomatic and Essential Complexity respectively. From now on, the rule will be that no design solution gets through a review (and if you are sensible you will say it does not even go for review), unless it makes the McCabe values better than they were before, or, if new functionality, has values of 20 and 4. Given the environment you have these targets are reasonable and you can always reassess the situation in six months time and make the targets tighter.

Effectively, I suggest that McCabe metrics be used as control gates. The actual values you use for those gates are less important than the fact that you are asking engineers to think about the results of their actions.

But do such approaches work? Are McCabe metrics worth anything? I have already mentioned the experience of one organization that got zero defects when it piloted these techniques. I can also tell you that Hewlett-

Packard has published data that shows a 0.9 correlation between Cyclomatic Complexity and defect reports across a large number of applications. That is pretty impressive no matter what reservations you have about correlation statistics.

The best example I have come across to support the use of McCabe metrics is somewhat back-to-front. A while ago I was asked to pilot Complexity metrics in an organization as part of a quality improvement program. I was given a particular application and team to work with and initial discussions indicated that McCabe metrics would be the best approach. I asked what the current quality levels were in terms of defects only to be told that this application did not have defects, at least so few that it was almost zero. Needless to say I asked for proof and this was not available. Being something of a cynic I suggested that we put in a defect reporting mechanism on the current project, a fairly straightforward five thousand line enhancement job.

This was done and I returned expecting to find a good few defect reports awaiting me from the link tests and from the user acceptance or system tests. There were three defect reports. Two of these were due to data and could not be blamed on the programming team. This meant I had a system that appeared to be exhibiting a reliability level better than 0.001 defects per thousand lines of code changed. Bear in mind that the best norms we have to work with suggest 4 defects per thousand lines for US and European software.

Why was this? Well the team was not large, consisting of three individuals. Those individuals were quality staff to their toenails. As the team leader said, those three defects should not have got through, and she meant it! They had a very close and good relationship with their user. Obviously it all helped but the thing that really battened it down was that most of their system components conformed to the ten/two rule. They were applying McCabe concepts automatically and they were getting the results.

Incidentally, this team had one individual who manually analyzed all the components associated with that 5K project and it took him three days. I would not recommend that McCabe analysis is regularly carried out by hand but it shows that it can be done.

Of course everything is not perfect, even with these metrics. There can be problems with recursion, that is when sections of code call themselves, and with fall-through, where one component passes control down to another and so on so that there is no single entry/exit point. However, most managers steer clear of recursion, wisely I believe, and fall-through is fortunately quite rare so I tend to ignore these concerns.

More important are the people worries that sometime arise. Some managers are very concerned about the use of such metrics because they see that use adding to development time. In my mind the results speak clearly in favor of their use but it should be remembered that a McCabe analysis, when done as part and parcel of the day-to-day work, adds about five or ten minutes to a component change that typically takes a minimum of an engineering day when you allow for familiarization, re-documentation and all the rest of what makes up IT.

McCabe metrics do also seem to open some other interesting doors.

There are a number of tools around that support McCabe metrics. These are easily found through the web. Some of these tools also enable the automatic production of unit test cases. This can offer a significant saving on testing effort.

Even more interesting are some of the reports that came out of the United States some time ago. It seems that some people have been using McCabe metrics and the automatic generation of test cases to identify redundant code within systems. By redundant code we simply mean modules that do the same job as other modules in the same system. For example, you may need a sort routine and so may I. Assuming you write yours for release 1 is it very likely that I will check things out before writing my own for release 2 or 3? The answer seems to be, 'no, I will write my own.' For further information about this experimental technique see McCabe (1).

Based on the work done so far, it seems that we could expect systems to exhibit about a 30% level of redundancy. That is an awful lot of code to be there when it does not need to be!

To summarize, McCabe metrics are a well established, well proven foundation for techniques to manage complexity and, hence, reliability and maintainability. Like them or not, many people have found that they work.

5.3   INFORMATION FLOW METRIC

The other set of metrics I would like to place under the ADM umbrella are generally known as "Information Flow" metrics. At the conceptual level Information Flow metrics are not difficult to understand; it is when you come to apply them that the fun can start. Having said that, a pragmatic approach, as always, works wonders.

The basis of Information Flow metrics is founded upon the following premise. All but the most simple systems consist of components and it is the work that these components do and how they are fitted together that influence the complexity of a system. If a component has to do numerous discrete tasks it is said to lack "cohesion." If it passes information to, and/or accepts information from, many other components within the system it is said to be highly "coupled." Systems theory tells us that components that are highly coupled and that lack cohesion tend to be less reliable and less maintainable than those that are loosely coupled and that are cohesive.

Sometimes definitions of terms like cohesion and coupling help so I present the following as working definitions of those terms:

> *Cohesion*   *The degree to which a component performs a single function.*
>
> *Coupling*   *The term used to describe the degree of linkage between one component and others in the same system.*

Now, what is a "component?"

> *Component*   *Any element identified by decomposing a (software) system into its constituent parts.*

This systems view maps to software systems extremely easily as most engineers today use, or are at least familiar with, top-down design techniques that produce a hierarchical view of system components. Even the more modern "middle out" or rapid engineering design approaches produce this structured type of deliverable, provided documentation is produced and maintained. Here again, Information Flow metrics can be used.

Information Flow metrics model the degree of cohesion and coupling for a particular system component. How that model is constructed can justifiably range from the simple to the complex. I intend to start with the most simple representation of Information Flow metrics to illustrate the basic concepts, how to derive information using the metrics and how to use that information. I will then expand this basic IF model.

Just before I do this I would like to put the credit for these metrics and the approaches I outline here where it is due. In terms of applying Information Flow metrics to software systems the pioneering work was done by Henry and Kafura, Henry (1). They looked at the UNIX operating system and found a strong association between the Information Flow metrics and the level of maintainability ascribed to components by programmers. Other individuals who tried to apply these principles did find difficulties in using the Henry and Kafura approach. Further work was done in the UK by Professor Darrell Ince and Martin Shepperd, Ince (1), among others, which resulted in a more practical IF model. This work was complimented by Barbara Kitchenham, Kitchenham (2), who addressed the same problem and who also presented a clear approach to the question of interpretation.

The author had the good fortune of having the assistance of Ince, Shepperd and Kitchenham when he was first attempting to use these metrics. What is presented here is a distillation of that assistance.

Information Flow metrics are applied to the components of a system design. *Figure 5.5* shows a fragment of such a design and for component *A* we can define three measures, but remember that these are the most simple models of IF.

Figure 5.5   Aspects of Complexity

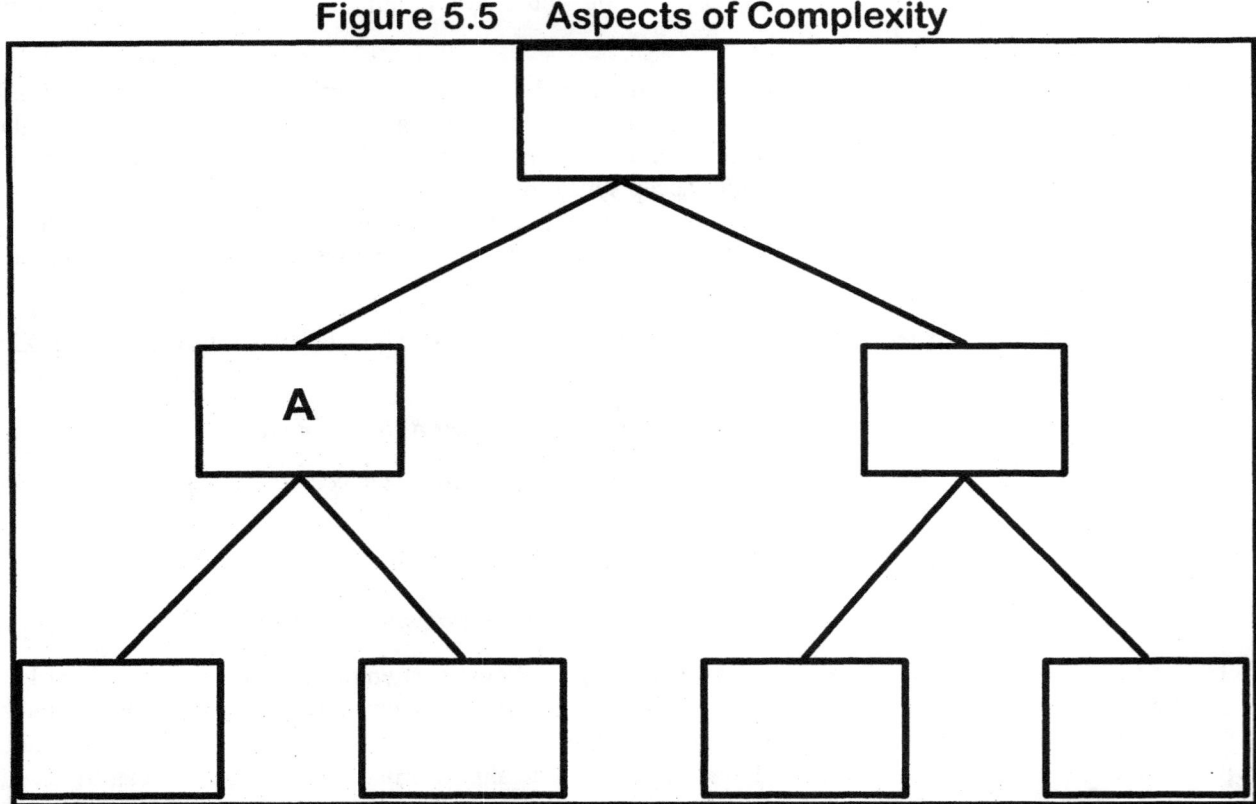

The first measure is "*FAN IN*." This is simply a count of the number of other components that can call, or pass control, to component *A*.

The second is "*FAN OUT*." This is the number of components that are called by component *A*.

The third measure is derived from the first two by using the following formula. We will call this measure the INFORMATION FLOW index of module *A*, abbreviated to *IF(A)*:

$$IF(A) = (FAN\ IN(A) * FAN\ OUT(A))\ ^2$$

The formula includes a power component to, as most texts on Information Flow metrics put it, "model the non-linear nature of complexity." The assumption is that if something is more complex than something else then it is much more complex rather than just a little bit more complex. Given that assumption we could raise to a power three or four or whatever we want but on the principle that the simpler the model the better, then two is a good enough choice. From my point of view, raising to two makes it easier, as you will see, to pick out the potential bad guys. That is a good enough reason and I will leave it to the purists to worry about the finer detail.

Information Flow metrics can be applied to any functional decomposition of a software system. Examples of these include structure charts, Data Flow Diagrams and SDL Block diagrams. Obviously you may have to tailor your terminology to suit the notation being used. For example, in a Data Flow Diagram you do not have "calls;" instead you have data flows between processes. The principle is the same. One of the easiest applications I have come across is to use Information Flow metrics on the hierarchical tree that forms a basis of some configuration management systems. This is a good example of the synergy that can sometimes be found to operate within software engineering.

Given that Information Flow metrics apply to these forms of functional decomposition they come into play from as early as the high-level design stage and serve a useful purpose right the way down to low-level design when you can start to use McCabe metrics.

Given your functional decomposition you will notice that there is one additional attribute possessed by each component, namely its level in the decomposition. The following is a step-by-step guide to deriving these most simple of Information Flow metrics.

1.   Note the level of each component in the system design.

2.   For each component, count the number of calls to that component, this is the FAN IN of that component. Some organizations allow more than one component at the highest level in the design so for components at the highest level which should have a FAN IN of 0, assign a FAN IN of 1. Also note that a simple model of FAN IN can penalize reused components. As a pragmatic rule, if a component calls no components, its FAN IN is greater than seven and it is deemed to be "small," and this last point requires the discretion of the designer, then assign a FAN IN of one.

3.   For each component, count the number of calls from that component. For components that call no other, assign a FAN OUT value of one.

4.   Calculate the IF value for each component using the formula above.

5.   Sum the IF value for all components within each level. I will call this the LEVEL SUM.

6.   Sum the IF values for the total system design. I will call this the SYSTEM SUM.

Which brings us to the analysis phase, so to continue:

7   For each level, rank the components in that level according to FAN IN, FAN OUT and IF value. Three histograms or line plots should be prepared for each level.

8.   Plot the LEVEL SUM values for each level using a histogram or line plot.

This may sound like a great deal of work but for most commercial systems that I have come across, provided you have the documentation, this data can be derived and the analysis done within one engineering day. If your systems are larger than the ones I have seen then it will obviously take longer but remember that once done it is very easy to keep up to date. Depending upon your environment you may even be able to automate the calculations.

Having got the information, you now need to do something with it. You must realize that, for Information Flow metrics, there are no absolute values of good or bad. Information Flow metrics are relative indicators. This means that value for your system may be higher than for a system I have but this does not mean that your system is worse. Nor does a high metric value guarantee that a component will be unreliable and unmaintainable. It is only that it will *probably* be less reliable and less maintainable than its fellows.

The rub is that in most systems, less reliable and less maintainable means that it is potentially going to cost you significant amounts of money to fix and enhance. Potentially it could even be a nightmare component.

A nightmare component is the one that the system administer has nightmares about because he or she knows that if anyone touches that component, the whole system is going to crash and it will take weeks to fix because Fred designed it and Fred was weird. Fred also left five years ago!

So the strength of Information Flow metrics is not in the numbers themselves but in how you use the information.

As a guide, the 25% of components with the highest scores for FAN IN, FAN OUT and IF values should be investigated. Now in practice you may well find that you have a certain number of modules that stick out like a sore thumb, especially on the IF values. If this group is more or less than the 25% guide then do not worry about it, concentrate on those that seem to be odd according to the metric values rather than following any 25% rule slavishly.

High FAN IN values indicate modules that lack cohesion. It may well be that you have not broken out the functions to a great enough degree. Basically, these components are called often because they are doing more than one job.

High levels of FAN OUT also indicates a lack of cohesion or missed levels of abstraction. Here you stopped design before design was finished and this is reflected in the high number of calls from the component.

Generally speaking, FAN OUT appears to be a better indicator of problem modules than FAN IN but it is early days yet and I would not wish to discount FAN IN.

High IF values indicate highly coupled components. You need to look at these components in terms of FAN IN and FAN OUT to see how to reduce the complexity level. Sometimes you may hit a "traffic center." This is a component where, for whatever reasons, you have a high IF value but cannot improve things. Switching components in telecommunication systems often exhibit this. Here you have a potential problem area which, if it is also a large component, may be very error-prone. If you cannot reduce the complexity then at least make sure that you test that component thoroughly.

Looking at the LEVEL SUM plot of values you should see a fairly smooth curve showing controlled growth in Information Flow across the levels. Sudden increases in these values across levels can indicate a missed level of abstraction within the general design. For systems where the design has less than ten levels then a simple count of components at each level seems to work equally well.

The final item of information you have is the SYSTEM SUM value. This gives you an overall complexity rating for the design in terms of Information Flow metrics. Most presentations on this topic will say that this number can be used to assess alternative design proposals. At which point you often get wry chuckles from the practitioners in the audience who feel they never have enough time to develop one design let alone alternatives. My sympathies have always been with the practitioners but let me just state that I have come across a number of teams in different organizations who do prepare alternative designs at this kind of level for enhancement projects. Information Flow metrics give them the opportunity to increase confidence in the choice they eventually make by quantifying aspects of complexity. Score one for the so-called practitioners who discount this as impossible!

We have looked at the most simple form of Information Flow metrics but the original proposals put forward by Henry and Kafura were more sophisticated than the control flow based variant discussed above. As I said earlier, Ince, Shepperd and Kitchenham have done a great deal of work to help in the practical application of Henry and Kafura's pioneering proposals and it is a distillation of that work that I will now summarize into the more sophisticated IF model. You should also realize that this is a model and it will need to be tailored to your own organization's design mechanisms if it is to be used. Such a tailoring process should not take more than two days for counting rule derivation and documentation of these rules provided you use a well-defined design notation and use a competent engineer who knows that notation.

The only difference between the simple and the sophisticated Information Flow models lies in the definition of FAN IN and FAN OUT.

For a component A let:

a = the number of components that call A.

b = the number of parameters passed to A from components higher in the hierarchy.

c = the number of parameters passed to A from components lower in the hierarchy.

d = the number of data elements read by component A.

Then:

$$FAN\ IN(A) = a + b + c + d$$

Also let:

e = the number of components called by A.

f = the number of parameters passed from A to components higher in the hierarchy.

g = the number of parameters passed from A to components lower in the hierarchy.

h = the number of data elements written to by A.

Then:

$$FAN\ OUT(A) = e + f + g + h$$

Other than those changes to the basic definitions the derivation, analysis and interpretation remain the same. I must say that my advice to any organization starting to apply Information Flow metrics would be to build up confidence by using the simpler form. If these work for your organization then leave it at that. If and only if the simpler form fails in your environment — in other words, you are confident that no significant relationship exists between the simple measures and the levels of reliability and maintainability — only then spend the effort to tailor and pilot the more sophisticated form.

You can be encouraged by the fact that there have been a number of experimental validations of Information Flow metrics that seem to support the claims made for them. These results have been encouraging. Programming groups that have been introduced to Information Flow metrics have been able to make use of them and also report benefits in the area of design quality control and system management. They seem to work but there does seem to be some reluctance in the industry as a whole to make use of Information Flow metrics. Perhaps one reason is because managers feel they are a bit "techie." Perhaps others feel that they are not yet ready to use sophisticated techniques like Information Flow metrics. I hope that this brief explanation of the measures has shown that they are practical and pragmatic method of ensuring quality.

5.4   SUMMARY

To summarize this chapter, it is based on the assumption that avoidable complexity costs our industry a great deal of money. If we can design avoidable complexity out of our systems before we deliver them to testing groups or, worse, to the end customer, then we will save much of that money. The simple metrics-based techniques offer an opportunity for organizations to start that designing-out process.

You may ask if the models behind these techniques are complete, and the answer would be no. Complexity itself is complex as it operates in at least four dimensions. There is the complexity that results from the way a system's components are connected which we can call coupling complexity. There is the complexity that results from the black-box view of a component, basically how cohesive it is.

Complexity also derives from the white-box level. How does a component do what it is supposed to? We can use Information Flow metrics to model the first two dimensions and McCabe Cyclomatic and Essential Complexity metrics to model the third. None of these models are a totally accurate representation of a complexity dimension.

I have also completely ignored the fourth complexity dimension, data complexity which itself can cause major problems with live systems. Complexity is almost certainly a function of these four variables and there may be others, one candidate being the degree of concurrency in a system. Unfortunately very little work seems to have been done in this area and one can only hope that further research into the different aspects of complexity and how they relate to one another will be undertaken in the near future.

The metrics and the associated techniques in this chapter do not give a total solution to the problem of complexity but they provide a start, and one that does not cost an arm and a leg to take advantage of!

6

Project Control

Key Points:
Using measurement based techniques to help manage projects
Metrics to help assess feasibility
Metrics to help manage risk
Data based progress tracking

The final chapter of this section looks at the topic of project control. This is often seen as being outside of the scope of a metrics initiative or it may not even be considered during the requirements analysis stage of implementing a metrics program.

If the reason for this is that the organization has projects under control then I have no argument with the position that this is not part of the remit for a metrics program. If, however, the organization has a requirement for project control that is not being addressed by another part of that organization then it makes sense to me to put project control within the program's terms of reference. I believe that I can justify this position with one sentence: Software Metrics initiatives are there to improve the quality of products and

PROCESSES, and if that means enhancing the project control mechanisms then so be it. This concern merely demonstrates the difficulties we face in defining clear functional boundaries for "metrics."

And talking of boundaries I should define what I mean by project control. Consider this situation: you receive a customer's statement of requirements — the wish list — and you carry out your initial estimation and submit the bid. Notice that you still have not managed to convince the customer or your own organization that you should actually bid for the requirements definition phase first but you are already working on it! Now, despite all expectations to the contrary you get the contract.

What happens next? Usually a whole group of people start beavering away on that requirements definition. Hopefully you also get some sort of a project plan together with the obligatory milestones. Oh yes, this is a "Quality Organization" now because the top man said so a couple of months ago so we had better have a quality plan. OK, that has got the overheads sorted out now let's get those people cutting code! Let's just hope things go better than last time. Remember what happened, two weeks before delivery and we had to tell the customer there was a six month delay. That was embarrassing. Especially as we had spent two years, elapsed, on the project!

The chances are that you do not have a situation that is as bad as that, do you? Let us run a slightly different scenario: We have won the bid and we have got first-cut project plans which we will refine after we get more information from the requirements definition stage. The first-cut plans have been through a feasibility check and the refined plans will also be checked in this way. We have also pulled in the standard quality plan for this class of project and made any modifications we feel necessary. Of course, these have been checked and agreed to by our project control people and, perhaps, the customer. After all, we do talk to the customer more these days since the quality initiative made us realize we had such a thing as a customer. We have also put together our risk management plans and prepared contingency plans and, of course, all of the team leaders know how progress is going to be monitored across the life of the project. Now we have increased overheads, or have we simply increased the chances of success, and we have also increased the probability of delivering on time.

This is a scenario in which project control is operating. Looking at the components that go to make up the picture, we see the following. There is project planning and feasibility checking of those plans, quality plans, risk management and progress checking.

Project planning is a well established discipline and I do not intend to address it here. There are many good reference books that deal with work breakdown, scheduling, logical task linkage and critical path analysis, for example **Project Management, a Managerial Approach** by Meredith and Mantel (2003, John Wiley and Sons). Your own organization may well have standard approaches to these areas. There are also numerous commercially available project planning tools.

Quality planning is also an area that is relatively well established especially in organizations operating a Process Improvement policy. If not fully established, at least the concepts are well understood and I could do no better than to direct you to Humphrey (2), and for the view taken from the software engineer's perspective to Humphrey (3).

The areas I would like to discuss, quite briefly, because each is a subject in its own right, are *feasibility checking*, *risk management* and *progress checking*.

Before we go any further I would like to touch on the implementation of the techniques we are about to discuss because a common reaction is to throw ones hands up in horror at the additional costs implied. If your situation is that you operate with, effectively, one project at a time over long durations, typically between five and ten years, then these techniques are certainly applicable and justifiable. In fact, they are almost mandatory. However, this type of environment is very rare outside defense work.

More commonly, you will be operating in a mixed environment of maintenance, which includes enhancement, and development. New developments typically take no more than two years elapsed time or even much less but the majority of the available effort is spent enhancing existing products through new releases once or twice a year. Within your IT function you could easily have one hundred projects on the go at any one time.

You do not reinvent the wheel every time you start a new project. Standard approaches to feasibility checking, risk management and progress checking should be implemented and, after a bedding-in period, the deviations from these standard approaches should be minimal. Note that justifiable deviations should be allowed and are the responsibility of the project manager.

6.1   FEASIBILITY CHECKING

Feasibility Checking is a very close relation to cost estimation but in this case you have the estimates for cost and the planned duration contained in the project plans and you want to assess the probability of achieving those estimates.

Given the relationship to cost estimation it should come as no surprise to find that you can manipulate the public domain models to get this kind of feasibility check. In its most simple form the check is performed by plotting effort or duration against size, holding all other variables such as programmer skills constant, and then seeing if the estimates for your project at its given estimated size lie above the plotted line. If they do then you are, according to the model used, in the feasible region. If your estimates lie below the line you have a problem. Putting it diplomatically, you plan to do your project more effectively than the model predicts you will. Remember that you need to use a model calibrated to your environment. More sophisticated models can be set up, based on industry data or your own experiences and there is an obvious potential here for automating those models.

Of course, you may wish to apply a more humanistic approach to feasibility checking. There is no reason why project plans should not be reviewed or inspected just like any other deliverable. These plans should satisfy two requirements. They should be complete in that everything that is expected is present, for example, the Critical Path if that is normally used. They should also be, in the opinion of the reviewers, feasible. This may mean discussing the assumptions that underlie the estimates and also implies that the review team should have project management experience.

So you see that both simple and sophisticated techniques do exist to administer this aspect of project control but if you have a plan that looks good, what about when things go wrong? That brings us to Risk Management.

6.2   RISK MANAGEMENT

Risk Management is a topic that really does require a book in its own right and like many other topics it is one that has strong links to Software Metrics. All that can be done in the space available here is to give a brief overview of the subject and to demonstrate those linkages between Risk Management and Software Metrics.

The process of Risk Management starts, as one might expect, with an identification of those factors that could cause problems for the project, identifying the "risks" themselves. These can range from the possibility of key individuals going sick to the satisfaction of requirements being more complex than was originally thought. Basically you should identify anything that your experience, and the experience of others, tells you could cause you problems, and by problems we mean factors that could result in missing milestones and delivery or exceeding your cost budget.

Each risk factor should now have assigned to it a probability of occurring. This brings us to the first link between Risk Management and Software Metrics. In an ideal world you would look back at your collection of project data, all partitioned by class of project, and within the relevant class you would identify each time that particular factor made its presence felt. Is it too much to ask how many of your last one hundred projects, reported absence due to illness of a key individual? Of course it is. As we said before, you probably do not have decent data on your last project, let alone the last one hundred. Sorry, this is not patronizing, you know your own reality just as I do.

So what do you do? Well one thing that you can consider is to use a Delphi approach to probability assignment. Get some of your team together and ask them, how likely is it that we are going to suffer from sickness? Alternatively make a guess yourself. This is not a perfect or even good solution but at least you are starting to think about managing the project rather than letting it manage you. Managers who let their projects control them rather than vice versa often state that they spend most of their time firefighting. The trick is not to let the fire start.

Of course there is something else that you can do. You can start to collect information on risk factors. But what about the fact that every project is different? Let us see if some of the commonly identified risk factors ring any bells with you:

Milestones being missed

Requirements volatility and growth

Staff loss and turnover, resulting in a lowering of application knowledge

Customer or management pressure on delivery dates

Morale loss due to external events such as a reorganization

Unanticipated complexity, sometimes called the "how-did-I- get-into-this-mess" syndrome.

If these do ring bells with you then you probably know projects where they have occurred. The chances are, unfortunately, that you will work on projects in the future where they will also occur. You will find that most managers will agree that these are probably risk factors on their projects wherever they are. That being the case you should be able to collect information from projects where those risks become problems and, equally, from those projects where they do not. This enables you, at some time in the future, to derive probabilities based on more than pure guesswork.

But why bother? You want those probabilities for a very pragmatic reason. There are only so many hours in the day and you do not want to spend time managing a risk that has a 1% probability of occurring as a problem. Much better to concentrate your efforts on those that are likely to become problems.

As a personal guideline, I believe that Risk Management principles should be applied to any risk factor with a 25% or more probability of occurring. Mind you, I am a great believer in Sods Law that says that anything that can go wrong will, at the worst possible moment!

Having decided what risk factors are probable (or at least *more* probable) to be the problems of tomorrow you should decide what you are going to do about them if and when they occur. In other words, you should prepare contingency plans. Personally I prefer two levels of contingency planning, what I call amber plans and crisis plans. My amber plans usually reflect the belief that I can still contain the problem, perhaps by working a little overtime or shifting a couple of priorities. The crisis plan is something else again. When a crisis plan kicks in, the bells go off, lifeboats are readied, break out the extra-strong coffee and cancel leave until we get it licked.

Never plan to run a crisis plan for long. Neither you nor your people can work at the pitch a crisis demands for long. If you try the chances are you will make the situation worse!

To give you an example of the two different types of plan let us look at a much simplified pair of plans. Let us say that I notice that morale is dropping because of concerns about a reorganization. The first thing to do is "go public." A memo goes off to my manager saying that the lack of information is causing me problems. I might also decide to take everyone out for an extended lunch, the idea being to get them off the battlefield and somewhere they can talk more freely. I may also start to run a "happy hour" for the last couple of hours on a Friday.

Now what if things still go from bad to worse? The situation is that people feel so browned off that work is not getting done. What is getting done is shoddy and, because of an increase in rework, it really looks like this project is going to miss delivery, exceed its budget and be seen as a failure. Assume I also KNOW that the cause of this is the way the reorganization is being handled. First rule again, go public. Start banging the drum so hard that someone has to take notice. Advise the most senior director you can get access to, advise the customer, at least of the effect if not the cause. Run a containment action. The team members are so fed up that it is affecting their work, so maybe we should stop work, get them off-site for a couple of days and talk it through as a group. Maybe nothing can be done to fix the problem but we can certainly start to feel better about the way we handle the problem.

Now, you may not agree with the bare bones of the approach I have outlined to handling the particular problem I chose as an illustration but you should realize one thing: none of the reactions outlined was a spur-of-the-moment thing. They were all planned in advance and were there ready and waiting to be called into play when needed. This approach means that you are able to worry about containing the effects of the problem rather than worrying about how you are going to achieve that containment.

The trick of course is to know when to kick in those contingency plans and this brings us to the next link between Risk Management and Software Metrics: the risk factors must have measures associated with them, and these measures must be monitored. Additionally, there should be predetermined levels at which the contingency plans, amber or crisis, come into play.

6.3   PROGRESS MONITORS

How you measure the risk factors is an area of great interest to those in the metrics discipline but what it really comes down to is setting in place monitors with which you are comfortable. In many cases these will be subjective and you should remember that there is nothing intrinsically wrong with subjective measures. Certainly, the last time I purchased a car, a not insignificant personal investment, the only hard measure involved was that of price. The rest of the decision was purely subjective.

Looking at a couple of the risk factors I have claimed are fairly common across projects you might decide to measure morale by having your project team members fill in a questionnaire each month. When I first ran this as an experiment to see if it was feasible to collect soft or environmental data in this way I was pleasantly surprised that I was able to detect changes in morale across the team by asking about things like promotion prospects and training. I was also surprised at how happy the team members were to take part in the exercise. They felt it gave them a chance to point out the good things and the bad things in their working environment and, hopefully, to have an effect on that environment.

Complexity could be handled in much the same way. You could ask each of your designers to simply state if they think recognized complexity is now less than it was last month, the same, or greater than last month. Add in a couple more options to give them more scope and if 50% or more of them say it has grown you could have a problem. Watch out for creeping growth. If you get a small increase each month you can end up with a big increase over the life of the project.

Wherever possible it is best to use hard measures and this is certainly possible for some risk factors. The occurrence of many risk factors shows itself in a reduction in progress. Monitoring progress against plan is one of the most effective ways of controlling a project — especially when this is tied into an effective Risk Management strategy.

There are a number of ways that progress can be monitored. If your milestones operate at a fairly low level (normally this means that milestones are being passed with no more than a fortnight's gap on each major plan stream), then milestone monitoring can be an effective progress check. All you need do is monitor the milestones that should be achieved during a particular time slice against what has actually been achieved.

Another, somewhat more complicated, approach is to use *Earned Value Analysis*. This is well described in most project planning books but the basic principle is that by the time it is delivered a project will have spent a certain amount, say in terms of engineering hours. At a particular point in time you compare what has been spent to what should have been spent, also building in how much is still to be spent. The formulas get a bit messy but most project planning tools that allow for the recording of actual effort spent will calculate Earned Value for you. Earned Value is fine as far as it goes but it does assume that the plan is realistic. This is not always the case.

An approach I particularly like is known by the inauspicious name of the *RAG Technique*. RAG stands for RED, AMBER and GREEN which gives a good clue as to how this approach works. The principle is one of project classification and one of the major benefits of the approach is that it allows managers to concentrate their efforts where they will do most good. The technique works where there are a number of projects running simultaneously or where a large project can be subdivided into smaller elements or sub-projects.

Each project should have a project manager and this individual is tasked with filling in a questionnaire each month, or perhaps fortnightly. The questionnaire can be as long and complex as it need be but remember that someone has to spend time filling it in. Personally I believe ten or twelve questions should be ample for most environments.

Question and answer pairs are of the multiple choice variety and the responses are run through a very simple scoring algorithm. If for example you had a question that related to resource usage things might look like this:

Q: Compared to planned budget expenditure for this project, how much has actually been spent to date?

> 20% Underspend	Scores 5
< 10% Underspend	3
As planned	0
< 10% Overspend	1
> 20% Overspend	5

and the score is added to a running total.

When you have a final score you simply use this to classify each project as being at status GREEN, AMBER or RED.

The nice touches in this technique are that GREEN projects are allowed to go on their merry way because, after all, everything seems to be fine with them. They are hitting milestones on time, spending what they said they would and the project manager is happy. Why should a more senior manager waste time formally reviewing a project that is running well? Of course, that manager should make sure that the truth is being told.

AMBER projects do not have serious problems but should be watched. The easiest way to do this is to have a rule that says projects at AMBER for two months out of three will go to RED status. Again, the system can be abused, but what system can't?

RED projects get special attention. Where this approach works is when the project manager whose project has gone RED is not hit over the knuckles like a naughty boy. The chances are that the problems are totally beyond his or her control as they may stem from another department or they may be the fault of, for example, more senior managers. Having recognized that a problem exists the thing to do is to contain and remove it, not to make someone feel bad. To do this the project manager, his manager and someone from the project control office who administers the RAG system should get together. Of course, if someone continually has projects that perform poorly and the fault seems to lie with them then that is a particular type of senior management failure: the wrong person may have been put in the wrong job.

You should also note that a project manager should always be given the option of asking for the project to be made red even if everything currently looks okay. Typically, RAG questions relate to progress and could include the following examples:

What percentage of milestones due have been achieved?

Are any deliverables due from external sources behind schedule?

British Telecomm is possibly the largest private business operating within the UK and it would be foolish to say that RAG is used in every part of the organization but they have presented did some interesting claims for the success of RAG including dramatic reductions in re-plans and late deliveries.

One of the best things about RAG is its simplicity. It costs little to administer and can really give you a handle on project control.

6.4   SUMMARY

The topic of project control illustrates the wide range of areas that include and benefit from an element of measurement. It is a fact that projects that are not controlled or not managed have a high probability of failure in terms of overrunning on cost and duration budgets. Control cannot function effectively if it depends upon gut feel. This is, in microcosm, the problem faced by all managers. The particular problem facing managers in the software engineering industry is that managing by gut feel or flying by the seat of your pants is the norm. This is one reason we have so many problems and they will not go away unless we do something about them.

The other thing to remember about project control is that it is already seen as a necessary piece of bureaucratic control by most engineers. This means that you can introduce things in this area, such as questionnaires, with a lot less controversy than in some other areas. If, however, you also spend some time talking to the engineers, involving them and getting them to help shape the bureaucracy they start to own it. People are generally more careful of things they own than they are of things they do not.

SECTION 2

Building and Implementing

a Software Metrics Program

In this section we will look at approaches to putting a measurement regime in place within an organization such that we can reap real benefits from the techniques and specific metrics applications previously discussed

7

A Lifecycle for Metrication

Key Points:
A project based lifecycle for developing and implementing a measurement program
A brief overview of the constituent parts of that lifecycle

This chapter introduces the second section of the book. This section discusses the development and implementation of Software Metrics initiatives or programs within business organizations. The intention is to provide a route map that will take a practitioner from the initiation of such a program all the way through to its first stage of implementation. At that point it is a question of expansion and further implementation and all the points that will have been discussed by then apply for the future.

The framework upon which this section is built is a lifecycle model and I would like to spend some time discussing that model. I appreciate that you may be very familiar with the concept of lifecycle models and if this is the case you may wish to simply skim this chapter to familiarize yourself with my use of various terms or pass over it completely. The following chapters put the meat on the bones by discussing each of the lifecycle stages in more detail. The work involved in each stage, the problems that may be encountered and, most importantly, some possible ways of overcoming those problems will be described.

7.1   THE LIFECYCLE MODEL

The lifecycle is a generic model. This means that you may need to tailor it to your own specific environment by adding a further level of detail. You may also need to add some additional activities that are specific to the way in which your organization operates. The most likely area where this will be necessary is in the budget approval tasks. You may even be able to skip some of the specific tasks described later.

The model is described by means of a data flow diagram (DFD) type of notation used to describe a process rather than to model a computer system's behavior. I have found this to be an extremely useful way of modeling processes. The notation is quite straightforward:

Circles represent processes, tasks or activities. Essentially these show elements of work that need to be carried out by people.

Directed lines show the inputs to or outputs from processes. These are objects, resources or deliverables consumed or produced by the processes.

Parallel lines indicate stores of information. Conventionally these are files or database entities within a computer system but in our model they have a wider meaning. They can be electronic stores but they are also used to indicate paper files, any type of repository and even generic stores such as "literature."

Rectangles retain the conventional DFD meaning of terminators. In this model they represent objects or entities with which the Software Metrics implementation process must interact.

The model is layered with greater detail being added to each layer. We start with the highest level of the model, the context diagram of *Figure 7.1.* Notice that I will use the term "Software Metrics Program" to describe the development and implementation of a measurement initiative.

Figure 7.1   Software Metrics Initiative Context Diagram

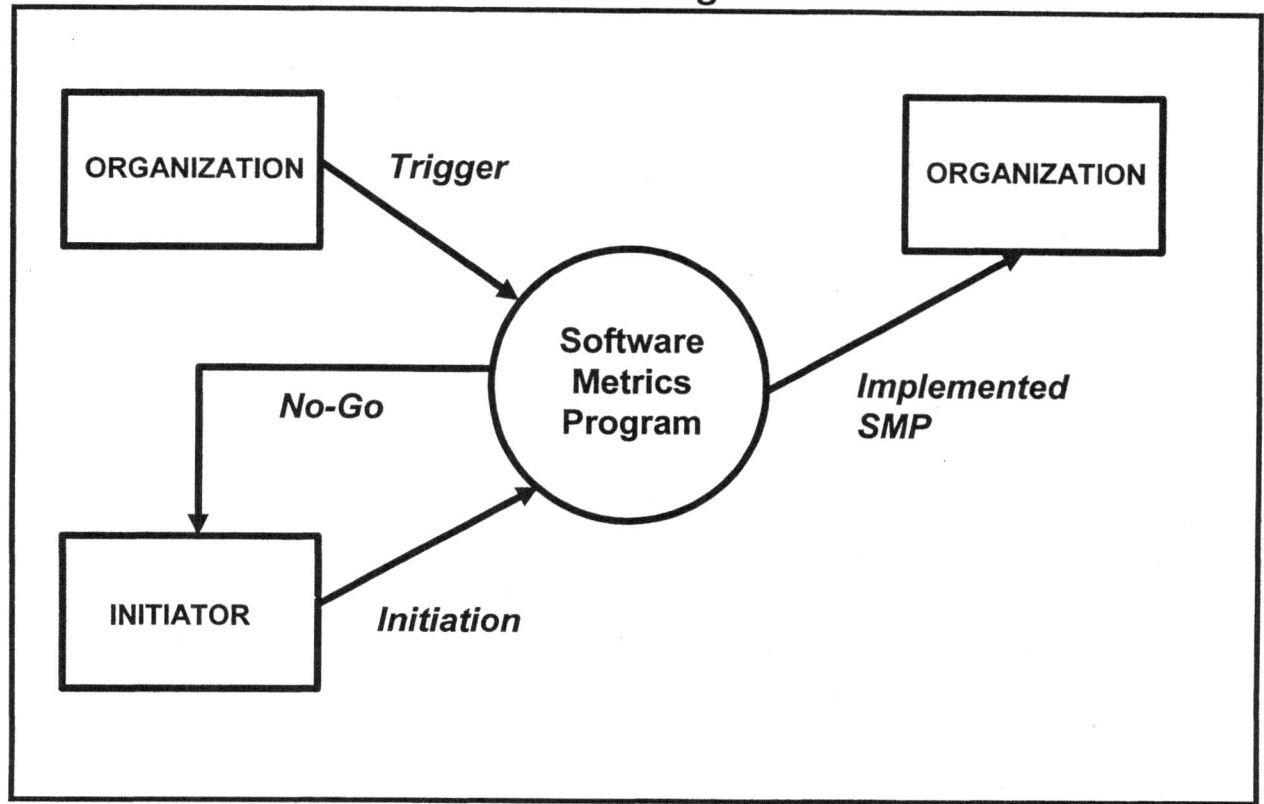

This describes the system boundary of our implementation program. It shows that the program is a process in its own right that takes, as input, some trigger from the organization and delivers, some time later, the results of the implementation back to the organization. I have deliberately shown the initiator of the Software Metrics program, which I will sometimes refer to as the SMP, separately because, as you will see in the next chapter, this individual or group of people is a major element in determining the scope of the program.

The context diagram is useful at the conceptual level because it recognizes that the trigger, the situation or situations that give rise to a need for a measurement initiative, the initiator and the eventual customer or recipient of the Software Metrics program are external to the process of developing and implementing that program. The key word is "customer" and this theme of the program serving the needs of customers will recur many times.

Something else we need to be aware of is that a decision not to proceed with the SMP is possible. We will try to avoid this situation — but forewarned is forearmed.

If we move down one level and explode the SMP process bubble you see, in *Figure 7.2*, that the lifecycle model looks familiar. It bears a close resemblance to simplistic system design lifecycles common in the computing industry. This is quite deliberate.

Figure 7.2   Level 1 Lifecycle Model

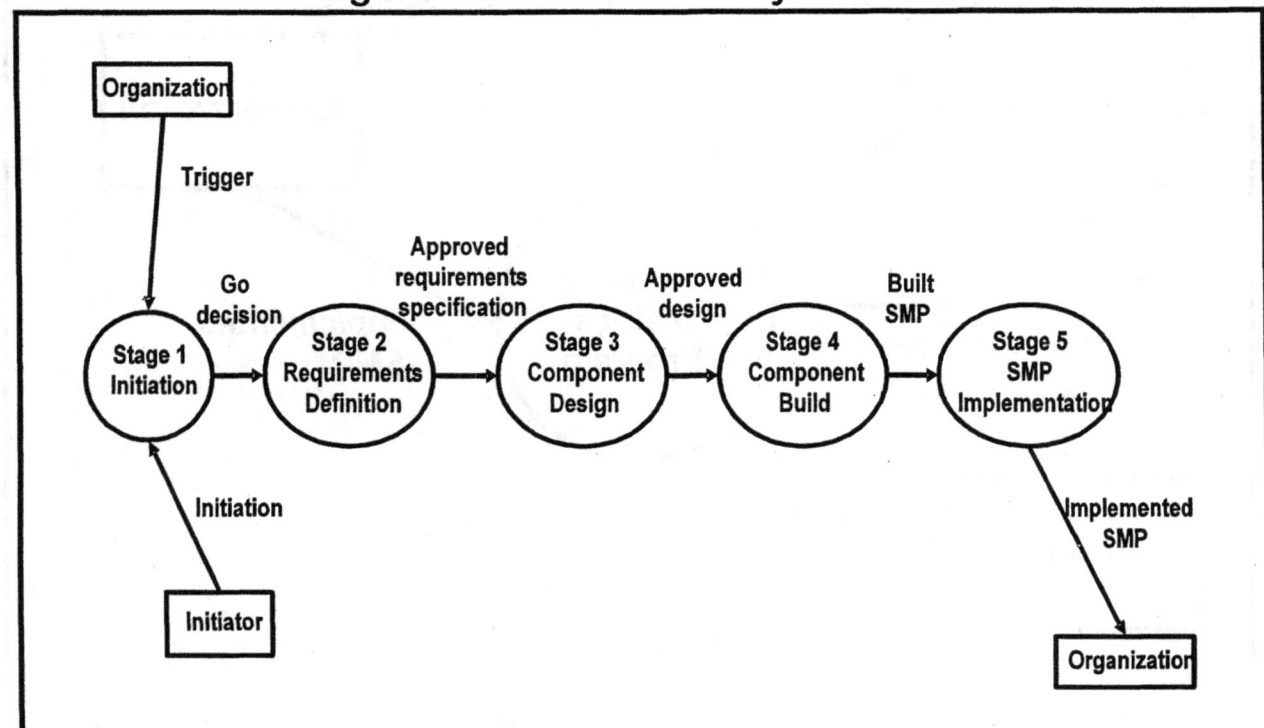

Introducing the use of Software Metrics to an organization demands the same approach as any other project whose aim is to develop a system. Ignoring this fact, or missing out one or more of these high-level stages, probably accounts for more failed Software Metrics programs than any other single mistake.

Everything starts somewhere, so we recognize this with an *Initiation Stage*. Decisions taken during this stage set the scene for the rest of the program and can form the foundation of a successful program — or sound its death knell before it ever really gets going. It is a question of designing for success rather than designing to fail, and we probably all have experience of projects where the latter was the case.

Requirements gathering and specification, which I have referred to as *Requirements Definition*, is the next stage and is so often ignored. It is not enough to simply read the literature and then to blindly impose a program on the organization. It is very easy to define and develop a Software Metrics program that addresses productivity measurement only to find that the most senior customer for that program is concerned about user satisfaction and not with productivity. The Software Metrics Program needs to address the problems of the organization and we cannot do this unless we know what those problems are. Please remember that one person's view of those problems will never give you the total picture. There are always different viewpoints within an organization and these will have different problems as well as different requirements. I will talk more about this later, but let me stress the importance of this by saying that recognition of these different viewpoints is another important step towards a successful measurement initiative.

Design is also necessary. The *Design Stage* encompasses both the choice of specific metrics; notice that it is only now that this is considered, together with the design of the infrastructure that will support the use of those metrics. Many programs fail because they concentrate on the metrics at the expense of this infrastructure and one of the areas that seems to let many such programs down is in the area of feedback. Many programs seem to assume that this will happen automatically once data has been collected, but it will not. This aspect of the Software Metrics program needs to be addressed in as much detail as the derivation and specification of the metrics themselves. Both aspects of the program are important. I have used the term *Component Design* to indicate that there are different streams within the program, perhaps concentrating on cost estimation and on management information as an example.

The *Component Build Stage* is the easy part, at least speaking relatively. Provided the design is correct and is based on effective requirements capture, the build stage is equivalent to coding from a good software design; it is mechanistic. That is not to say that there will not be a considerable amount of work to do. You will not only have to do the equivalent of coding in terms of writing operational procedures, you will have to build the full system from the ground up from welding the case together to writing the user guides! A lot of work, so make it as easy as possible by getting the earlier stages right!

Implementation is where it gets difficult again. This is where you will be putting your theories into practice. You will meet many problems that you will not have thought about before; this is a fact of life. You will be working closely with other people who may not immediately see the benefits of your proposals. You will be changing the culture. Anyone who has been involved in the introduction of a new computer system will be only too aware of the vagaries and upsets that can occur during this stage but will also be aware of the satisfaction that comes with success.

And if we succeed, then we do it all again while expanding our system across more of the organization and tackling the requirements we put off until the "second build." Do you really want all this grief?

If you do; if you become responsible for the introduction of Software Metrics to your organization, then be prepared for a roller coaster ride. Like a roller coaster you will find things start off slowly as you climb the first slope. But once you pass the summit of that first slope you will be moving so fast through the ups and downs that you could often feel things are out of control. You may well experience real fear at some of things that happen and the things that you see but you will also see a lot more than those on the ground. The trick is to keep control of yourself and the program. When you finally get off the roller coaster you will have a real sense of achievement. Welcome aboard!

8

Stage 1 - Initiation

> **Key Points:**
>
> Typical triggers for a measurement program
>
> The impact of ownership (technical versus business)
>
> Setting up your measurement team
>
> Getting past the first hurdles

This is the first point that we start to see the customers we, as the developers and implementors of a measurement program, will have to serve. This orientation, almost fixation, on the customer angle that you will find running through this section, has its basis in reality. Too often, measurement initiatives fail because they are developed in ivory towers totally removed from the software engineering environment or the people involved in that metrics program development pay lip service to the concept of customer service and then proceed to ignore that interface.

If you remember nothing else then remember that your purpose is to make things better for others within your organization. The organization, with its many facets, is your customer. The organization does not exist for your benefit or for the benefit of your measurement program..

Having said all that, this is also the first point that you begin to realize what you may have let yourself in for. I have a theory that people are appointed to Software Metrics teams when they are ill, on leave or absent from work for some other reason. Surely nobody actually asks to join this bunch of madmen and madwomen who, for some strange reason, actually seem to enjoy trying to do the impossible, for the ungrateful, with practically no resources!

And it all starts with the initiation stage of the process. *Figure 8.1* contains some detail about this and the format I will adopt is that you get the picture early and we can then discuss things in text. As the diagram shows, everything starts somewhere, even Software Metrics programs.

Figure 8.1   Initiation Stage of a Software Metrics Program

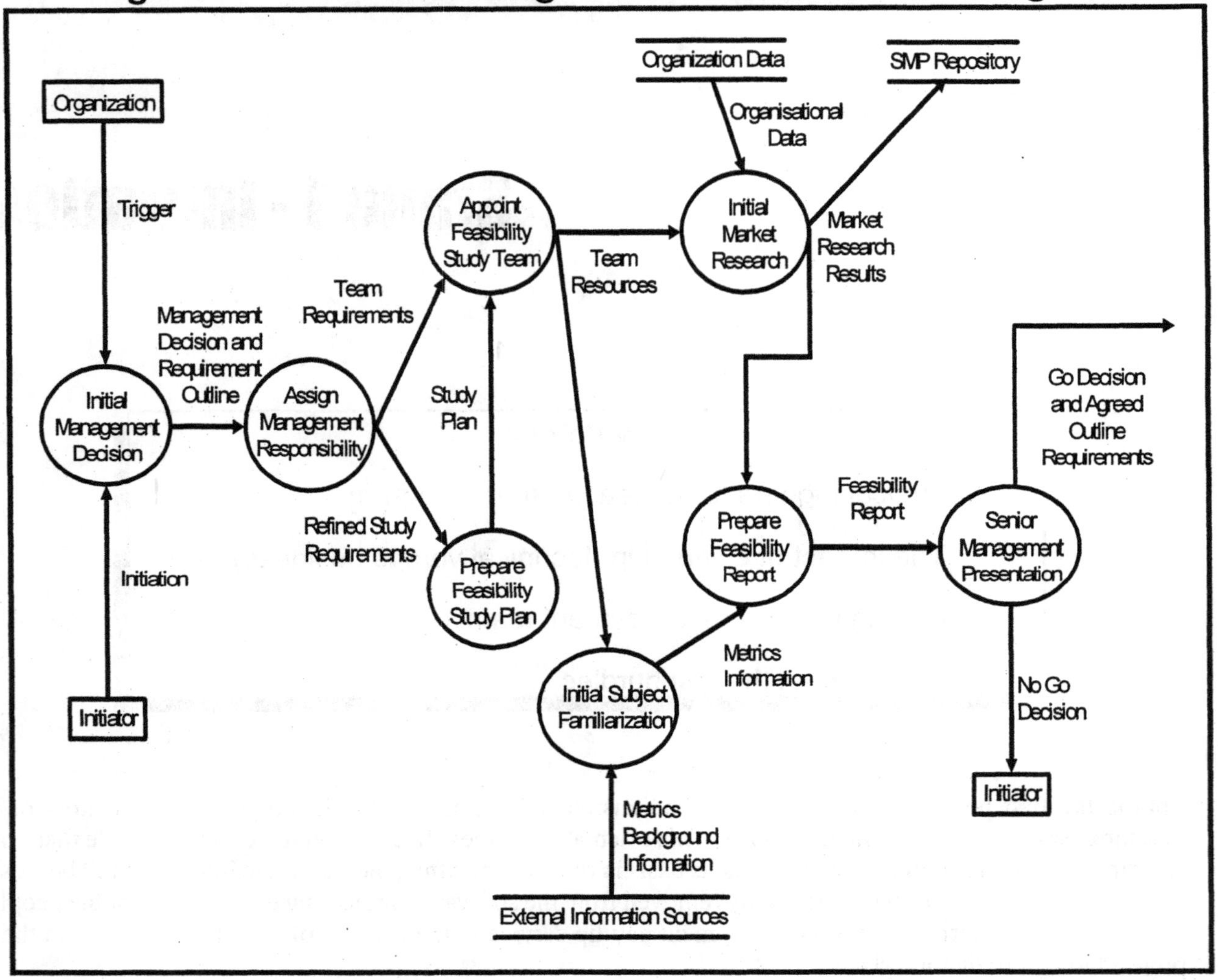

8.1 THE INITIAL MANAGEMENT DECISION

Two things lie behind the start of a Software Metrics program: an *organizational trigger* and an *initiator*. The trigger comes from some need within the organization. The initiator realizes that the need exists and seeks to satisfy that need.

Software Metrics programs can be triggered by many different situations or events and some of these are listed in *Table 8.1.*

Table 8.1: Software Metrics Program Triggers

General quality or productivity concerns
Concern about customer complaints
Customers requirements for increased information
Knowledge of competitors' activity in the metrics area
Process improvement programs
A cost-cutting environment
Management pressure for more information
A consultancy recommendation
New awareness of the possibility of measurement, perhaps as a result of someone attending a conference or seminar

One point that should be recognized is that it is rarely possible to attribute a single trigger to a Software Metrics program. The reality is that there tend to be multiple triggers for such an initiative. This can be both a blessing and a curse. A blessing, in that it tends to widen the scope of the work so that difficulties, and even failures in one area, can be outweighed by successes in others. A curse, because widening the scope of the work can slow things down — and one problem with any metrics program is that the lead time, as it were "the time to market," can be seen as a liability by an organization.

This problem is often a result of limited understanding of Software Metrics within the organization. "After all, we are only talking about a putting in a bit of measurement aren't we? Other industries measure so it can't really be that difficult. We should be able to get something going by next month." Well of course we can. It will not work, will probably cost money and will also probably result in at least part of the organization being turned against metrics for the foreseeable future!

It is vitally important that a Software Metrics program is not seen as a quick fix. Software Metrics is about fixing the process rather than patching to fix the fault.

For example, it will take a certain amount of time to develop and implement a productivity measurement program, some time to collect data and a small amount of time to interpret that data. This is not a rapidly deployed defense against the threat of outsourcing within the next two weeks! Depending on the scope of the program and the size of the organization there will be a minimum elapsed time necessary before the program can be implemented and the lifecycle that lies behind this book will enable a manager to assess that minimum time for his or her organization. After all, if you know what needs to be done you stand a much better chance of estimating how long it will take.

Recognizing the trigger or triggers is important because they can affect the Software Metrics program by driving it down a particular road. For example, it is no good advising people how to measure software usability if the sole trigger is concern over productivity levels. When you start to plan your own Software Metrics program, it is a useful exercise to list the triggers acting within your organization as you see them. This gives you your initial focus but bear in mind that this is not cast in stone. You will be gathering specific requirements as you progress through the lifecycle and these can broaden the scope of the program.

We can now consider the initiator of the program. I view the initiator as someone who is external to the Software Metrics Program but someone who will still interact with that process especially during the earlier stages of its lifecycle. Generally, an initiator identifies a need for measurement, determines that something will be done to satisfy that need and then promptly delegates the responsibility for development and implementation to someone else. This is generally known as management! Seriously, such delegation makes sense. Initiators tend to be in positions where they are affecting strategic positioning whereas the developers and implementors function at the tactical and operational levels.

The initiator sets out the scope of the work and will often obtain or even give the initial authorization for that work. The initiator's role is important because he or she sets out the boundary of the eventual system, thus bringing in the first set of constraints. At the same time, the initiator will not be a Software Metrics expert and so should not aim to constrain the program too tightly. In many ways, the initiators role is akin to the person who chooses a site for a new building. Picking rocky terrain will mean that the builders will have their work made more difficult by external constraints, they will have to cut through solid rock. Pick shifting sand, by giving no guidance on the initial direction, and there will be many false starts.

The initiator must draw a balance between constraining or tightly defined requirements and a vague problem definition that is liable to drastic changes. Different initiators tend to lean one way or the other as illustrated by *Table 8.2*:

Table 8.2

Initiator		Too Rigorous	Too Vague	
Chief Executive or Director		X		
QA Function				X
R&D Group				X
Customers or Users	X			
A Technocrat		X		
Management Consultant			X	
Auditors			X	

As a guideline, during the initiation stage it is better to tend towards vagueness rather than rigor. After all, at this stage we do not really know what we are getting into, so a rigorous definition will probably be incorrect anyway. Notice that I said "tend towards vagueness." Make sure that you, as the initiator, do not put your people on shifting sand by at least giving them the space to define their own terms of reference. These can then be reviewed by you to ensure that they meet business goals.

The people responsible for the development and implementation of the Software Metrics program will probably have little to do with the early part of the initiation stage so let us now assume that a decision has been taken within the organization to do something about Software Metrics. Now we get down to the real work.

8.2   ASSIGN MANAGEMENT RESPONSIBILITY

Somebody has to take responsibility for the work being done. Ideally, this will not be the people doing the work but rather somebody with authority within the organization and someone with access to senior management. Access to senior management is important because the final activity within the initiation stage concerns a proposal for further work. This further work will involve a cost and will need to be authorized at some level. Many programs flounder because they cannot get a fair hearing from senior management who control the purse strings, and since we are going to face enough problems anyway, design to succeed from the start by making sure that you can get that fair hearing.

There are many terms used to describe the individual who takes on responsibility for a work item; the sponsor, the champion and the customer authority are some common examples. Personally, I prefer the third choice as sponsors and champions can lack involvement, merely lending their name to the project while the term "customer authority" implies someone with a specific role, namely to act as the final arbiter for the project when decisions have to be made. Whatever term is used (and an organization will have its own preferences), a relatively senior individual should be appointed as the sponsor or customer authority for the Software Metrics program. As a general guideline, the more senior the customer authority the better, provided the involvement of that person can be assured. Do *not* go for seniority at the expense of involvement!

It is generally advised that the customer authority should not change during the life of the a project. Reality often means that such a change will happen, possibly more than once. We all know the pain that severe changes to requirements can cause a project, so if your customer authority does change, endeavor to ensure that the new sponsor accepts and agrees to the requirements, designs, etc. that have already been signed off. This can involve some effort but it more than pays for itself. Notice that this implies that such things are documented and retained. It is no good having the terms of reference in peoples heads.

8.3   APPOINT FEASIBILITY STUDY TEAM

The initiation stage involves the concept of a feasibility study. The organization has demonstrated an awareness of Software Metrics by initiating the implementation project but it may well need to be convinced that the effort will pay back the cost. At the very least there will be some senior managers who have doubts about whether it is possible to control the software development process through measurement. They will need to be convinced that there is some merit in going forward and this should be done as early as possible. This is one of the things we hope to achieve at the end of the initiation stage. Now, who is going to do this work and convince these doubters?

The feasibility team should be small. Even in a very large organization it should not consist of more than three or four people. For most organizations one or two people, reporting functionally to the assigned customer authority, should be sufficient. Although there is considerable debate about whether metrics team staff should be full or part time, I firmly believe that the team should be assigned their responsibility on a full time basis or the work will be patchy, shallow and will take too long.

It is unlikely that an organization will possess a "metrics expert." It is also true to say that Software Metrics is not yet so well established that recruiting the services of someone who is experienced in the area will be easy. The use of consultants can help overcome this but it is important that any consultant be employed on the understanding that one of their main tasks is to transfer knowledge to the organization. At the risk of offending some people I have found consultants to be like little boys. When they are good they are very, very good but when they are bad they can be truly awful! Remember, even good consultants will need help from someone who understands the business of the organization.

Which brings us to the skills we need in the feasibility team. We cannot expect to get a Software Metrics program that works well for the organization if we do not understand the business, so we need someone who knows the business or who can get that knowledge quickly. We will also need someone who can get valid and useful information from other people so we need an effective interviewer. A good systems analyst can often supply these first two skills and is a godsend to any Software Metrics team. We also need to be able to present our ideas to other people so a good communicator, both in terms of writing skills and the ability to talk to different types of audience is important.

Finally, measurement is about numbers so a good understanding of mathematics is desirable. We are really talking about applied mathematics rather than pure math on the one hand or "sums" on the other because, in many cases, it is the application of mathematical techniques to new and different areas that is necessary to make Software Metrics work.

The initiator and the customer authority should ensure that they appoint good people to the feasibility team. Do not be tempted to assign dead wood to this group. Once again, design to succeed, do not design to fail — or you will!

8.4   "WE NEED A PLAN!"

The feasibility team will also need to be given an initial direction. In other words they should be given a high level plan or requirement for at least the rest of the first stage. This is the responsibility of the initiator together with the customer authority and should encompass the following points:

> **The scope of the work.** Are they to look at the whole organization or only part of it? What are the main drivers or triggers that the organization wishes to address through the use of Software Metrics? In other words, what problems are we trying to solve?

> **The requirements.** The feasibility team should be tasked to determine the needs of the organization though some initial market research. They should also be tasked to bring knowledge of Software Metrics to the organization by familiarizing themselves with the subject and to highlight possible benefits to the organization. Finally they should be tasked to provide a plan for the way forward geared to the needs of the organization.

> **The timescale.** In an ideal world the feasibility team would be able to prepare their own low level plan and this should determine their timescale. In reality there will be time pressure on the feasibility study and on the whole implementation program. The feasibility team will need to familiarize themselves with a new subject as well as identify the relevance of this to the organization.

The customer authority should be realistic and flexible but should give guidance to the team about when results of this first stage will be expected.

8.5   SUBJECT FAMILIARIZATION

Once the team is assigned, the work of the feasibility study can begin in earnest. We have to realize that we will only be able to fully convince the organization of the benefits of Software Metrics by demonstrating the successful use of those metrics within the organization itself. This activity is really piloting the use of Software Metrics rather than demonstrating their feasibility.

To demonstrate feasibility we will need to show that Software Metrics can potentially be used by the organization, the key word being "potentially." The easiest way to achieve this is to show that the way in which others have successfully used metrics is applicable to our own organization. This involves three distinct tasks:

*   First we have to become aware of what others have done;

- second, we have to establish the needs of our own organization; and, third,

- we will have to map what others have done to our own organization's needs and present this information in some form.

The team will almost certainly have a very limited understanding of Software Metrics when they start the work so they will need to gain a broader and more detailed appreciation of the subject. Books and technical papers are obvious sources of information. These will provide valuable background information about Software Metrics in theory and, to a more limited extent, in practice. The books and papers will also provide pointers to other sources of information that can be explored.

One of the best ways of learning about the practical use of Software Metrics is to talk to other practitioners. One of the most pleasant aspects of working in this field is that people are almost invariably willing to share their knowledge and experience, even to the extent of arranging visits to their own organizations to discuss the topic. Take advantage of this as I have and you will have the privilege of sharing time and experiences with some of the best people around..

Other sources of information are certain of the so-called "academics" who are often more practical than they are given credit for and, of course, consultants. Talking to both academics and consultants can be a very cost-effective way to gain an introduction to the subject area.

There are a small number of formal training courses that have recently appeared that deal with the subject of Software Metrics. These tend to concentrate on the theory of the metrics themselves rather than the implementation of a Software Metrics program but, again, they can provide a useful introduction to the subject.

8.6   INITIAL MARKET RESEARCH

Having gained some understanding of Software Metrics and how they can be used, the feasibility team will need to establish the needs of the organization and the potential market for the use of metrics within that organization.

The users and customers of the metrics program will be varied and will impose different requirements on the program. This is a very important point. Many Software Metrics programs concentrate on one group of these customers and this can cause problems later on as you realize that you need the cooperation of other groups within the organization — but that you are offering them nothing in return for this.

During the initial market research activity, the first thing the team will have to do is to broadly identify the potential customers of the Software Metrics program. To do this it is best to divide the organization into a number of functional groups. At this stage, a high level division will be sufficient. One such grouping is:

Senior management

Project managers

Support groups such as the planning department or the project control group

Any process improvement teams or groups in the organization

- The software engineers or programmers.

This last group is important but is often ignored. The success of your Software Metrics program will depend, at least in part, on information supplied by engineers, a term I prefer to programmers. If you ignore their needs then you may well find their co-operation difficult to obtain and the data you are given suspect. After all, why should an engineer, for example, carefully record the way his or her time is spent if they get nothing back from that additional work?

Another group of potential users of the Software Metrics program are the organization's own customers or the internal users of software that is produced. It can sometimes be difficult getting access to these people but they should be added to the above list. A strategic decision must be taken by the customer authority, namely should the organization's own customers be approached at this point or not? This will depend on the relationship between the organization and the customers but I feel that they should be approached unless there are good commercial reasons for not doing this. At the very least you can make them aware of your organization's commitment to improved service. However, be careful not to build false expectations of rapid improvement. Change takes time.

Having identified the potential users of the Software Metrics program the team will need to go and talk to these people. Obviously, the team will not be able to talk to every single potential customer: after all there may be hundreds of engineers alone. The team should identify a representative sample from each group and arrange interview sessions with these individuals. The team should also concentrate on people they think will be receptive to new ideas but should not totally exclude the ones they think may be less positive. You might as well get an appreciation of the problems these people will raise as early as possible.

Each interview should address three areas:

- The interviewer should be prepared to provide a brief introduction to the subject of Software Metrics and the reasons why the organization is looking at the topic. This should not be prescriptive because you do not want to constrain the interviewee but you will have to provide a reason for the interview and an initial direction.

- The second point that must be addressed concerns the problems faced by the interviewee in his or her work. One way to get this part of the conversation going is to ask the interviewee to briefly describe his role in the organization. This will usually bring up areas that can be explored in more detail given the high level requirements placed on the Software Metrics program.

- Finally, the interviewee should be asked what additional information they feel would be beneficial in their work. The interviewer will often need to drive this part of the session and should link the way other organizations have used Software Metrics to the role of the interviewee.

The results of the interview should be documented. I will call the store of this, and other information, the *SMP Repository*. This is no more than a convenient name for what may, in reality, be no more than a filing cabinet or electronic folder (don't forget to back up!).

Another area that the initial market research activity should address is the size of the potential market. How many groups or teams are involved in developing or enhancing software or in supporting applications? Each of these groups is a potential customer. How many projects are each team involved in? How many engineers are in each group? How many senior managers or management groupings are there? How many organizations are customers for the software produced? How many support groups, for example planning departments, are there and how are these organized? How is the process improvement group organized and how large is it?

Surprisingly, a considerable amount of effort may be required to get this information but it will pay dividends in the future. "Know your market" is a good maxim that we often ignore.

8.7   PRESENTING THE RESULTS

Having gathered all this information and knowledge we now need to make use of it to get authority to proceed. The information needs to be presented, at the very least, to someone with the necessary authority to sanction the future work, possibly to a group of senior managers. This is where the customer authority can help immensely. Get access to the most senior manager you can and present the feasibility report. The more senior the recipient of this report the briefer it should be but it should contain:

> Identification of the problems associated with software development in the organization. Refer to the triggers identified earlier.

> A statement of the business priorities of the organization.

> A definition of Software Metrics and a brief description of the scope of the subject.

> A mapping of Software Metrics to the business priorities and the problems of software development. This states what high level requirements it is planned be addressed.

> A strategy for implementing a Software Metrics program. This can be based on the following chapters of this section.

> A request for authority to proceed.

It is also a good idea to make a personal presentation to management. This presentation should summarize the report and it may be that the presentation is the vehicle for getting the necessary authority. Spend time on this to make it as professional as possible. Make sure that you know your audience. Make sure it relates to the business needs of the organization. By all means include examples from other organizations but be aware that you will only convince people, fully, when you can demonstrate success within your own organization. Make it brief!

8.8   MAKE IT A SUCCESS!

It is quite common for the feasibility aspect of the initiation stage to be missed completely. In this sense, the members of the metrics community may be victims of their own success. It is less difficult these days to convince people of the feasibility of measurement in a software engineering environment, but this brings other problems. The initiator, responding to a trigger or triggers, appoints a team, provides outline requirements and expects results. This is fine provided that time is given for subject familiarization, that the potential, internal market is identified and that, based on this, sensible plans are made.

The biggest dangers with this approach are that the initial requirements are so constrained to one area that they do not address the overall business needs of the organization or that, through ignorance of what is involved, impossible budget or resource constraints are imposed on the responsible team.

8.9 SUMMARY

The Initiation stage of a Software Metrics program, generally speaking, is out of the control of the practitioners who will have to develop and implement that program. It will be caused by some trigger and it will be driven by an initiator. It is the time when the initial scope of the program is defined. Remember that this scope will almost certainly change over time. The best advice I can give to anyone involved in the initiation stage is to *listen*. Listen to the various individuals in your own organization who will be on the receiving end of your program and listen to those outside of your organization who have been involved in measurement programs and who have probably made many of the same mistakes which could trip you up.

9

Stage 2:

Requirements Definition

Key Points:

Establishing your marketplace

Introducing a model organization

Laying firm foundations - learning what the organization needs

Establishing the shop front — the Metrics Coordination Group

At this point, I would like to do three things. First, I want to highlight and elaborate on some key points that have been made in the previous chapters so that you keep them very much in your mind as you read on. Second, I need to talk about some things that are common to each of the development and implementation life cycle stages we will be discussing. Finally, I need to set up a fictitious organization to which I can relate elements of the lifecycle model . This fictitious organization will be as generalized as I can make it but you will, of course, have to map elements of it to your own organizational structure.

Once we have looked at these items we can go on to discuss the activities and tasks that need to be carried out during this Requirements Definition stage of the development and implementation lifecycle.

9.1   THINGS TO REMEMBER

Software Metrics is a large, multidimensional subject. It covers management information, cost estimation and the use of metrics based techniques to improve quality, control complexity and to assist with system management. It is, and in fact must be, applicable to both new, green field developments and to enhancement or maintenance projects including application support. It has links to project control, configuration management and customer relations.

If you consider any standard software development life cycle, you can add an additional, parallel stream to show the relationship to software metrics as shown in *Figure 9.1*. Notice how information flows to and from

Figure 9.1   Relationships Between a Standard Lifecycle, Software Metrics and Project Management

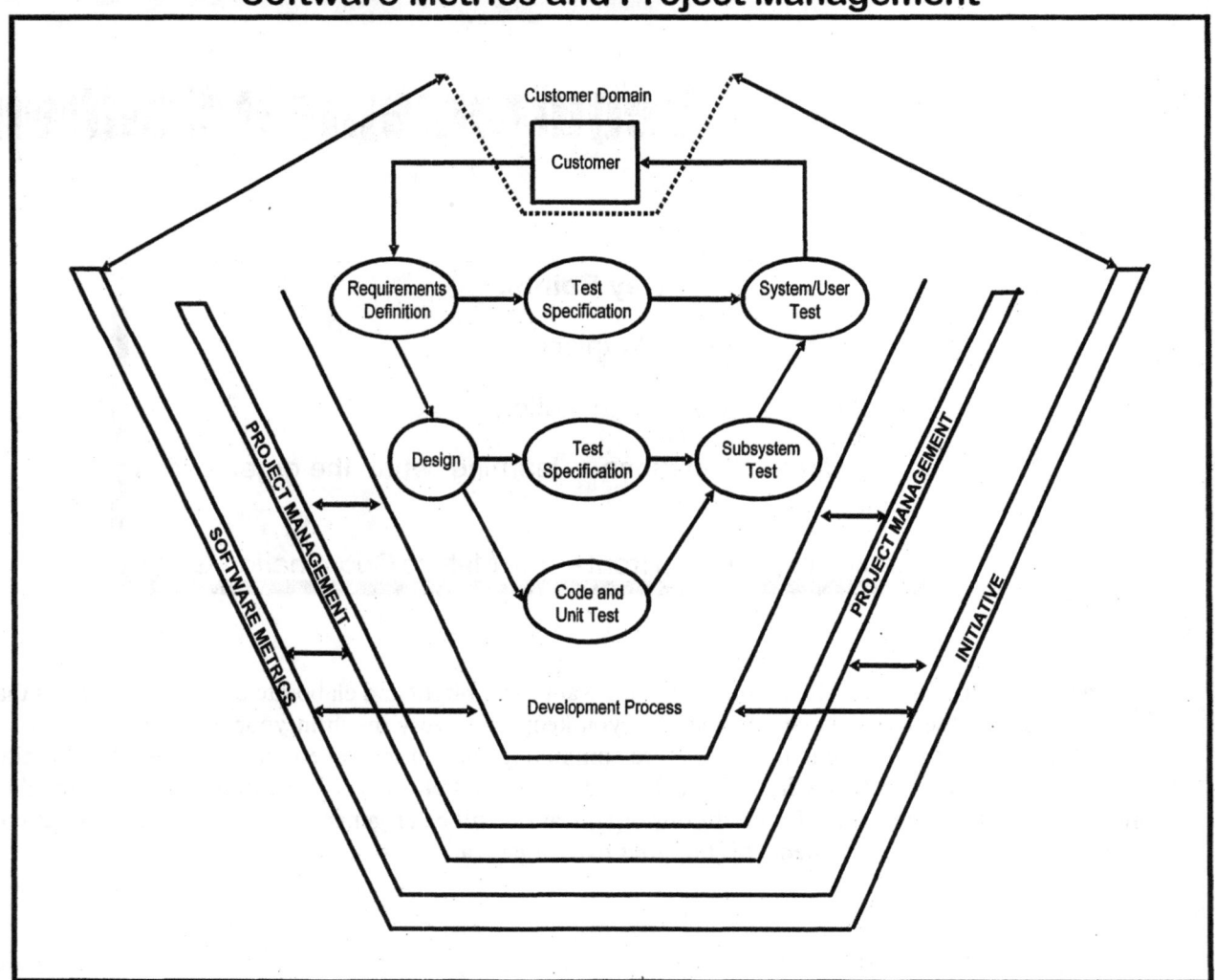

the project management process across the interfaces with the development process:

Notice also that information is communicated between the project management process and the Software Metrics initiative as well as between the Software Metrics initiative and the development process directly. There is also an interface between the customer or system user domain and the measurement program.

The next point to consider is that to attempt to introduce the use of Software Metrics in any kind of ad-hoc way simply will not work. It must be handled as a project in its own right with each of the usual project stages, i.e.:

> Requirements Definition

> Component Design

> Component Build

> Implementation.

One very useful concept that was highlighted by a QA Forum working party report of which I had the pleasure of being party to some years ago, "Implementing a Software Metrics Programme," Irvine (1), was that of multiple sub-projects within such programs. This simply states that the Requirements Definition stage may identify a number of requirements that the organization wishes the metrics program to address. After these requirements have been identified it is possible to establish a separate sub-project that takes each of these requirements through the design, build and implementation stages. This makes the management of the SMP much easier and allows an organization to concentrate on those areas where it sees a quick return while still directing some effort towards satisfying those requirements that may provide a significant pay-back in the mid to long term.

This idea can be further developed by introducing the idea of "phasing." There are a number of ways that this can be done. I have said that Software Metrics is a big subject area. Normally, there is another element of "bigness" that will affect the program, namely the size of the organization that seeks to apply metrics. Most software engineering organizations or departments consist of a number of project or product teams. Often this number is large. To target all of these at once can make the management of the Software Metrics Program a nightmare.

Phasing can help with this size problem in two ways. First, the software metrics topic itself can be partitioned and these partitions addressed by different phases of the metrics program. Second, the implementation process itself can be phased so that only a manageable number of project teams or work areas are targeted within a particular time slice.

Figure 9.2 illustrates the first type of phasing and shows effort ramping up at different times against different topic areas.

The actual partitioning can be considered right at the start of requirements specification, provided an organization is very clear about its business objectives and what areas will give the best short term pay-back. For most organizations, however, the detailed phasing is best left until the end of the Requirements Definition stage.

To summarize, Software Metrics covers many areas and will impinge on the total development process. It can also affect every member of the software development organization. Software Metrics is also a technical subject. Because of this, the introduction of Software Metrics should be treated as a project in its own right. Finally, different types of phasing can help manage the implementation of metrication.

9.2 COMMONALITY

We are going to be discussing a number of stages of the SMP development and implementation process over the next few chapters. There are two elements of commonality across these stages.

The first relates to the normal management procedures that should be applied to any project stage. An outline plan should have been prepared during the initiation stage and this should have been agreed as part of the decision to proceed. However, each stage will require some detailed planning. Organizations differ in when this is actually done, some preferring to carry out detailed planning for a stage as the first task within that stage, others prefer such planning to be done as the last task of the preceding stage. Provided this planning is done, I do not believe that it matters which option is chosen.

The second element of commonality has to do with staffing. In an ideal world, a project team would be assembled and this group of people would see the whole thing through to full implementation. There would be no staff turnover and no constraint on resources so that all team members went through the familiarization

Figure 9.2   Potential Phases of a Software Metrics Program
(Not to scale)

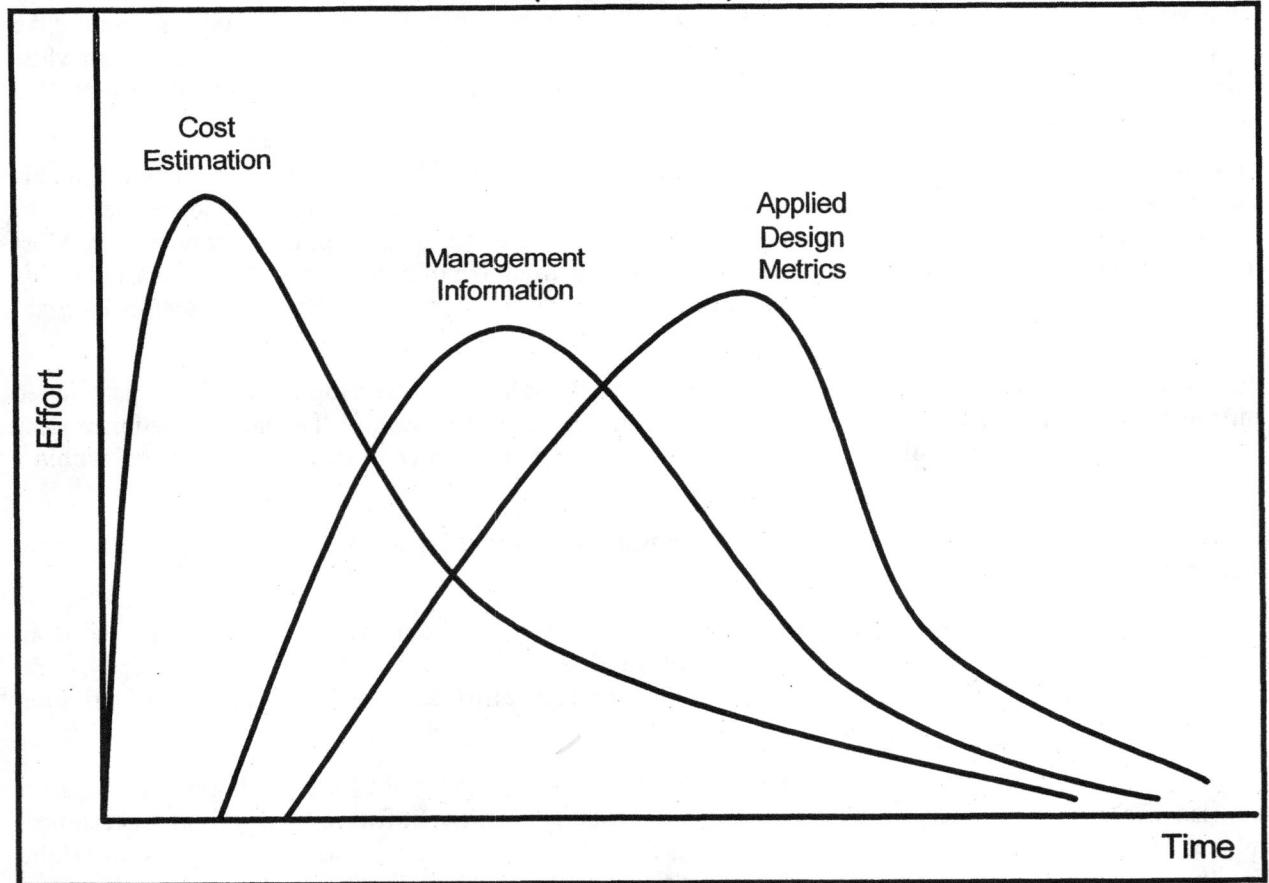

process at the same time even if this meant that some team members were then underutilized for a period of time. We live in the real world!

The reality is that, at any point in time, some staff may leave or be reassigned, as may managers. This implies that task bubbles covering staff/management appointment and subject familiarization can be added to any of the stages we will be discussing. Bear this in mind and, if you expect staff turnover, be prepared to manage this risk. One way of doing this is to ensure that the metrics team consists of at least two people, even if one of them is part-time.

In this way you can at least maintain some degree of continuity if your "expert" leaves.

Neither of these areas will be explicitly discussed during the next few chapters but remember that they can be present.

Some people may feel that a review task, that is, the work associated with reviewing deliverables of a particular stage, should also be seen as a common element across all stages. I have deliberately left that task out of this immediate discussion because I have found that the type of review process differs depending on the stage you are in at a given time. I intend to discuss the review processes explicitly as necessary.

9.3   A COMMON FRAME OF REFERENCE

To help with our discussions over the next few chapters I have concocted a fictitious organizational structure and business model that we can use as a common frame of reference. There are a number of reasons for doing this.

One of the major stumbling blocks when discussing software development, and it seems metrics in particular, is the use of words, or terminology. I remember wasting a full day of fairly intensive effort because of a misunderstanding about the word "interface." More recently I had a very interesting discussion with a colleague concerning the use of compiler preprocessors. It was just a shame that we were both discussing different things, both called preprocessors! The models discussed below will provide a common terminology for use within this book. I am not trying to impose my terminology on your organization.

While touching on the area of terminology I will point out that I will use expressions like "software engineering," "product development" and "software development" interchangeably. In all cases I am referring to the work that is carried out to develop new systems, to support existing systems including corrective maintenance and to enhance such systems. The context of the expression should make the meaning clear.

Figure 9.3　Level 1 Engineering Process

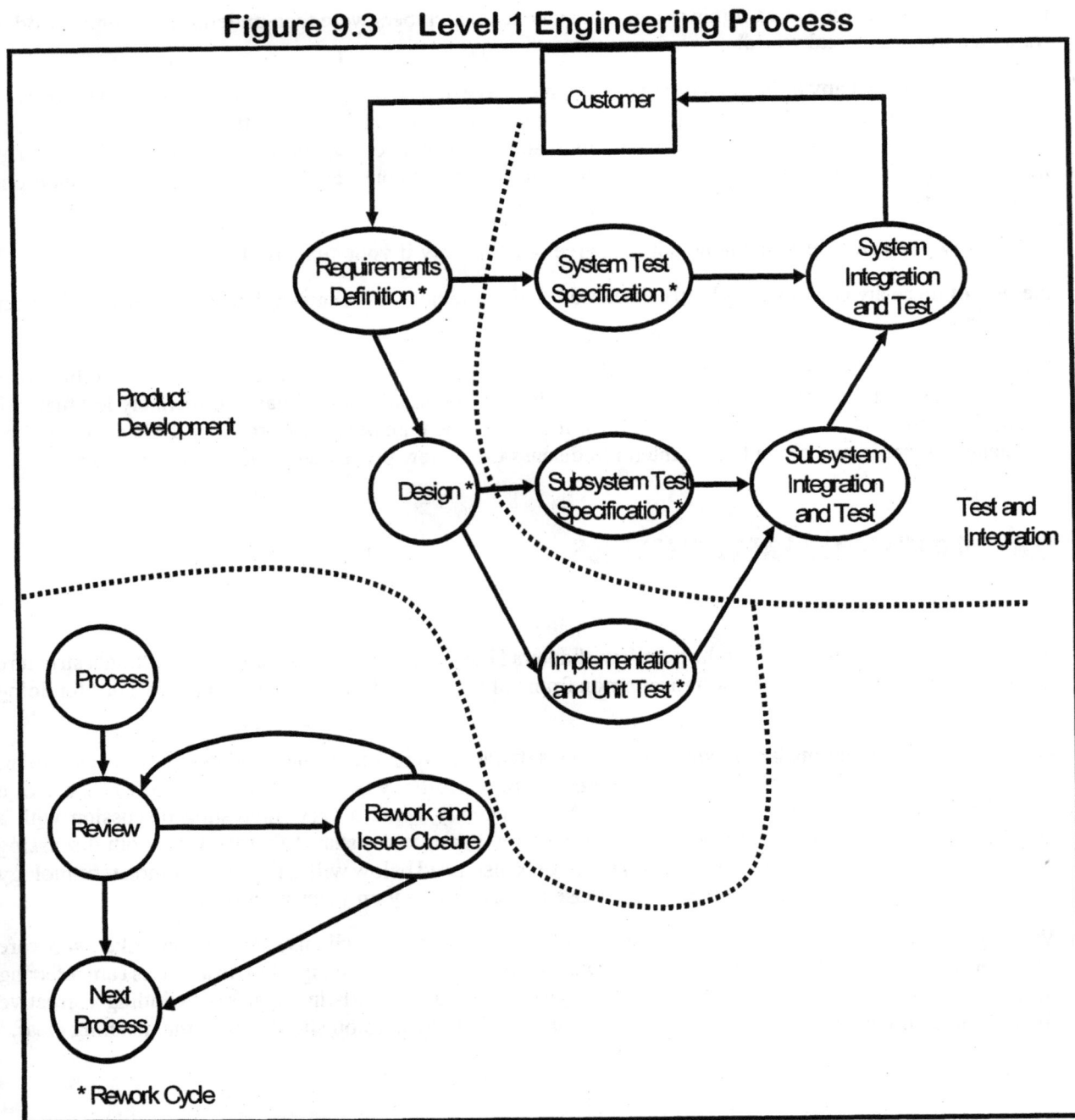

When you get into the area of software development life cycles things tend to get even worse. What I call design, others may call requirements specification; what I call low-level design, others may call implementation and include the task with coding and compilation. I offer the "V" model-based development life cycle in *Figure 9.3* simply as a common frame of reference for the purposes of this book. I do not see it replacing the Waterfall, Boehm (1), or Spiral, Boehm et al (1), models or even the newer Agile development environments if these are what you prefer. *Figure 9.3* describes the software development life cycle model

I shall use within this book. As usual, circles or bubbles indicate processes while the connecting arrows indicate deliverables or products of those processes. Please note that each process bubble marked with an "*" includes a review and rework cycle and that rework as a result of testing or proving activities have not been shown although, of course, they will be present.

If there are many representations of the software development lifecycle there are also many types of organizational structure and, again, terminology can be confusing. I will now suggest an organizational structure, not claiming that this is better than that employed by your own organization or even that it is a good structure, but simply to give us a common frame of reference. Let me stress that the organization I will depict is only used by me for the purpose of discussion and examples within this book.

Figure 9.4 shows an entity relationship model for our reference organization. This is simply a diagrammatic representation of various functions and their associations with each other within the organization. It shows Systems Development as a major function within the organization and that this function consists of two components, Product Development and Support Development both of which may consist of more than one established team.

Each Support Development team is responsible for producing a tool that will only be used internally within Systems Development. These are delivered to the Operational Support team who will then manage its use by a number of Product Development Teams.

Product Development is the revenue-earning arm of Systems Development. In this case, I will assume that this revenue is earned by selling software products to external customers although it is very possible that the organization itself may be the customer of its Systems Development Function. I will ignore the complication of bundling software and hardware together into a product that is then sold so as not to over complicate the model. From my experience, this does not have a major impact on the implementation of a Software Metrics Program although there are obviously ramifications to be borne in mind.

Figure 9.4   Functional Linkage

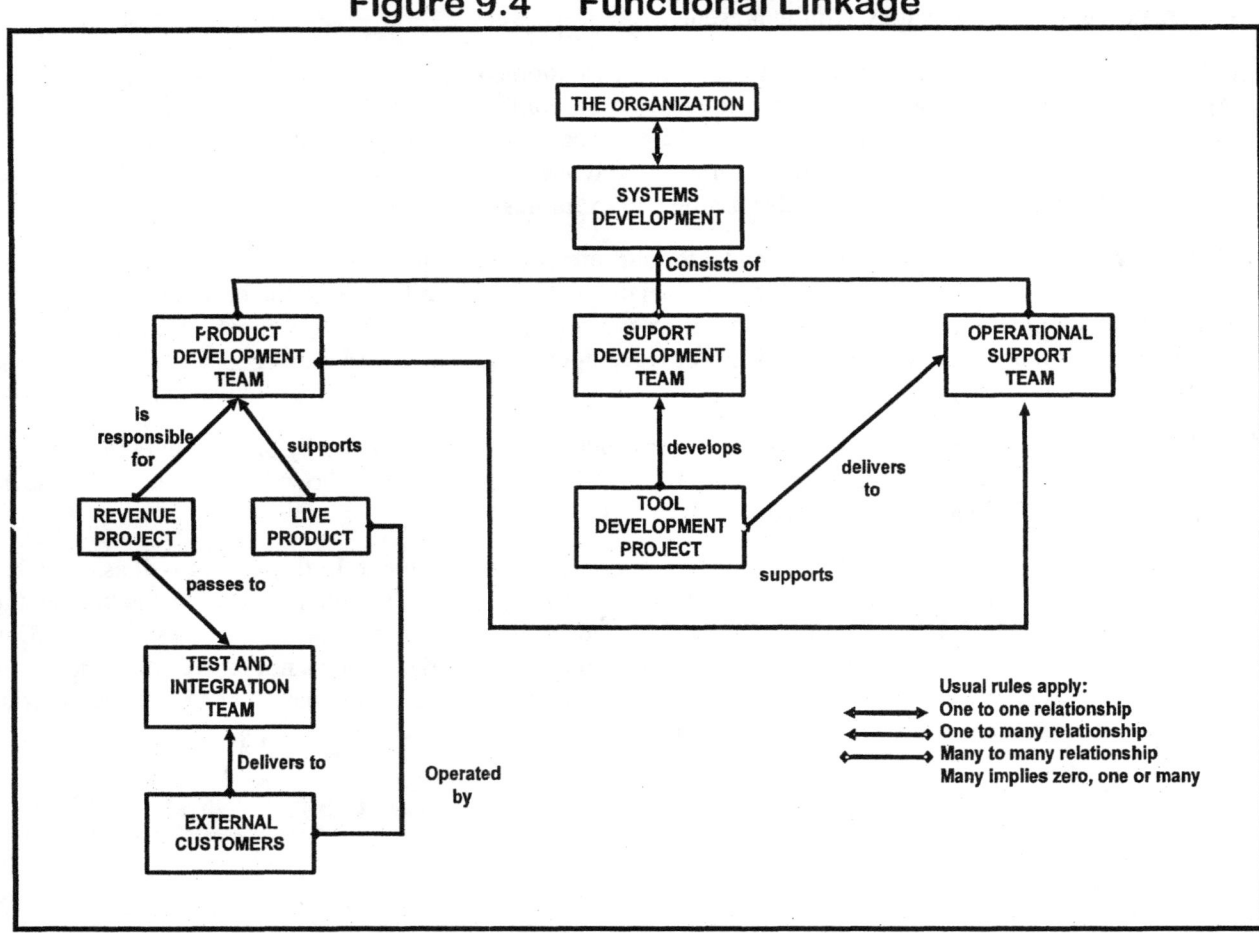

Notice that each Product Development team can be working on a number of revenue-earning projects at one time. This reflects reality where part of the team can be working on the implementation phase of the development lifecycle while another part of the team can be specifying requirements for another project. Please note also that I include enhancements to existing software products as revenue-earning projects in their own right. The maintenance of products currently in the field, which I have shown as also being the responsibility of the Product Development teams, I see as being the correction of faults that cannot be put of until a future, full product release, the operation of help desks, etc.

I have also separated out a test and integration team, who can provide this service for a number of revenue-earning projects. There may be more than one such team. Relating this back to the software development lifecycle in *Figure 9.3*, the Product Development teams are responsible for all of the left-hand portion of the "V" model through to unit test and integration, together with unit test specification. The Test and Integration team are responsible for link and system testing, system integration and the associated test specifications.

Figure 9.5 shows a traditional organization hierarchy for the model shown in *Figure 9.4*. We have a Systems Development manager operating at director level with three functional managers beneath. The Support

Figure 9.5: Traditional Organization Hierarchy

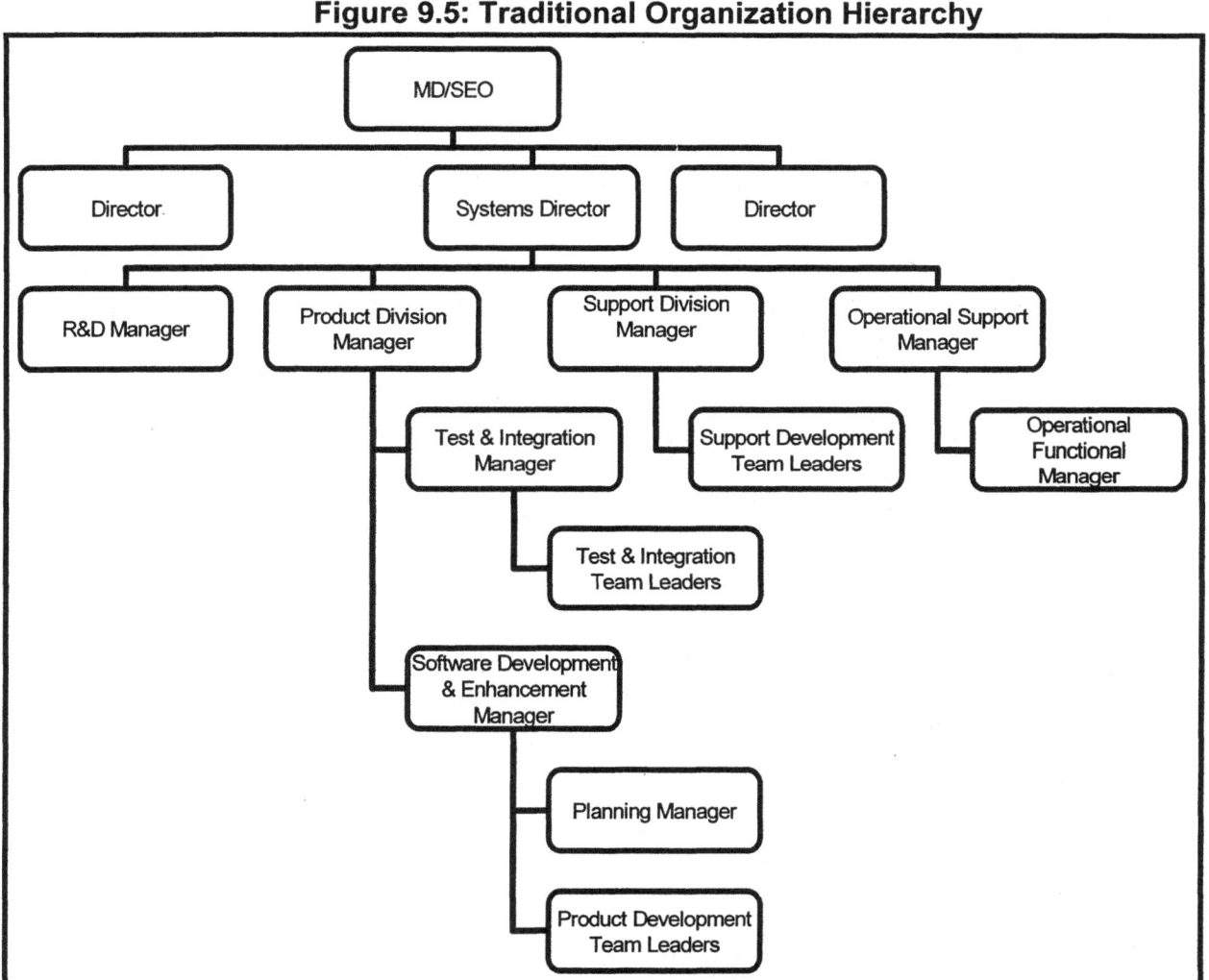

Development manager is responsible for a number team leaders who will have line management responsibility for software engineers and a project management role. The Operational Support manager is responsible for a number of functions covering the development environment.

In this organization the Product Manager is responsible for the largest part of the Systems Development function. As this is the revenue-earning component within Systems Development this would seem to make sense! I use the term "Product Manager" because he or she is responsible for the development of new products, the enhancement of existing products and the maintenance of these. So, he or she has two managers reporting up, one responsible for Test and Integration the other responsible for Software Development including enhancement. Both are responsible for a number of team leaders who, again will have project management responsibilities.

I have also introduced two additional functions, R&D and Planning. The reasons for this will become obvious later.

The models in *Figures 9.4* and *9.5* are simplistic. In reality, organizations tend to be complex beasts and the relationships between functions within the organization tend to reflect this complexity. Size alone may well add complexity as it can introduce an additional level, or multiple levels, to the organizational hierarchy. However, these two figures do give us a common frame of reference with sufficient complexity to illustrate some of the problems that will face a Software Metrics Implementation project.

Which brings us to the final component in our reference frame, the Software Metrics Project itself. As we have already discussed, such a project can come about for a number of reasons and can be actioned in a number of ways. It may be decided, as a result of the feasibility study described as stage one, that a pilot will be undertaken within one Product Development team and will be their responsibility; it may be that the program will be driven by a number of external consultants reporting directly to the Systems Development Director; or, it may come about as part of a Process Improvement Program and be the responsibility of a Software Engineering Process Group or manager.

All of these options, and the many others that exist as a result of the diversity between organizations have an impact on exactly how the Software Metrics Project is structured and operated. The purpose of this book is, among other things, to present a generic model for the implementation of Software Metrics within organizations that can be tailored and used to help real-life organizations with such an implementation.

So, I am going to make certain assumptions to set up a situation within our hypothetical organization and this will be used to illustrate such an implementation. I have chosen this model of a Software Metrics Project because I believe it to be a very common approach to metrics implementation and because it does lend itself to illustrating a range of problems that can occur as well as to possible solutions. Where I feel it necessary I will mention some of the situations that can arise in other styles of approach.

My first assumption is that the stage one feasibility study has been carried out by an individual within the R&D group. Remember what I have said about terminology: the actual name of this group does not matter but it is, typically, divorced from software development and its role within Systems Development is to improve the software engineering process. A presentation has been given to the Systems Development Director and his first-line managers resulting in approval to proceed with the development of a suitable Software Metrics Program. Notice that at this point we only have authority to develop the program, not to implement it. The reason for this is quite simple: in this hypothetical case the other first-line managers are not yet convinced that they will get a good return on the investment they see themselves having to make. Mind you the Operational Support Manager is on our side but that is to be understood because he or she is not really affected by this program, not yet anyway. Notice I am assuming that the scope of the program covers Product and Support Development only. In fact, such a program may well be confined to Product Development at first.

And who has responsibility for this new project? I will assume that the responsibility has been placed back on the R&D manager who, in turn, has given that responsibility to the person who did the feasibility study. Of course there is no reason why the project could not be placed under the Product Manager, the Support Manager or even the Planning Manager. Well there are reasons, not least given the scope of the project and the cross-functional problems that could arise. At least R&D may be seen as independent of the other functions within the organization and may be perceived as having less of an axe to grind.

There are also problems in placing the project within the R&D function. These arise from such things as a lack of credibility R&D staff can suffer from, the ivory tower syndrome and the "not invented here" reaction which can occur within software development functions. There is much that can be done to overcome these problems, but not yet! Having got our sanction to proceed the first thing to do is to make sure we know how to proceed. Planning is the next thing on the agenda.

To reiterate: we have authority to develop a Software Metrics Program that will be applied, subject to authorization, to both Product and Support Development. The high-level requirements on the project are that a Software Metrics Program provide information about the software development process and its products and that it improve that process in a cost effective way. If you can get a tighter initial requirement, so much the better but this rather vague description of what we need to do does enable us to discuss the various aspects of a Software Metrics Program within the context of implementing that program. Oh yes, we have also been given a time scale. It does not matter how long it is, it will not be long enough!

At this point, the Software Metrics team may have been expanded so that there are now more resources available than during the feasibility study. Equally, the "team" may only consist of one person working part time on the problem. I have already given some indications of my views on resourcing such a team. I will refer to those who have responsibility for the development and implementation of the metrics initiative as the "metrics team."

I said that we need a plan for the future work but I do not intend to describe that plan at all. As stated earlier, this stage of planning activity is seen as being common to all stages. Instead, I will describe the work that needs to be carried out during this and subsequent stages of metrics program development and implementation around which you can develop your own plan. Please remember that this is not a theoretical discussion. The approach described in this book is one that has been tried in practice and is one that has proved to be successful on more than one occasion and in different types of organization and industry.

Figure 9.6 summarizes the work, tasks and linkages within this stage.

Figure 9.6   Work, Task and Linkages
Within the Requirements Specification Stage

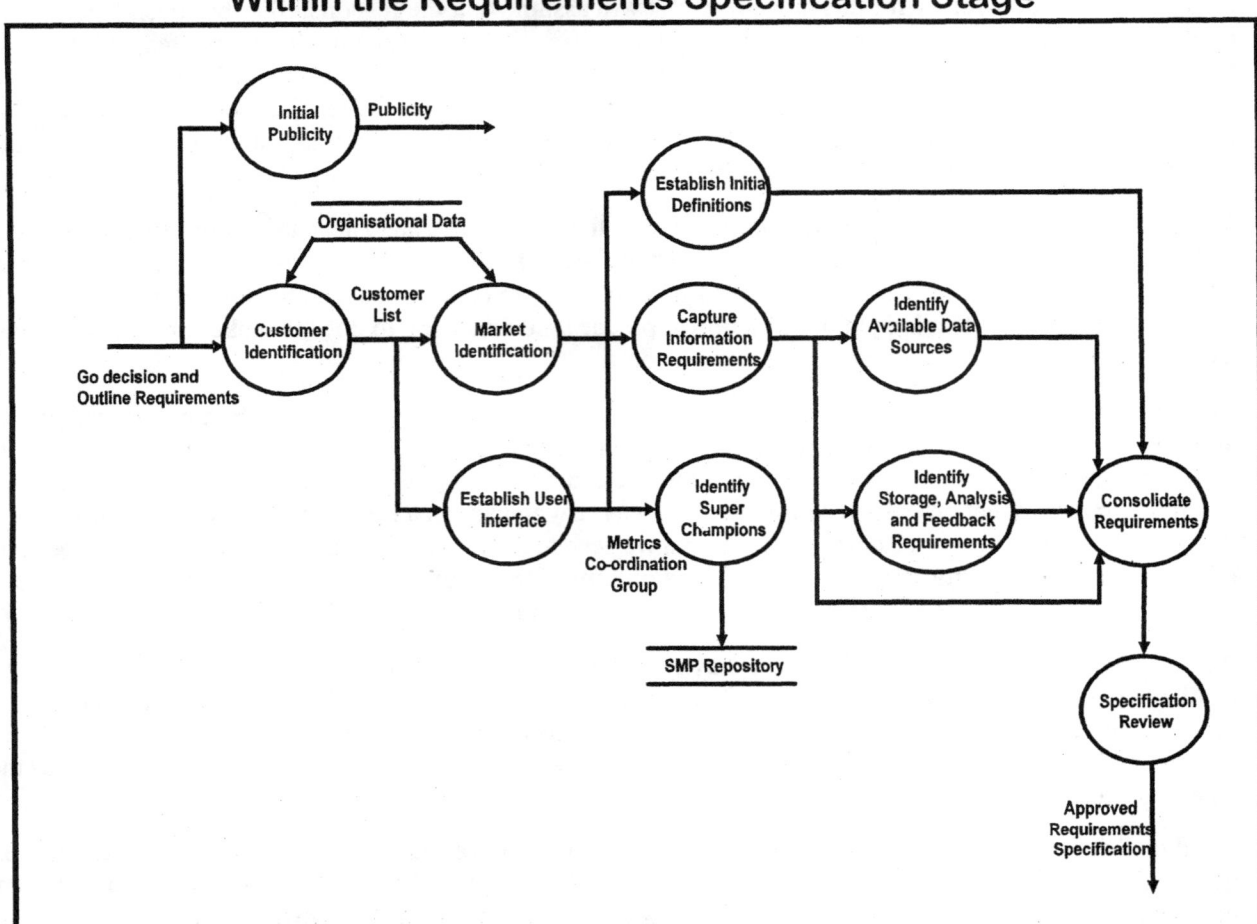

9.4   INITIAL PUBLICITY CAMPAIGN

Having prepared the project plan we will have a good idea of what needs to be done, at least at a relatively high level. It is very tempting to get your head down and get on with it; after all, you can always let the business know what is going to hit them when you are ready to hit them with it. But stop and think for a moment!

Any Software Metrics Program relies heavily on the cooperation of many individuals within the software engineering functions. It is always a good idea to let these individuals know that such help is required as early as possible but you probably will not know exactly which individuals you need this help from. One way to counter this problem is to inform as many people as possible of the fact that a Software Metrics Program now exists.

Apart from just raising the profile of the project, an initial publicity campaign can also be used to start the education process within software development. You may be convinced, from talking to other people outside of your own organization and from your reading during the feasibility study, that a metrics program has a valuable contribution to make to improving the software engineering process, but you will almost certainly be in a minority. A great deal of time and effort is going to be spent convincing others of this fact.

You may also be in the fortunate position of having convinced a senior manager that the organization should adopt the use of Software Metrics immediately. This individual may also believe that mandating that use will be sufficient for it to happen. Don't believe it: a successful Software Metrics Program depends on the active participation and cooperation of the people to whom it is being applied. Time spent convincing those people that such co-operation will be worthwhile is time well spent and will repay your efforts ten fold.

A word of warning: beware of overselling the program. At this point in time, you have nothing that the development function can make use of so there is no point making exaggerated claims that you cannot back up. Also, these people have probably heard it all before. The IT industry does tend to suffer from "flavor-of-the-month syndrome." About twenty years ago third generation languages were going to solve all our problems. Then it was automatic code generators, then the ill-fated Integrated Project Support Environment.

Formal methods, object-oriented design or coding and software reuse have all been hailed as panacea to all of our problems, yet the problems still exist. Do you really expect people to believe that Software Metrics will be any different? And in many ways, this cynicism is justified, even when it is applied to Software Metrics.

Software development is largely about people. Software Metrics, per se, will not necessarily improve things directly, but the changes in the way people work and think that Software Metrics helps bring about can generate immense savings and improvements.

So, how should such an initial publicity campaign be handled?

First, consider another question. What do we want the campaign to achieve? There are four points that we should address with such a campaign:

- we need to make people aware that the topic, Software Metrics itself, exists.

- we need to tell the organization that the Systems development function has initiated a program aimed at monitoring and improving its own processes and products.

- ideally, we should also generate discussion; and, finally,

- we should alert everyone in the software development function that this new project may well need their help in the near future.

Does the organization have an in-house magazine? If so you can use this as a vehicle for publicity and education. Bear in mind that you will be introducing a topic that is new to most people and that the subject is both wide-ranging and complicated by people issues. Because of this, you may wish to consider a short series of articles starting with a brief introduction to the areas that Software Metrics can address and followed by separate articles addressing each of those areas. Your "campaign" may be as simple as a briefing note sent out as a general email from your sponsor to all staff.

Remember not to build up false hopes. There is little point in discussing, say, McCabe Metrics if your program is only addressing the measurement of productivity. Also remember not to make exaggerated claims about the benefits of using Software Metrics as you will stretch credibility.

Another vehicle that can be used for publicity is site notice boards if your organization uses these. A simple poster, perhaps using humor, can be a good way of getting a message across. One example I have seen consists of a sword-wielding king, with a few hard-pressed knights nearby. Behind this group is a salesman holding a machine gun. The comment is "Don't bother me now, I've got a war to fight." Give the king a standard labeled "Software Development" and put the words "Software Metrics" on the guns ammunition box and you have an effective advert for your work. Alternatively, you could get some simple announcement on the company Intranet.

Perhaps your organization holds periodic, open briefing sessions. If so you may like to consider staging such a presentation. Alternatively you may have some sort of networked advertisement scheme on your development machines that you can utilize.

A presentation to senior management, can be tempting at this point but do beware. One of my previous managers gave me some very good advice some years ago regarding such an audience. He said, "Keep the presentation short," which I am sure you already know but he went on, "tell them what the problem is, tell them the options then tell them what they are going to do." This is a good guideline and while you may be able, even at this early stage, to tell them what the problem is you are unlikely to be able to give them the options nor are you yet in a position to tell them what to do. So, tempting though it may be, it is probably best to avoid such events at the moment unless you need their approval for the work; but remember, we are assuming that this has already been obtained.

Do not expect senior management to mandate every step of the metrics initiative development and implementation process.

There is another technique that can be used to both stimulate interest in a Software Metrics program and that can provide a vehicle for education: a Software Metrics workshop can do both of these things. Please note that this is not a traditional training course. It is true that such an event will contain many similarities to a training course and it will be "driven" by the presenter but it is essentially a two-way exercise in communication. You as the presenter need to provide information about the subject, what it is and what it can achieve, but, equally, you are seeking information that will enable you to identify potential champions and that will help you focus on their needs.

A Software Metrics workshop does require a significant investment on the part of the organizer and the presenter. Also, running such an event can be very demanding so you may feel that this is best left until you are comfortable and confident with the detailed use of metrics.

The publicity and education process within a Software Metrics Program is continuous. Use it to help maintain momentum as well as to introduce new ideas to the organization.

Finally, realize that staging a publicity campaign, even one that is only intended to introduce the topic of Software Metrics, does take time and you will need to budget for it in your plans. It does help to get rid of the "ivory tower" syndrome which could plague Software Metrics programs. This is because the key element in such a campaign should be a statement of intent saying, very clearly, that the program will include the people involved in the day-to-day work of the software development function from an early stage. We will now discuss how this involvement can be achieved.

9.5   CUSTOMER IDENTIFICATION

One element that adds complexity to a Software Metrics Program is the number of customer types that the program must satisfy because the various customers have different requirements.

You may still be unsure about the use of the term "customer" in this context so a few more words about this may be appropriate. I am convinced that all projects, be they to develop software, to introduce a new development tool or to implement Software Metrics, should have a customer or group of customers associated with them from the earliest possible stage. Now it may be that the customer is only a pseudo-customer, as in the case of a marketing group when a new software product is being developed as a speculative venture, but the customer still exists.

Why is the customer so important? Unless you recognize your customer you cannot effectively capture the requirements for the project deliverable and this is as true for Software Metrics as it is for anything else. The customer requirements should always drive the project, otherwise there is a very real danger that the deliverable will not have a market and that the effort expended on the project will be wasted. Conversely, a project that recognizes its potential customers and that involves those customers has a much greater chance of success and needs to spend less effort in marketing its products.

While the specific customers of the program will differ between organizations there does seem to be very definite similarities between programs. I have used these to develop an approach to customer identification. The first step is to model the organization that the program will service in terms of major functional groupings.

Looking at the organizational structure of our example we can easily see a number of clearly identifiable groups. First we have the senior organizational management group. This consists of the managing director or CEO and his or her first-line reports including the Systems Development Manager. This group will probably possess certain characteristics that should be noted. Some senior managers view Systems Development or IT as a "black hole" into which they pour resources for very little quantifiable return. They also tend to view Systems Development, rightly or wrongly, as something that is very poorly managed. There are some good reasons for these views.

Historically, the drive for IT within organizations has been to put systems in place regardless of cost. Often, it has been thought that if systems were not developed then the competition, if they developed IT systems, would gain such a competitive edge that the very survival of the organization would be in doubt. This led to a "blank check" style of systems development that has cost many organizations a great deal of money, often justified by the flimsiest of cases, for little return.

In addition to this fear-driven investment, there has also been an element of "momentum drive" acting on organizations. Momentum drive is something that has probably never been experienced before in the history of commerce but which has typified the IT industry. Information Technology appeared within the last sixty years or thereabouts but within this relatively short period of time has impacted almost every walk of life and has truly brought about a second industrial revolution. You know that this is true, but have you considered the effect?

The most dramatic effect has been on time. Time, unlike most physical dimensions, is not fixed. We perceive time differently in different circumstances and the effect of the IT explosion has been to dramatically speed up our time perception. For example, acceptable time-to-market is now much shorter than it was ten years ago, product lifespan is much reduced and even in our personal lives we are no longer willing to accept delays in, say, transatlantic telephone calls that were previously considered normal. What all this means is that many organizations have invested in IT, at high cost, with little or no control. They have been pulled along by the momentum of the second revolution.

The second major push to the momentum drive came with the Internet and this is accelerating at an ever-increasing pace. While most organizations have already addressed the obvious applications of IT the focus in commerce today is often on E-commerce, often with great diversity. At the more technical end of the industry the impetus comes from the capacity of the technology to deliver ever more functionality, often for less unit cost. Simply consider the cell or mobile phone explosion.

But there was ever such a slight lull, a slowing down. For some parts of our industry this came at the point when the majority of basic applications had IT systems associated with them. The end of the cold war gave a pause to the defense industry. Non-IT managers had just a short time when they could think without the full pressure of the momentum drive bearing on them.

They took stock and started to insist on greater control over their Systems Development functions. This is true for organizations whose Systems Development functions service internal requirements and it is equally true where such functions earn the organization revenue. Senior management is demanding that greater control be applied to such divisions to reduce risk and maximize return on investment.

Another driver towards greater control is the appalling reputation that the IT industry has concerning cost and time scale over-runs. Senior management who, previously, accepted this state of events, will no longer accept this.

So senior management at the organizational level will become important customers of the Software Metrics program and we can guess that they will see the program as a vehicle by which greater control can be obtained.

The second customer grouping is the Systems Development manager and his or her first-line reports. Note that the Systems Development manager is in both of the groupings identified so far. Such an overlap or intersection almost always identifies a key player!

While this identification can be trivial, such a diagram does highlight the fact that someone like the Systems Development manager will, in fact, be relating to the program in different ways to others in the groups of which they are part.

The Systems Development manager may well wish to use the Software Metrics program to gain greater control over his own managers, especially the Product and Support Development managers. However, the Systems Development manager will also see the metrics program as something that may provide a defense against the bullets other directors fire his way.

Some organizations initiate a Software Metrics program to gather information to protect themselves from what they see as the threat of outsourcing. However, the decision as to whether or not to outsource an IT function is often a political one rather than one that is taken based on objective, quantified information. To be frank, if you initiate a Software Metrics program in response to such a threat you probably have insufficient time to gather the necessary information before the decision will be made.

For the moment I am going to include the Software Development and the Test and Integration managers as part of the Systems Development senior management group. This group is typified by the fact that its members are not responsible for the day-to-day activities of specific projects. They are a functional management group rather than a group focused on specific projects.

Which brings us nicely to our third customer grouping, the project managers, who in terms of our example organization are the Team Leaders. These individuals are right there on the firing line. They are responsible for the day-to-day work on specific software development projects. These people tend to be technically oriented. Given our industries propensity for taking good technical staff and then putting them in positions where they have to manage people — which often demands a very different skill set — you should not be surprised to find some interesting interactions occurring between this group and the Software Metrics program.

Project managers tend to fall into three camps. They may latch onto Software Metrics as something that can actually help them get control over their projects and enable them to communicate facts to their own managers. Alternatively, they may be the kind of technician who insists on proving the theoretical concepts behind every idea or suggestion. This can cause problems because of the immaturity of many Software Metrics techniques. Finally, they may be pragmatists. Of the three camps this is the one I find it easiest to work with. A pragmatic project manager knows he has problems and has tried to address these, often with limited success simply due to a lack of available time for thought let alone action. He also knows that life holds no guarantees but because he does not have an answer to a specific problem he is quite willing to listen and to try something new.

A pragmatic project manager will often gratefully accept a new idea, the use of a metric or a metric-based technique. Typically, you as a consultant, internal or external, go back to that manager one, two or maybe three months later to find that he is doing things that you never even thought of. Now you become the pupil and he or she becomes the teacher. This is one of the most satisfying times within a Software Metrics program.

Not only have you succeeded in getting something useful in place but you now have a practical application that can be used to convince others and, as a bonus, you probably have new ideas developed in the field.

It is often said that senior management commitment is THE prerequisite for a successful Software Metrics program. I disagree! It is a prerequisite but I believe that identifying project managers who are sufficiently open-minded and who are prepared to work with you in implementing Software Metrics is equally important.

Another important group is the support units. These are functional specialists whose role is to facilitate software development within the organization. This group covers departments such as marketing, planning and project control offices. An R&D function can also be included as can the process improvement function. In many cases groups like these need information such as productivity and quality levels to be able to function effectively but such information is often unavailable. Once they see that the Software Metrics program intends to make such information available to them, support groups can become good customers of the SMP.

In particular, you may well find that the process improvement function welcomes such a program with open arms. The process improvement philosophy is relatively new to western business as a whole and yet it has become very popular over recent years. All implementations of such a philosophy, whether they are based on the Capability Maturity Model, International Standards, the Business Excellence Model or even if they have their roots as far back as Crosby or Deming, emphasize the need for measurement; but most process improvement functions struggle with the application of measurement on a broad scale.

For example, the application of Statistical Process Control in its traditional sense is difficult within software engineering functions because of the general skew of data sets from that environment and because of the need to get a reasonable data set to be able to apply this technique. However, the link between this and Software Metrics is obvious: Software Metrics is a specialty that can satisfy the requirement for measurement within a practical application of Statistical Process Control and such a link should be exploited as much as possible.

And so we come to our final group of potential, internal customers of a Software Metrics program. This group is often overlooked yet their involvement and acceptance of a Software Metrics program is vital to its success. The group I am talking about is the software engineers, or programmers.

I vividly remember one occasion when I spent half an hour going through my standard introduction to Software Metrics with such an engineer. He nodded in all the right places and even asked one or two pertinent questions. He saved his real bombshell until the end when he simply asked, "what's in it for me?" This really drove home the point. Why should engineers take time to supply information, accurately, when they get nothing directly back in return? This important group exists and, please, do not ignore them. Simply taking the time to talk to and involve as many engineers as is practical could pay handsome dividends. But do be honest, the engineers may not get much benefit directly from the Software Metrics Program until the data that comes from it is used to improve the working environment by setting, for example, more realistic timescales for projects.

Having talked about internal customers, that is groups that are involved in the production of software within an organization, we really must consider external customers of the metrics program. I mean now the actual consumers of the products of software development. In the case of our example this means true customers, individuals or organizations that pay real money for the products of software development. But customers can also get their hands on such products without paying real money.

We all have customers even if we never speak to or see anyone who is not part of our employing organization. For example, our organization model contains a number of support development teams who generate products that are used by the product development group. These people are customers in almost every sense of the word. I consider it so important that we consider our customers as just that, be they external, paying customers or internal users of our products, that I do not intend to distinguish between them.

Customers will not generally be involved in the day-to-day use of Software Metrics, but they can be considered as a specific customer group for that program. They may even be driving that program but, more often, they will be more passive during the early stages. Depending on the commercial environment in which you work you may have to make some assumptions about their requirements.

Once you have derived a high-level breakdown of your potential customer set you should consider this in more detail. For example, within the Systems Development Senior Management set we have two levels to cater for, the Test and Integration and the Software Development managers. Also, the actual number of support groups seen as customers of the program will be dependent on the program's terms of reference and the detailed organizational structure.

I do not intend to discuss the derivation of the lower level breakdown as it is so dependent on these factors but please let me emphasize that performing such an analysis is worthwhile and should not be ignored. I have produced a table, **Table 9.1**, showing one lower-level breakdown that could apply to our model organization.

Table 9.1

Organizational Senior Management
Managing Director
*Systems Development Director
Finance Director
Personnel Director

Systems Development Senior Management
*Systems Development Director
R&D Manager
Product Manager
Support Development Manager
Operational Support Manager
Test and Integration Manager
Software Development Manager

Support Groups
R&D
Planning
Project Managers
Engineers

Notice that this breakdown can include functional groups or individuals where they carry out a functional role. One way to derive this lower level identification of customers is to merge the reporting hierarchy such as is shown in *Figure 9.5* with the functional linkage chart shown in *Figure 9.4.*

9.6   MARKET IDENTIFICATION

Having identified the potential customers of our program, we should consider the potential market and the size of that market. This activity is similar in scope to the initial market research work done during the feasibility study. The difference lies in the amount of detail, this market identification being more than a sizing exercise. Surprisingly, this is an activity that is often ignored within Software Metrics programs yet it is important. To all intents and purposes you are going to be establishing a business within your own software development function that will service the needs of that organization. If you were setting up an external business, one step that you would most certainly consider is to establish the potential market. There is no reason why you should not do the same for an internal business!

There are various questions that should be addressed by this activity and the answers you obtain will form the basis of a "business plan," as opposed to a project plan, later in the program. It can be argued that market identification does not need to be carried out until you get nearer to implementation but, from my own experience, the earlier that you start to address this issue, the better. The information you gather during this activity will also directly affect the next job, establishing a user interface.

You may be surprised how difficult it is to get some of the information you require. It never ceases to amaze me how little basic management information is available within software development functions of any size and, if nothing else, this activity will give you a better understanding of the organization in which you work.

Typical questions that should be asked during this activity include:

How many sites is software development carried out on and where are they located?

Is there any functional specialization between sites? For instance, does one site concentrate on integration and testing of software developed on other sites or are different products developed on different sites?

How many project teams are in existence at the current time?

How many software engineers do we have?

Do engineers work exclusively on one product/project at a time?

Are projects grouped under functional headings? For instance, do we have a team leader managing more than one project team, each developing say a build of a current product?

How many project teams do we plan to have at the start of the next three financial years?

What is the relationship between the planning function and the project teams?

You may find that some of this information is readily available from organizational data. Other items of information will certainly require some digging. You may also find that these questions, in turn, raise other questions. For example, what do we mean by a project? Does the project team include the team leader? Has anyone ever defined our development process?

When in doubt remember the first principle of Software Metrics: be pragmatic. At this stage you are trying to get information that will allow you to proceed with the Software Metrics program. This does not have to be correct to three decimal places nor will it be used in any way that involves significant business risk. Yes, you may well need to define what is meant by a project and have that agreed by your customers but that comes later so use any sensible definition at this point.

Having obtained this information you can now proceed to the next activity:

9.7   ESTABLISH USER INTERFACE

One of the great problems with any activity aimed at changing an existing process is that the attempt can be made without the involvement of those people who will be affected. Such attempts are very prone to failure!

Software Metrics programs are as likely to suffer from this "ivory tower" syndrome as any other culture changing process and conscious steps must be taken to avoid it happening. Yet, at first glance, it is not easy to involve the process owners, especially when the team that is trying to effect the changes to that process are not directly involved in it. This is certainly the case in our model organization where the Software Metrics team is part of the R&D group and it is also true of the vast majority of industrial Software Metrics programs of which I am aware, both in Europe and the United States as well as elsewhere.

One of the problems is often the large number of process owners because, as I view things, anyone who is involved directly in a process has a vested interest in that process and can be seen as an owner of it. How can you involve this large number of people in the work of changing the process? How can you ensure that the process owners also own the process of 'process change?'

One of the best pieces of advice I have ever seen regarding the implementation of Software Metrics came from the Grady and Caswell book, _Software Metrics: Establishing a Company Wide Program_ (Prentice Hall PTR). They introduced the concept of a "Metrics Council" and I have used a very similar concept when implementing metrics initiatives. Names vary: the council could be called a user group, a working party or, my own favorite, a _Metrics Coordination Group._

The role of this group is simple: they act as the steering committee, they guide the direction of the program and, most importantly, they ensure that the program does not fly off into flights of fancy that do not address the business needs of the organization.

The role of this group does depend, somewhat, on the involvement and strength of the customer authority. If the customer authority is both strong and involved, the high-level requirements for the Software Metrics Program will have been set out relatively clearly but even these will probably benefit from having fresh minds applied to them. In most cases the high-level requirements that will have been placed on the metrics program will be fairly vague and, in this case, the Metrics Coordination Group will be responsible for setting the more detailed direction of the program. The group will decide if the program covers both productivity and quality measurement, for example. Should any attention be directed towards measuring soft or environmental factors? Is there a need for more effective cost estimation techniques?

The Metrics Coordination Group is there to demonstrate that the users have been consulted from the start. Establishing and involving such a group is one step towards ensuring that the Software Metrics program is owned by its users rather than being seen as an imposition on them. As you will see, achieving this ownership is an important success criteria.

The group can also act as the final review body for any products from the Software Metrics Program. This is an extremely useful way of overcoming objections from the potential market for such products, be they reports, measures or training courses. It helps combat the "not invented here" attitude of some teams. Using the phrase, "approved by the Metrics Coordination Group" can be a powerful weapon in the war to get a Software Metrics Program accepted.

The group will also help in other ways. There is a phenomena I have labeled "reverse synergy." This is where the constituent parts of a group are more powerful than the group as a whole. Unlike Grady and Caswell, I do not expect the Metrics Coordination Group to do "real work" during its meetings although I fully accept that, with the right people, a set of metrics can be defined, for example, as they describe in their book. Personally, I prefer to use the group meetings as an opportunity to share information and a time for general discussions of strategy. However, I do use the members of the group as local champions and as doorways into different parts of the organization. They provide me, as the facilitator or the leg man, with the contacts and the introductions that are so necessary to the work of a Software Metrics program. If you are able to get the right people on the Metrics Coordination Group you will quickly find many centers of interest developing within the organization. All you have to do is change centers of interest into centers of working expertise. Not an easy task but infinitely easier than trying to carve your way through the organization single-handed.

So, who should be members of the Metrics Coordination Group? There is a great temptation to insist on senior managers From our model for example we may target the R&D, the Product, Support Development and Operations Support managers. Possibly we would add in the Software Development and the Test and Integration managers as well. Great if you can get them all in one room for a day but I doubt that you will. In many ways it is unfortunate that these individuals cannot form such a group as they are the "shakers and makers." They have the power to make decisions and see those decisions acted upon quickly. I repeat, you will be very lucky if you get the level of representation, in terms of seniority, that you would like. The one exception to this is when you are completely external to the organization, i.e., a consultant. In this case you may well be able to insist on access to senior management and this is one reason why consultancy-led programs can often move a lot faster than internal programs. There is a down side to this: consultants are transitory beasts, they are not there for long and there are few consultants who can effectively accomplish the transfer of technology or knowledge that is necessary for an organization to be able to proceed under its' own steam without any slowing down.

However, even if you cannot get senior managers onto the Metrics Coordination Group all is not lost. Provided that the majority of the group members are open-minded, constructively critical and believe that process improvement is both necessary and possible, the group will still be effective.

There is even an argument for establishing two groups, one consisting of more senior managers who determine strategic direction and another made up of project managers who work on the tactical plans and oversee the introduction of operational procedures. This is certainly workable but be very aware of the costs you are incurring and the bureaucracy you could be accused of generating.

Use your own and other peoples' knowledge of the organization to target individuals. Ensure that you have at least one representative from each of your customer groups. With luck you should be able to get at least one senior manager involved. If your organization is split across sites try to get a representative mix within the group and do not forget to include your customer authority or sponsor.

Approach the targeted individuals to sound them out and, if you are happy that they will contribute positively, get their line managers' approval for attendance. This is also a good time to let senior management know that this group exists.

The first meeting is important and will really be driven by the metrics team itself. In fact this is going to be the case right through development to implementation. Ensure that you set out the terms of reference for the group and the individuals. Remember they are to act as local champions, and use the first meeting to discuss the program components and the strategy as it is perceived at this stage. If necessary, use the results of the feasibility study to underline the importance of Software Metrics and what can be achieved. Tell them what the organization, in this case the metrics team, is going to do and be prepared to discuss time scales even if you avoid the question of detailed costs for now. Above all, get their agreement to your proposals even if this means modifying those proposals. Remember, the involvement of many individuals often means that compromise is necessary.

The first meeting of the Metrics Coordination Group can be seen as the true launch of the metrics initiative. After the initial meeting, I have found it best to hold meetings at need rather than on a regular basis at least during the development of the metrics program. Once you get to implementation, the role of the group changes to become more of a true user group. At this time regular meetings, say quarterly, are probably justified.

One final point: keep in mind that the members of the Metrics Coordination Group will be helping you. Make sure that you thank them for that help; publicly and often! Remember it is their program not yours, at least it will be if you succeed. If it is not then you have failed!

9.8   IDENTIFY POTENTIAL SUPER CHAMPIONS

Within the Metrics Coordination Group there will be what I call potential "super champions." A super champion is a person who not only lends his or her name to an initiative but who wholeheartedly adopts that initiative, becomes part of it and starts to drive it forward down new routes. Such individuals are worth their weight in gold as they become, not merely centers of expertise and enthusiasm, but centers of excellence. The real beauty of it is that they are always owners of the process that is being changed and that they are doing the changing!

Both through the Metrics Coordination Group and through other interactions with the organization as a whole, you will become aware of potential super champions. It is up to you to cultivate these people to ensure that their potential is realized.

9.9   CAPTURE INFORMATION REQUIREMENTS

This is the core activity of this stage. It is important because there are various techniques that can be used to derive a set of Software Metrics that can then be used by the organization. One technique is to go into a development team, a project or the data from a previous project and then to measure everything you can possibly think off. This is the data hunters strategy. Having got a vast array of base data you then apply various statistical techniques to find out what all this information is telling you. Your hope is that it is telling you something useful that can then be used to improve the development process.

One problem with this approach is that the very quantity and diversity of information can produce apparently meaningful results, information that in reality is telling you very little. For example, you may find that the number of comments per thousand lines of code is running at about 30%. Let us say that you are really clever and that you find the spread of this comment density ranges from 1% to 75%. What conclusions can you draw from this? The answer is very little.

Now it can be argued that by relating comment density to error-fixing productivity you may be able to show that high comment density relates to high productivity. In some ways this may make sense if your engineers are using the code comments as the primary source of system documentation! Before throwing your hands up in horror, go and ask them if this is the case. You may be surprised. However, the very quantity of data that you will be collecting will probably mean that you cannot form that relationship from a statistically significant number of projects or observations within a project. Essentially, the data collection costs when working under the data hunting approach are simply too high because you do not know which base measures will be useful.

Alternatively, you may give the matter some thought and then go and measure everything that seems to make sense. Under Murphy's Law, the one thing you do not measure will be the thing you should have measured. I state this from bitter, personnel experience.

In one installation we measured every element of a system design that we felt could possibly be a valid predictor of software size, and hence development costs. The collection and analysis took quite a while and the results were interesting. In fact the best predictor seemed to be the number of pages in the functional specification. Try selling that one to senior management!

By the by, it is worth pointing out that we were using a relatively formalized, diagrammatic documentation technique so perhaps we should not be too surprised by this result. But the bottom line is that when we presented our results a member of the audience asked why we had not measured a particular design attribute. The answer was that we had not thought about that one, so we agreed that we would try it out. Of course that attribute, the number of data dictionary definitions, turned out to be the best predictor of all, at least for new systems which was our area of interest at that time.

Fortunately, there was also a need to get a size measure for enhancement work as well and the data dictionary model broke down when we tried to apply it to that sphere of engineering. We managed to save face to some degree!

Believe me, measuring everything in sight is fraught with difficulty and is not a cost effective method of deriving Software Metrics.

Fortunately there are other approaches that can be used. The most widely recognized and respected approach to metric derivation is something called the *Goal/Question/Metric*, or GQM, paradigm and this is discussed in some detail in *Chapter 10* which describes the Component Design stage of the SMP development and implementation lifecycle.

The foundation of this approach, developed by the Software Engineering Laboratory in the USA, Rombach (1), and is aimed at making practitioners ask not so much "what should I measure?" but "why am I measuring?" To be able to answer this question you need to be able to answer the additional question, "what business needs does the organization wish its measurement initiative to address?"

Capturing and specifying measurement requirements uses the same procedures as classic systems analysis, i.e., interviews, workshops, prototyping. And the foundation of good systems analysis is preparation.

Taking requirements from a number of sources you will probably identify certain similarities between requirements that will enable you to focus on those for which there is a general need. In this way you will be able to group requirements into particular classes. The benefit of doing this is that it reduces the amount of duplicated effort that may otherwise be expended. I offer the table below as one possible set of headings that can be used to group metrics requirements and these can be used to focus an interview or workshop session:

Table 9.3

Project Metrics
Business Entity Metric
Cost Estimation
Quality Assessment
(Applied Design Metrics) and Prediction
Project Control

I define **Project Metrics** as being *any measure of a process or product attribute where the source data and the subsequent application is confined to a single project or product and the associated team.* For example, consider field reliability of a product. The primary customer for such metrics is almost invariably the project manager.

Business Entity Metrics can be defined in the same way as project metrics except that the source data is drawn from a number of areas that, together, form a managerial unit. In terms of our example organization, a business entity could be the Test and Integration Group, the Product Division or the whole of the Systems Development area. An example of a business entity metric requirement would be of a product group manager wishing to monitor the general reliability levels of their products over time as a group rather than as a set of individual products. Another example would be where the management board wished to monitor return on investment for the whole of the IT function. In both cases the requirement could be met by aggregating information from measures taken against individual products or product groups respectively.

These areas have been discussed in *Section One*, project and business entity metrics coming under the general heading of Management Information.

Having obtained a set of requirements and grouped them into classes you may well see that you have two macro classes. The first will be requirements for information, the second will be for techniques that can be directly used to improve the development process in some form or another. Each macro class requires a slightly different approach.

Although these two approaches are really part of the Design stage of our metrics program I will briefly introduce them here. Requirements for information will mean that you need to adopt a model, either by using one that is generally well accepted and with which you feel comfortable, because there is no reason to reinvent the wheel, or if the wheel does not exist you will have to go through the modeling process yourself. The model will provide you with a composite metric which in turn will lead you to a set of base metrics. To define these two terms, composite and base metrics, a *Composite Metric* is a mathematical formula, the solution of which will provide you with quantitative value which in turn satisfies, through analysis, the initial requirement. *Base Metrics* are the items of raw data that need to be collected in order that the mathematical formula within the composite metrics can be applied.

If this sounds complicated the following may help.

Imagine that the product manager has asked you, as part of the metrics program, to supply information that will tell him or her how productive software development is within the revenue earning part of the organization. Obviously, the source data for this requirement will be drawn from more than one project or product area so we would seem to be talking about a *Business Entity Metric*.

Productivity is a relatively well understood economic measure that is widely used within most industries and it is generally defined to be:

$$Productivity = Work\ Product\ /\ Cost\ to\ Produce$$

To satisfy our current requirement this does require some additional definition. We may choose to define Work Product as "Function Points" or even as Lines of Code. In other words, the size of what we produce in terms of functionality or "volume" in the same sense as a car production line output measure may be defined as the number of cars produced during one shift.

Before anyone gets too upset at this let me stress that we need to be very careful in our definition of, say, lines of code, and the definition of other parameters in our model. We must also accept that productivity is not a magical, overall measure of process effectiveness. As you will have realized, we could produce lots of Lines of Code whose quality is lousy. However, productivity can be used as a high level measure of organizational performance and I will have more to say about how we derive valid measures later on.

Likewise, we could define our cost parameter as "effort" in terms of engineering days booked to a particular project. Now as this is a Business Entity Metric we could decide to sample a set of representative project/product teams or we could total across all teams. I will assume the latter case for this example.

We end up with a composite productivity metric defined as:

$$Productivity = (Total\ Project\ Lines\ of\ Code\ Delivered\ to\ Test\ and\ Integration$$
$$during\ financial\ year\ x)\ /\ (Total\ project\ effort\ booked)$$

From this we can see that our base metrics, the raw data that must be collected to be able to derive our productivity metric, are:

- Project Lines of Code delivered to Test and Integration

- Project effort.

For now think about the terms used and the derivation method, not about the metric itself.

For the other common macro class of requirements, direct process improvement, the technique is slightly different. First we need to identify, at a conceptual level, what will be done, perhaps what we feel should be done. This is often based on examples taken from other organizations or on our own personal experience within the organization.

Conceptual models are a necessary step but they seldom provide the answer. The elements of the conceptual model need to be grafted onto the development process within the organization. In other words we need an Application model that will describe how we will do what is described within the conceptual model.

Again an example will help. Given a requirement to improve the effectiveness, i.e., the accuracy, of our cost estimates we may decide to use a proprietary cost estimation package. Conceptually we should realize that the package will need to be calibrated to our own environment before we can use it properly so our application model, based on that calibration, may say something like:

"At the point when requirements analysis has been completed, use the requirements specification to complete the estimation input form. Submit the form to the estimation team who will, in turn, supply you with a modified, package-based estimate and confidence level."

Again an oversimplified example but it illustrates that just deciding to use a cost estimation package is not enough. The application model addresses a great many issues that the conceptual model can ignore.

Of course, all of this assumes that you are able to obtain your requirements. This is not always as easy as it may seem so let us consider this area now in more detail.

Obtaining the set of specific requirements that will drive the Software Metrics program is not a task that can be easily defined because it involves interaction with people. What can be defined is the types of information that should be contained in such a requirement together with some approaches and techniques that can be used.

Essentially there are two techniques that can be used to define the specific requirements within the metrics program. The most obvious is to adopt a systems analysis approach by identifying specific, key players within the customer set. Structured interviews are then carried out involving these individuals.

My personal preference is a two pass approach. For each player, the first interview aims to identify their particular role within the organization as they see it; what processes they are personally involved in and what those processes entail; what responsibilities, in terms of deliverables, they have; and, most importantly, what they perceive to be the weaknesses in the processes they operate. This can be quite a tall order!

Do not minimize the importance of this activity. Talking to people takes time and to get the most out of the time you have available you will need to plan and structure your interview sessions. One plan which certainly appears to work goes as follows:

- Start the session by briefly describing the purpose of the interview which is to ensure that the deliverables of the metrics project really address the personal needs of the interviewee and the business needs of the organization. Do not try to sell metrics too hard. You are there to listen and learn, not preach! By all means explain the high-level requirements of the program as this will help to set the focus of the interview session.

- Ask the individual to explain his or her role within the organization in their own terms and be ready to spot "key terms" such as project, build or vagaries such as "size," "complexity" and "quality." You will see why this is important shortly. This part of the meeting is vitally important. You really need to listen to what is being said, and, perhaps more importantly, to what is *not* being said. Can you start to see areas that you think may benefit from measurement or from other metrics techniques you know of?

- As the interview progresses, take notes. If you are unsure about what is being said, ask questions. Simple actions like this demonstrate interest on your part and provide a positive stroke to the other person's ego. Don't knock it! You need this person to work with you so you use everything you can to develop a rapport with him or her. One warning: a single question asked by you can drive the interview off at a tangent if you interrupt a persons flow of conversation so perhaps you should simply note a point and return to it later.

- The interviewee will be involved in processes. As the interview progresses start to build a model of those processes on your note pad, perhaps using a Data Flow Diagram notation similar to that used in this book. Look for sub-processes that do not seem to be triggered or for information that is consumed but not used. Use points like these to drive the interview if it seems to be flagging.

- Make sure that you have got it right. Play back your understanding of what has been said regarding the interviewees work. If you have got it wrong then do not argue, change your model. Remember, you are trying to find out how things are done. Do not try to impose text book solutions on your interviewee. If he says that they do not carry out any review of code designs then feel free to query it, but if that is the case then accept it.

- As you talk, note the areas where there seems to be problems. If he is involved in estimation how do they do it? Can they supply information about the last project or product delivery in terms of how big a job it was, what the quality levels were, how effective the process was at getting rid of defects?

- Now we get to the difficult part. You need to find out how Software Metrics can help the interviewee, so ask him. Now if you simply put the question you will probably be met with a blank look. You will need to steer this part of the interview by suggesting ideas to the interviewee. Would some assistance with estimation be appreciated, perhaps a centralized estimation group or some training in techniques? Are there some problems because of more senior managers asking for embarrassing information such as productivity levels — possibly embarrassing because the manager does not have the information? Do new tools need to be justified? Explore the possibilities with your partner, and I use the word deliberately because the interviewee should now start to feel part of the metrics project, a partner in it.

- Finally, try to arrange another session with your new-found friend but also try to leave the date flexible. Why? The reason is that you will now have some serious work to do. First, you have to hold similar sessions with other individuals so that you can identify a macro set of requirements. You also need to check some of the points raised with other people. Is it really true that effort data is recorded accurately by all project team members as perhaps the manager believes or are the engineers making a wild stab at the figures at the end of each month? You will also find, almost certainly, that your first few interviewees raise even more fundamental questions that need to be answered. Be honest: if you do not have an answer then defer it by noting that it needs to be addressed and by telling the interviewee that various basic definitions and ground rules will be defined before the requirements are baselined. This will not be an alien concept to most people involved in software development.

Before we consider this last point, a few more words on initial requirements capture using this interview-based approach. How long should such an interview take? I seldom schedule more than two such sessions during a day even if I can only get the interviewee to agree to give me a hour. The reason is simply that people like to talk about themselves and it is amazing how quickly time passes in such a situation. In some cases, you may well find yourself sharing lunch and going on in the afternoon when you originally planned to finish by ten in the morning. Do not worry, this is time well spent.

Another point about scheduling. There is always a temptation to "start at the top." Don't! There are two reasons for my saying this. First, you will not be as well prepared as you should be when you do that first interview. In fact, it may take three or four sessions before you really start to get to grips with what you are doing so it is best to minimize any risk at this point. Second, the case when this relaxed, open format interview technique does not work is with the people with whom it would be most useful, senior managers. Senior managers, say the Systems Development manager, do not have the time to chew the fat with you, and even if they do they certainly do not want to seem as though they do.

Time with senior managers is difficult to get and is therefore valuable. To make the most of this time I can only suggest that you adopt the approach mentioned earlier with one modification: tell them what you think the problems are, what the options are and what you intend to do. The modification? Then ask them if they have any specific problem areas that they want addressed or if they want any of the identified action areas given a particularly high priority.

Of course, all senior managers have already identified the immediate business requirements and their priorities for the next five years as advised by all the management books. If you believe that, watch out for flying pigs! Even with senior managers you will need to control the interview but remember again, you are there to learn, not simply to make an impression; that comes later.

To be able to talk to senior managers sensibly using the approach outlined above means that you need to have an appreciation of the problems as perceived by the business, i.e., the very senior managers you will be talking to; you will need to have some idea what areas need to be addressed; and, you need to have a high-level plan even if this is then modified by the manager. Obviously, you cannot go and talk to the senior manager first before you have talked to anyone else.

One final point: do remember to consider business etiquette. Within your organization you may need to approach a senior manager before approaching any of his or her staff. From the previous stage, this permission may have been implied. It does no harm to politely get that permission again, explicitly.

Getting the requirements through individual interview is certainly one technique that can work effectively. There is another technique that can work more quickly in terms of elapsed time but, depending on the culture of the organization, it can involve a greater risk of getting it wrong, often because you do not get the key players involved.

Sometimes the approach is called brainstorming, or meta-planning or centers on a workshop. Essentially it involves a group of people simultaneously working out a set of requirements for the metrics program. It requires a fair amount of planning and coordination and also a strong meeting leader, who is more than a chairman, to control events as they occur.

On the positive side, it can give you a set of agreed requirements very quickly.

To use this approach within the type of organizational model I am using to illustrate the metrics program development and implementation lifecycle would mean that you need to prepare some material that could be used to introduce the topic of Software Metrics. This material needs to define what is meant by the term Software Metrics; it needs to introduce the principles of measurement and relate these to a software development environment; it should show examples of the effective use of Software Metrics; and, it should relate the information shown to the identified business needs of your own organization which, of course, form the basic, high level requirements of your own Software Metrics program. Avoid the use of mathematical formulae in this material as it can confuse the issue.

Once you have the material you will need to identify the key players that you intend to use to define your specific requirements. You will need to arrange some form of management sponsorship to ensure that you can get the people you want to the workshop. Ideally, the Systems Development director would agree to attend the meeting. You will have to plan out the structure of the session in some detail to ensure that you maintain control and get from it what you need.

On the day (and you will need at least a half day, ideally a whole day), be up front and honest. Explain that the purpose of the workshop is to derive a specific set of requirements that will be used to drive the metrics program. Present your introductory material in a strong way and be prepared to handle difficult questions from the participants in a realistic and sympathetic manner. Try not to be too defensive. After all you want their participation, so be prepared to modify your own ideas and concepts in the light of their contributions. Above all, do not come across as someone who claims to have the perfect answer to all their problems. First, they have heard it all before and are probably quite rightly cynical. Second, you do *not* have all the answers! What you do have is an approach that can help them, as managers of software development work, to help themselves.

If you have managed to get a full day, be very sure that you steer discussion towards the requirements definition by the start of the afternoon. It is very easy to get caught up in deep discussions about, perhaps, the true meaning of system size, and to find that it is five o'clock and you have half an hour left to sort out the requirements. If things start to get bogged down then try asking if they would like to try any of the approaches outlined in your examples within their own areas or you could even ask, 'what kind of information would you like that you don't get now?"

Prototyping is an approach I know has been used by one U.S.-based organization in the area of management information. The case was different from the usual situation in that the individual driving the program had a significant amount of experience in the application of Software Metrics, was well respected in the organization and had a strong supplier/client relationship with her customer. This approach worked for her and I could see it being very effective in phase two or three of a metrics initiative as a means of generating management commitment when you expand your program implementation. I have some doubts about applying it during the first stage when the metrics team will probably be learning about the topic themselves.

Whatever approach you use you should end up with a set of specific requirements that have come from the business and that the business wishes the Software Metrics program to address. Looking at these you may well find that they fall into a number of categories. First, you may see some that you feel you have a reasonable answer to and that will provide a quick payback for relatively little effort. You may also spot some that could be called research issues. Yes they are important but you know, from your earlier work, that there are no immediate answers just waiting to be put into place. You will also find some requirements that are obtuse. They are either very specialized or appear so convoluted that you could spend the next ten years just getting to grips with what is wanted. Avoid these like the plague.

In fact, you will almost certainly have too many requirements to address all at once so you will need to prioritize. One systematic approach to this is to look at the available data sources, together with the storage, analysis and feedback requirements. Address the areas where data is available already and where the storage, analysis and feedback requirements are clear first. How to identify what data is available is discussed shortly.

Very often, the Metrics Coordination Group are an ideal forum for determining priorities in terms of requirements to be addressed.

One other thing that you may well discover is that you need to establish some initial definitions.

9.10 ESTABLISH INITIAL DEFINITIONS

You may wonder why you will have to spend time deriving a set of initial definitions for use within the metrics program. After all, you probably have development standards that address these very points. The answer is twofold. First, standards, almost by definition, are documents that sit on shelves and that are very seldom read. Second, even if they are read, they seldom define basic terms in such a way that interpretation and modification do not occur. This means that when you use terms like "fault," "defect," "size" and even "project" other people will often put their own meanings on things. Time and again, I have found terminology to be one of the biggest barriers to understanding.

Let me try to illustrate this by example. Consider the term "defect." Does this mean a perceived difficulty as reported by the user, does it mean a problem with a delivered product even if the defect has not yet been detected or does it mean an identified problem with a product detected, verified and located? Any of these definitions are possible but what you mean by the term "defect" can have serious ramifications when you try to measure the things.

It gets even worse when you consider a term like "fault." Is a fault the same as a defect? Is there a relationship between faults and defects? Can you have multiple defects causing one fault, or multiple faults causing one defect? Confusing, isn't it?

A dictionary is not much help either. Collins English dictionary defines the noun "fault" as, "something that mars; flaw; defect." A defect is defined as, "lack of something necessary for completeness" or "an imperfection; blemish." Now we seem to be approaching another key problem as these defect definitions take on a similarity to definitions of quality.

If you would like to spend a fruitless but entertaining half hour, gather together three or four individuals who are connected with software development. Ask them to define what is meant by "software quality," sit back and watch the fun! At the end of half an hour, or the day if you have that much time to waste, you will not have an agreement but you will be very aware of the problems terminology can cause. One word of warning, do not let yourself get drawn into the argument or you may well be surprised at the strength with which you will defend your own corner. Defining quality is like politics and religion, such discussions are best suited to late nights with good wine and trusted friends.

Just to round off this section of despair, what about the term "project?" We all work on projects, projects have become our master in the past, we have meetings and reviews of the project. I will bet that even this term in your organization is not clearly defined.

So, what is the answer? Remember the first principle I discussed in *Chapter 1*, that of pragmatism and compromise. You will need to be able to define certain basic terms within your metrics initiative simply because you will be talking to many different people and you will be using these terms. It is important that you identify the terms that cause your organization problems and this is one reason why I have left this activity until now within the SMP development model. By talking to your users you will have identified the terms that you need to define. It is also important that you define them in a meaningful way, in a way that is acceptable to the organization and not as theoretical, abstract concepts. How can you obtain the necessary agreement to your definitions? I suggest that you present them to your Metrics Coordination Group and have that group ratify them.

I suppose I should practice what I preach and define some basic terms myself for use within this book. In one sense, these definitions have to be slightly theoretical because the actual definitions you used can depend upon your organizations culture and current practice. Let us return to a previous example. There is a great deal of discussion about the meaning of the terms "fault" and "defect." People tend to view one as the manifestation of an error as perceived by the user of a product, the other is viewed as a flaw in the product that has caused the perceived problem. Obviously, one perceived problem can be related to a number of flaws and vice versa. The question is, which is the defect and which the fault? My answer is very pragmatic, it depends on the organization! If your user reports problems through a defect report, the defect is the perceived problem, the fault is the flaw! If the user reports through a fault report it works the other way round.

But what if your user does not use fault or defect reports? One organization I know of uses "incident reports." In this case, I would suggest that you start to use one term for the flaw that causes the incident report to be raised and stick to it. If other people use the other term then try to educate them, gently and slowly, to use the chosen terms as agreed with the Metrics Coordination Group.

For our purposes, I will use the term *defect* as the perceived problem, so our users raise "Defect Reports." A *fault* will be the flaw that causes a defect.

Regarding size, I will use two definitions of size:

Product size is defined as the quantity of the product currently in use and requiring support;

Project size is defined as the functionality that is added, changed or deleted as the result of a software development or enhancement project.

Notice that I am not yet assigning units to our size measures. This will be done later when we select the metrics we will be using.

Now, what about the project itself? I define a *project* as "*a consolidated unit of work managed as a single entity.*" A project has a recognized start date and end date and has associated with it a project plan. The project starts when the first component of the unit is identified; it ends when the last component is delivered to the product recipient. Note that, depending on your own development lifecycle, this product recipient may be a testing team or the end user or some integration group.

This definition of a project is somewhat cumbersome but it does allow for the case when work starts to be booked against a small work element which then has additional elements added to it over time, during which the project team ramps up to full strength.

What about *quality*? At a conceptual level I prefer the idea that quality is the satisfaction of user requirements. For practical purposes I view quality as a collection of characteristics that are addressed individually. Remember that the particular set of quality characteristics that you may have to address may be a subset of the totality of quality and may not be clearly specified by your users. As an example of the second point, many users do not specify requirements for maintainability when a system is being developed but they can get very upset if a product is later found to be difficult to maintain. *Appendix B* contains two sets of quality attribute definitions. The first comes from the ISO/IEC standard IS9126; the second is one that I used before that standard was available. The main difference, mentioned earlier, is the different view taken of maintainability and enhanceability.

Finally, remember to adopt or derive a high level development lifecycle model for your organization.

9.11 IDENTIFY AVAILABLE DATA SOURCES

We can think about prioritizing the various requirements we have collected essentially by how easy they will be to satisfy. Remember that business requirements and advice from the Metrics Coordination Group may take precedence over what has been considered to be important by either the organization in the past or by you, but available data sources should be identified in any case as it is likely that they will assist you in satisfying current requirements.

The first thing to do is to look at what is currently available in terms of data and where this data resides. To do this you will need to talk to people yet again and this is another case where the Metrics Coordination Group can help. You can also draw on your own experience and the experience of other contacts within the organization. Beware! It is very easy to think that the way you have done things in the past is also the way that every one else does things — but this is not always the case. I did have one example where I built a model for capturing defect data using what I believed to be a standard tracking system used by the organization only to find that this process was only used by one third of the organization — a classic case of not checking the facts thoroughly enough. Fortunately I had only wasted a couple of days but the situation could have been very costly and embarrassing. Imagine presenting a new system to a group of senior managers only to find that they had never heard of the process that lay at the core of your proposal!

You will find certain data collection mechanisms already in place within an organization although it must be said that the validity of this data may well be suspect. Typically an organization will collect data relating to field defects, that is as reported by the customer or the end user. This can be a useful source of information. The other most commonly collected form of data relates to time spent by development staff. Many organizations have little faith in their time recording systems!

There are various reasons for this. Often time data is collected weekly or monthly. Personally, I find it difficult enough to remember what I was doing during the morning if I do not record that information until the afternoon. Completing a timesheet at the end of the week or, even worse, at the end of the month usually means that the information is very inaccurate. Having said that, things do tend to even out. One organization I know of managed to set up an experiment that compared recorded time to actual time spent on a number of specific projects. Their findings were interesting in that they did indeed verify that the recorded time was terribly inaccurate, yet it was consistently inaccurate across the sample. The recorded time was approximately 30% less than the actual time for any one project.

Defect data tends to be less inaccurate in terms of absolute numbers. The problem with defect data tends to lie with inaccuracy in detail or information that you would like to be present simply not being collected. For instance, in one project I observed the number of defects that were attributed to coding faults was very high. This is a common occurrence but equally common, and the case on this project, was the fact that after investigating these defects more carefully I found that coding faults only accounted for less than half those originally reported as such. The rest were design or requirements faults. This can have fairly serious consequences as the data suggested the coding phase of development should be investigated when the reality was that the design phase was by far the more costly in terms of injected faults. This experience was duplicated by other individuals in the same and different organizations. In fact, this experience has happened so frequently that I would always be suspicious of such data.

This lack of care in recording information seems to be a direct result of the lack of feedback from these established systems. People record the information because they have to, because it is part of the organizational bureaucracy. Having recorded the information they never see or hear of it again, so why should they bother to take care? This observation led me to coin the phrase, "write-only database." A ludicrous situation in anyone's view, but one that unfortunately occurs with distressing frequency.

The problem with missing data seems to arise from design by committee and a distinct lack of effective requirements analysis when these systems are set up. Try getting people to ask the question "why are we collecting defect or time data?" rather than "what data should we collect?"

You may be tempted to put completely new systems in place but take care. Developing completely new systems from the ground up for a large organization can be very costly. It is often easier to change something that already exists than to start from scratch.

At this point you should be noting the type of information that is available and relating this to the various requirements that you have identified. This will give you an indication of what is involved in satisfying those requirements and will help you to prioritize them. For example, it is easier to satisfy a requirement for information about productivity if you already have a *reasonable* — and please note the use of the word reasonable — effort-recording system already in place.

9.12   IDENTIFY STORAGE, ANALYSIS AND FEEDBACK REQUIREMENTS

Almost all requirements associated with a Software Metrics program imply the need to store, analyze and feedback information. Taking a first stab at the scale of these tasks for each of the identified requirements is another way of determining what you will tackle in Phase 1, what you will put off until Phase 2 and the requirements you will do everything in your power never ever to tackle!

You need to ask questions like, "how much data will I have to collect and from how many sources?" "Are we talking about simple trend analysis on one independent variable or are we going to get involved in multi linear regression analysis on fifteen variables?" And if you are, then remember you will need a great deal of data and that will take time to collect. Is it really a good idea to do this during Phase 1 when you need to demonstrate some quick results? Also consider, "how many customers do I need to feed information back to, in what form and at what cost?" For example, if you are talking about senior management reporting you will need to spend time ensuring that you present your results in a businesslike and professional way possibly using desktop publishing facilities. Can you get a budget for this in Phase 1 even assuming that you can get sufficient data to derive meaningful summaries?

Some people will argue that we are entering into the design stage but you need to get some idea of what is involved in satisfying a requirement to be able to decide whether it will be satisfied immediately.

9.13   CONSOLIDATE REQUIREMENTS

Having got a good idea of what the requirements are and what they may involve you will need to pull it all together into a consolidated requirements specification.

The exact form of this will vary depending upon the culture of the organization, the profile of the Software Metrics project and your own personality. It may be that a structured, documented discussion session with your own manager, as the customer authority, will be sufficient or you may need to prepare a full requirements specification document with (heaven help you) a cost/benefit analysis that is supported by presentations at board level.

If at all possible, I would suggest that you aim for a middle ground. Going to the board of directors at this point can be dangerous because you have really only identified the problems that need to be addressed. You do not have solutions. Simply talking things over with your manager means that the requirements may be subject to fairly dramatic changes and this can cause serious problems later.

I would suggest that you group the various identified requirements into goals. For example, you may have the following set of identified requirements linked to specific customer groups:

> Improve cost estimation techniques for enhancement projects — Product Development Team Leaders.

> Improve cost estimates that feed into the planning process — Planning Manager

> Sort out our estimates, if we get hit by another fiasco like that last fixed price contract we won't need a metrics program because we won't be here! — Systems Development Director.

With any luck you have identified a common theme here. The goal or consolidated requirement becomes:

> *"To improve the cost estimation process."*

Alternatively, you may have identified requirements that go something like:

> We need some way to focus limited testing effort on the components that need testing most rigorously — Test and Integration Manager.

> We are discovering faults too late, we need to sort them out earlier — Software Development/Enhancement Manager.

> Our inspections are a joke. We need some objective criteria that will get rid of the subjectivity in deciding when a design is good enough — Senior Software Engineer.

> Why don't we use Information Flow Metrics like they said at university? — Junior Software Engineer.

Now this one is a bit more difficult to consolidate, but it does illustrate that you should have talked to all the levels in the organization. What it boils down to is something like:

> *"Identify and implement non-subjective techniques that can identify error-prone*
>
> *components at the inspection stage, or earlier, of the design phase."*

You may also make a note to ask that junior engineer what these Information Flow metrics are!

A typical set of consolidated requirements, expressed very loosely, may look like this:

> "Improve cost and size estimation."

> "Improve project control procedures."

> "Provide management information about performance, covering productivity and achieved quality."

- "Address the prediction of quality attributes prior to release."

- "Address the assessment of designs and requirements."

Of course this may not be an exhaustive set and each goal should be expressed more precisely, at least as precisely as the earlier examples. There may well be sub-goals or requirements within the high level expression, for example management information about achieved quality may be confined to reliability and maintainability or it may cover many more of the so called "-ities."

You should also link each consolidated requirement to a set of primary and secondary customers. The primary customer will effectively be the individual, or functional group, that will decide whether or not you have satisfied the requirement. The secondary customers are those who have a view of what you deliver and will be expected to provide information to help you satisfy the requirement. For example, the primary customer for productivity information may be the Product Group manager, he or she being the person who has asked for that information. However, project managers and engineers are also customers, albeit secondary in this case, of the system that will be put in place to satisfy the primary customers requirement. It is the project managers and the engineers who will have to supply the information that will eventually result in productivity reports to the Product Group Manager.

9.14   SPECIFICATION REVIEW

Having consolidated the requirements you will, of course, have them reviewed by your customer authority as a minimum. It is a good idea to present them to the Metrics Coordination Group as their approval will be useful later. At the very least it means that the "organization" has validated what you intend to do.

You have spent a considerable amount of time and effort ensuring that you know, and that the organization agrees that you know, what is required from the metrics program. Now it is time to satisfy those requirements.

9.15   SUMMARY

This stage is all about finding out what the various parts of the organization want from a Software Metrics program. It is about talking to people to derive these requirements and it is about establishing the foundation of an infrastructure that will be used by you, the developer and implementor of that program, as one vehicle for the successful satisfaction of those requirements. Finally, it is about communicating those requirements back to the organization so that agreement about the objectives of the program can be gained.

10

Stage 3:

Component Design

Key Points:

Three distinct streams of design effort

Metrics Definition

Introduction to the Goal, Question, Metric paradigm

Administration Design

Marketing and Business Planning

Let us recap on the situation. You now know a lot more about Software Metrics than you did when you started work on the program, you have obtained the authority to develop proposals for a metrics program, you have identified a set of requirements against the program linked to primary and secondary customers and you have some idea about what information the organization already collects.

You have also established a steering group, the Metrics Coordination Group. You may also have some ideas about how you intend to satisfy the various requirements you have identified. This is almost inevitable and is typical of the iteration and stage overlap that occurs in real life despite any lifecycle model that appears to impose sequential development. In fact this overlap can be very useful as it allows you to feed back as well as forward to later stages in the development process. Do take care to control feedback, otherwise you can find that you do work against a requirement only to have the requirement changed!

Control is really about baselining requirements with the agreement of your customer authority. This does not mean that a requirements change will never happen, but it does give visibility to those changes and allows their impact to be assessed. The very fact that change involves consultation and agreement to amend a baselined document often means that the need for the change is given more serious thought which, in turn, can limit the changes that occur. Like so many things, it is simply good practice and common sense.

I have called this stage "design" and I see it as consisting of four main streams or sets of activities that will eventually come together and result in a design proposal. The first stream is the definition of the metrics, tools and metrics based techniques that will form the core of our program. Let me stress again that it is only now, after the information requirements have been defined, that we start to think about the metrics! Next we have, what I call, the administration requirements. This covers elements of the program that are needed to use the metrics in a practical way. Another way of thinking of this is as designing the operational procedures and support mechanisms necessary for the implementation of a tactical approach. Examples of these elements include a metrics database and the data collection procedures that will be required.

The final two streams are, I believe, vital to the success of any metrics program yet they are more to do with the organization and the people in that organization than with technical issues. Any initiative that is intended to change the way people think, act and work must address the infrastructure that will enable change. I found a classic case where this was not addressed in one organization that was striving to motivate its staff and to draw on their recognized ability to make things better themselves. So far so good. A huge publicity exercise was undertaken linked to a very expensive set of training courses that, together, raised peoples expectancy in terms of their perception of the contribution they could make to their business. Again, so far so good. This program had a budget of some five million pounds sterling over one financial year so it was not a trivial exercise. And it worked! People became switched on to making the business more effective, to contributing to the business but there was a problem: one of the cornerstones of this initiative was that everyone in the business could and indeed should contribute to the business because the people best placed to improve things are often the ones who are already there. Unfortunately there was no infrastructure put in place to enable this to happen.

This was made painfully obvious to me when a secretary came to me with an idea that was beautiful in its simplicity and that could have saved a considerable amount of money, the problem was we had no idea how to take that idea forward within the change initiative. The infrastructure had not been addressed! We will discuss the infrastructure necessary for a metrics program.

Finally, we need to consider the way the program will be marketed and introduced to the business so we will look at how to develop a marketing and business plan. It is interesting to note how often Software Metrics programs become the responsibility of functional groups that are separate from the software development function. Effectively, the metrics team must act as internal consultants because they cannot, and indeed should not, impose their will on development teams. This implies that the metrics team must conduct themselves in the same way that a small business or external consultants have to conduct themselves, namely in a professional and businesslike way. I am afraid that you can have the best set of metrics ever devised, the most effective techniques for assisting development to produce high quality software and control mechanisms that would make the harshest project coordinator smile, but if you do not market them effectively within your organization they will never be taken up and used by the organization. This is a fact of life!

I will talk about the various streams in turn but do remember that the tasks they cover do have dependencies within the stream and on tasks within other streams. *Figure 10.1* gives my interpretation of these dependencies.

Figure 10.1 Tasks and Links Within Design Stage
(Showing Dependencies Between Streams)

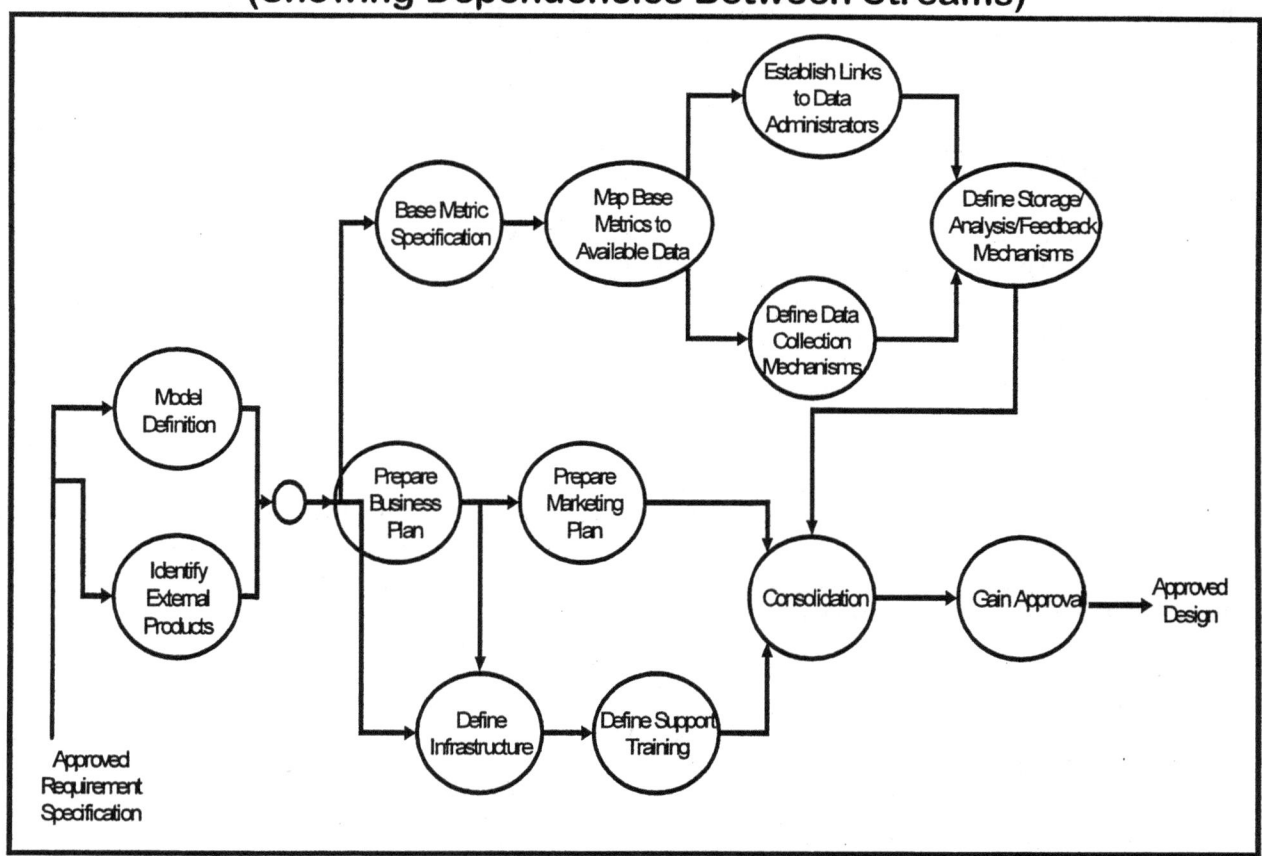

However, before we talk about the four main streams there is one set of activities that should be addressed, pilot projects.

10.1   PILOT PROJECTS

Pilot projects can occur for a number of reasons. It may be that, during the feasibility study stage, you have come across a metric-based technique that, for some reason, appears so elegant, so perfectly suited to what you know you want to do that you immediately see it forming part of your Software Metrics program. It may be that as you go through the design stage you identify another metric that you wish to test out within your own environment. Or, it may simply be that you wish to evaluate a set of tools, perhaps cost estimation packages, with a view to including one or two within the program.

For any of these reasons you may wish to run a pilot project at some point during the design stage. To be honest, pilot projects can be kicked off almost anytime although it would make sense to know what requirement the pilot is supposed to satisfy before committing time and resources.

Pilots should be small, targeted and of as short a duration as possible. You should carefully consider the experimental design of your pilot to be sure that you can get the results that you are aiming for, and of course that you are not guaranteeing the results by the design of your pilots. Experimental design is another specialty, just like statistics. My feeling is that I know enough to know I need specialist help and I try to check the design of pilots out with such a specialist unless I have done such a pilot before. If you do not know anyone within your own organization who can help, and if you have an operational research group I suggest they be your first port of call, then try the local educational facilities, colleges, polytechnics and universities. Academics can help you with this area and usually do some consultancy at very reasonable rates. One day's consulting could be money well spent.

Remember to review the results of your pilot and to feed them into your design process. Very often so called pilots are nothing less than the first stage of implementation with no feedback loop in place to affect the design. This is fine if you are just playing word games to get things rolling but you can find a genuine pilot becoming that implementation unless you specifically build that feedback loop. If you need convincing of this see if you have any development teams using rapid prototyping as a development methodology. If you have, ask them how many prototypes they throw away!

Done right, pilots can provide a wealth of useful information, especially about the amount of effort that will be involved in the full-scale implementation of an aspect of a measurement initiative, and can save considerable amounts of money. This is especially true of the pilot that appears to fail. In other words, when the results of the pilot is not what you hoped for, but is it not better to find out that something does not work in a contained, controlled experiment rather than twelve months down the line when you have invested more money than you should have?

I would like to give you two examples of pilots. In the first case, I was involved in the piloting of a specific sizing technique in a real-time environment. By analyzing historical data we were able to determine that our use of the size measure in that specific environment did not work. By that I mean that there was little correlation between size, as we were measuring it, and effort. It was much better to find this out at that point rather than to have started implementation of the sizing technique with all the training, development of storage mechanisms and the building of feedback loops that would have been involved. Such an exercise would have been costly and would have resulted in a major embarrassment if we had then found that there was no foundation for using the sizing technique.

The second pilot I will touch upon briefly involved the use of a simple cost estimation strategy. By piloting the strategy within one part of the organization, we were able to develop a familiarity with the techniques involved and, most importantly, we were able to obtain in-house examples that demonstrated the successful use of those techniques.

So, bearing in mind that pilots can be going on and feeding into the main design streams we will now start to talk about those streams.

10.2   METRICS DEFINITION STREAM

At last, do we get onto the core of the program, the technical part, the difficult but rewarding part? Wrong! Let me try a bit of heresy: defining metrics for specific requirements is the easy part. Well, most of the time it is although there are a couple of requirements that have stymied me in the past, but most of the time, the metrics are easy. The difficult part is getting them in place and in use within the business.

So, if it is as easy as I claim, how do you do it?

10.3   MODEL DEFINITION OR GOALS, QUESTIONS, METRICS

What I intend is to discuss the derivation of metrics or measures and to then support that discussion with a couple of examples. Remember where we are: we have identified requirements for information and metrics-based techniques linked to specific customer groupings.

These perhaps range from generalities such as "improve the cost estimation process" to very specific requirements such as "provide information to the Systems Development Director that quantifies the achieved productivity of all product development teams on a quarterly basis." The related primary customers could be the project managers (because they are the people who are fed up getting blamed for poor estimates) and the Systems Development Director respectively.

You have also been talking to people in the organization to derive these requirements so you have a great asset available to you: personal contacts.

You have, in terms of Basili and Rombach's Goal, Question, Metric paradigm, Rombach (1), the goals defined. You also have the means by which you can resolve the questions. Before you do this, do ensure that the goals you have identified are *measurement* goals. Individuals will often throw a general goal at you that is not suitable as a requirement within a metrics program. For example, a manager may claim that his goal is to increase development productivity by 25% within 2 years. Fine, as a strategic goal for that manager this is acceptable — but it does not help a metrics program at all. Unfortunately Software Metrics do not do managers' jobs for them and they need to realize this.

Acceptable measurement requirements within this managers strategic goal may include, "provide a mechanism by which the current and future productivity levels can be assessed," followed by "provide metrics-based techniques that can reduce rework within development."

This is not to say that measurement programs will not include some direct benefits to the development process, but only some parts of a Software Metrics program can do this. Examples include metrics-based techniques that can be used by engineers and managers on a day-by-day basis to directly improve intermediate or final deliverables; and, measurements that aim to identify the areas within generic products that are causing the majority of the problems, the idea being that these can be rewritten to reduce rework or testing effort. The other components of a measurement initiative, for example improving cost estimation and project control or providing general management information, will not directly improve things. What these components can do is enable managers to manage more effectively and it is this which improves the process.

So, be careful. Do not get forced into a situation where you have to shoulder what are essentially management responsibilities for development; you have quite enough to do just providing them with the tools they need to do *their* job.

Now, assuming that you have been careful about defining the requirements that have been placed against the metrics program, you can move on to the next step in model definition, *requirement classification*.

If you look at the various requirements you have identified you will notice similarities between them. These similarities will enable you to classify your requirements into a small number of major categories. A typical set of such macro-requirements was given in the previous chapter and is reproduced below:

- *"Improve cost, size and duration estimation."*

- *"Improve project control procedures."*

- *"Provide management information about performance, covering productivity and achieved quality."*

- *"Address the prediction of quality attributes prior to release."*

- *"Address the assessment of designs and requirements."*

Generally speaking the provision of information about achieved quality will be broken down into a number of specific "-ities."

The reason for this grouping of requirements is to enable the satisfaction of as many individual requirements as possible in the shortest time. In almost every case that I have seen, the number of customers and individual requirements that a Software Metrics program is expected to address far exceeds the available resources if those requirements are addressed individually. The only solution that appears to work effectively is to offer generic solutions to these requirements within the organization, which can be tailored to meet the needs of specific customers.

One question that this approach raises is related to the customer set that was identified earlier. What happens to these individuals and groups? Each customer who is linked to a generic or macro-requirement becomes a "viewpoint authority" for that requirement.

To explain this concept let us consider the case of cost estimation improvement. Various functional groups within the organization may have expressed this as a requirement and these could include:

>Project managers who have to prepare estimates. For now we will assume that this is one customer group currently using the same techniques and operating under the same constraints. While this is probably a simplification of reality it still enables us to illustrate the point.

>Marketing, who have to prepare bids for work.

>The Product manager who wishes to see better estimation.

The Systems Development director who is fed up with other directors telling him that the department is costing money by failing to meet promises to customers.

The external customers themselves.

Each of these groups has a vested interest in improving the cost estimation process and each will have input regarding the requirements for that improvement. It makes no sense at all to try to satisfy these individual requirements separately when a single, what we can call generic, solution will satisfy the majority of them. What we must realize is that each group will have a view of the requirement and the solution that is different to the other groups. In this sense, they all have a viewpoint on the requirement. We should also realize that each group may have subgroups within it and to reconcile these it is a good idea to identify or nominate a viewpoint authority. This individual is expected to express the needs of the group and to represent their interests during the process of satisfying those requirements.

There may well be conflict between the various viewpoint authorities and this can be resolved by identifying a customer authority who is the individual with the final say in resolving such conflicts. The ideal candidate for the role of customer authority is the primary customer for the specific requirement solution you have already identified.

One other advantage that comes from requirements grouping is that you can more easily use other peoples' solutions. You already have the concept of tailoring solutions for the various viewpoints but you can equally take an external solution, such as a cost estimation package that runs on a PC, and tailor its use for the organization. Requirements grouping helps because it makes the identification of external solutions easier.

Having carried out this requirements grouping you can start to go through the Question or modeling task of metrics definition.

Almost all requirements laid against a Software Metrics program relate to attributes of the development process or its products. In fact, the recognition of this was a fundamental step forward in the use of Software Metrics. Current thinking seems to have added in attributes that relate to Resources as well. This is more a large subgroup of attributes within the process/product split, but such a view can be useful. Do not fall into the trap of thinking that this solves all your problems or that this breakdown will automatically lead to metrics; it will not. Nor should you waste time trying to categorize metrics as product or process measures; it provides little added value.

What can be categorized is the requirement, but this is addressed by identifying the attribute of interest within that requirement — for example, the productivity of the development process as a process-oriented requirement.

Now for any attribute within a requirement, there are three items that need to be considered. The first is to determine what is meant by that attribute, in other words you will need to define the attribute. It may be that this has already been done when you were considering the set of initial definitions during the last stage but if this has not been addressed it is vital that it is done now. You need to be very clear about what is meant. The attributes that seem to typify the problem at the moment are "maintainability," "enhanceability" and "extendability." Any of these apparently innocuous terms can be used by different people to refer to the same attribute and individuals, including myself, will argue strongly for their own preference.

I am sure that the debate within the industry will continue for many years and may never be resolved to the satisfaction of everyone but you cannot afford to wait for such agreement. The approach I have adopted with a fair degree of success in the past is to define particular attributes within an organization. Even this can involve discussion and debate but it is practical to drive definitions for attributes, perhaps agreed and endorsed by the Metrics Coordination Group, in a fairly short space of time.

As far as the various quality "-ities" are concerned, some definitions are available from International Standard 9126, (ref. IS9126), and this can be used as the foundation of your own definitions.

Having defined the attribute you must now realize that there are two areas of interest for such an attribute. First, you may wish to monitor or assess the attribute. Alternatively, you may wish to apply prediction to the attribute. An example will clarify the problem. Software system reliability is an attribute that concerns many organizations. Reliability can be defined as:

> *"A set of attributes that bear on the capability of software to maintain its level of performance under stated conditions for a stated period of time"*
> (IS9126, 5th January 1990)

or my own definition prepared before I had sight of the ISO definition

> *"The capability of a software component to perform its functions to a level specified in the requirement, or defaulting to 100%, within a given environment."*

There may be a requirement in an organization to monitor the reliability of its software products in the field over time or across build releases. This information allows reducing reliability to be addressed before it becomes a disaster or, if reliability is increasing, it can be used to help market the revenue earning products.

Most organizations are also interested in building reliability into their products. This implies that conditions that exist within designs, for example, have an effect on the reliability of the delivered product. So the organization may wish to measure the extent of coupling and cohesion of components in design to predict the field reliability. It may even be as simple as using faults discovered and corrected during testing as a prediction of the number of faults that will be discovered by users or customers.

The approach used to satisfy these two demands are very different and I suggest that you treat the monitoring or assessment and the prediction of an attribute as separate requirements within the metrics program.

Refining the requirements in this way, through attribute definition and determining whether you are required to monitor or predict, will enable you to identify the processes you need to consider and, hence, the process products to which you will apply measurement.

The next step is to derive a model that will satisfy the requirement. To do this you need to identify what can be called the characteristics of the process or product that affect the attribute you are interested in. Modeling by its very nature is a human activity and is therefore somewhat subjective. Again, the best advice I can give you is to talk to the people who are best placed to answer the question, "what affects this attribute?" In other words talk to the people who are involved in the process.

Identifying the characteristics of interest may cause you to do still more definition, for example what is meant by size or complexity, but please remember to be pragmatic and to listen carefully. If you have doubts about presenting a definition, then call it a 'working definition.' You are not looking for perfection — you are looking for something that will enable you to satisfy a real and important requirement.

Once you have obtained a set of characteristics you can start to combine these in the form of a model. In this context, a model is *a mathematical combination of characteristics resulting in a function for which the dependent variable provides information about the attribute of interest.* The model can, and perhaps should, include a technique built around the analysis of that function.

As I have said, modeling is a human activity and also, by definition, includes an element of simplification. Do not try to form the "perfect model" or you will be firmly on the road to frustration and despair. The metrics you end up with are unlikely to tell the whole story about any attribute; the real question is, do they give you more information than you have now and is that information of practical use to the organization? This simplification may mean that you ignore some of the characteristics identified. Remember that simpler models are probably better than more complicated ones.

If you find that your models are not sufficiently sophisticated to be able to supply you with the information you require, perhaps because a characteristic is more important than you assumed, then CHANGE THE MODEL! Do not fall into the trap of believing that your models are perfect or, in some way "right," just because you have spent time and effort developing them. The great power of models is that they can be incrementally developed and extended.

Your model, or at least the component of the model that is a mathematical function gives you the composite metric that you will use to measure a particular attribute.

By looking at the components of the composite metric you can identify the base metrics, the raw data, that you will need to collect to provide information about a particular attribute. All that remains is to implement the use of the base and composite metrics and then to assess the results. The implementation step is the difficult one.

So as you can see, deriving the metrics is easy! Well, perhaps you still have some doubts, so let us try it with a couple of examples.

Suppose that we have a requirement from a product development team leader for a single measure to monitor the performance of software development. I have phrased this to ask for a single measure to deliberately simplify things as I wish to illustrate the modeling technique, not provide you with a new metric. In fact we are going to end up with a very old metric in this case! Such a requirement may come from a number of team leaders and similar requirements may also come from other customer groups such as senior management who wish to monitor performance across a number of teams. For the sake of illustration I am going to just talk about this single requirement source, a manager responsible for a number of teams, although the steps and principles are the same.

This requirement can be classed as a *business entity metric* because it relates to a number of projects for which the team has responsibility. All that this classification implies is that we can look at what other organizations are doing in the same area but, of course, to be able to see that we need to have some idea of what that area is. We can also identify the customer authority and the viewpoints for this requirement. The prime candidate for the role of customer authority would seem to be the manager as the request has come from him. Are there any other viewpoints in this rather simple example? There most certainly is at least one other viewpoint: the engineers who will be contributing to the measure! Depending on the size of the team, at least one viewpoint authority should be identified within the group. This individual will act as their spokesperson although others should also be talked to.

We now need to identify and define the attribute of interest. Development performance can be defined as:

> *"The effectiveness of carrying out software development activities within a given environment."*

Effectiveness can, in turn be defined as the degree to which a desired effect is produced. An effect is anything brought about by a cause, a result. I think it is time to go and talk to our customer and viewpoint authorities.

We may well find that the result they are aiming for is to deliver quality software at minimum cost. Discussion may also reveal that, of the two main elements within this target, they feel that quality is important and that they are taking continuous steps to improve this, but what they actually want to show is that they are also improving their ability to reduce costs. This could lead to a refinement in our basic measurement requirement to monitor development performance, the more refined version being:

"Supply a single high level indicator of development performance that describes the effectiveness of production."

Now we are getting to the nub of the requirement, we are talking about the effectiveness of production; that sounds like productivity to me. Well, I did say it was going to be an old metric!

Productivity can be defined as the degree to which economic value is produced.

What we now have is an identified attribute and a definition of what we mean by that attribute. Armed with this we can start to look around the industry, and other industries to see how they measure "productivity." We can also go back and talk to our customer and viewpoint authorities again to ask the question, "what is it that affects productivity, what do we put in and what do we get out?" In other words, what are the characteristics that affect productivity?

With many examples that you will come across there are two ways of answering this question about characteristics. One is to model them internally, the other is to find out what the "state of the art" or "accepted wisdom" is in other organizations and industries. For the purposes of this example, we will have a look at the first approach.

Productivity would seem to have two elements, what do we put in and what do we get out in terms of what does the software development process consume and what does it deliver? We put in people and time that we can call 'effort,' equipment, managerial support and organizational support covering things like the personnel department, accommodation and travel. Of these cost elements you will almost certainly find that the most significant is effort. You will also probably find that your accountants have techniques by which they can apportion the other cost elements down to effort costs to give a loaded salary for any individual or group. This simplifies things because we can, perhaps, just use the effort cost as the "what do we put in" component of a productivity measure.

Now what do we get out of software development? One way of looking at this is to say that we deliver a software system to the market and what we get out is the revenue from that system. This is complicated in two ways, if the team is involved in enhancement engineering then we may have problems determining the revenue from a particular build and many of the factors that determine revenue are beyond the control of the software development function, falling instead to, for example, marketing. Remember that we wish to keep it as simple as possible; so, take a look at the process for which software development does have responsibility. What is the product of that process? It would seem to be a software system including code, object or source, and documentation.

Now, what are the characteristics that contribute to what we get out? These could include the amount and detail of the documentation that is required; the size of the code and the complexity of that code. Talking to our engineers we may find that the documentation is relatively standard across projects and if this is the case we may decide to factor out this element. What about the code? We have now got involved in looking at how we are going to combine our aspects but you will often find that this overlap between characteristic identification and combination happens.

As far as the code is concerned, you may see the size of the system as being important and the complexity being equally important but, again, talking to the engineers and the team leaders may indicate that complexity between projects is fairly constant, especially in an enhancement situation. So in this case, could we simply use code size? You may decide to check this out by looking for a relationship between code size and development effort.

Time pressure, or more correctly varying time pressure, on projects is also seen as having a major impact on effort. If time pressure is applied and the project must be completed by a very tight deadline then, providing scope or requirements are not reduced, the only variable that can be adjusted is effort. Despite the argument that says throwing effort at a problem will not reduce duration, the reality is that this is the only option available and that large projects can be delivered relatively quickly by using more staff. The point to remember is that the relationship is not linear, in other words if a project is required in half the time then you cannot simply double the team size. You may need to quadruple the size of the team and add further resources just to tackle the communication problem. You will probably pay for this approach to system development in terms of reduced productivity.

However, you will often find that the time pressure operating on projects is relatively constant within, and this is important, a single environment, for example a tool development group or a specific product group handling ongoing releases. Again this effect can often be factored out. In this sense we can justifiably simplify our productivity model.

Alternatively, you may have looked at what other organizations are doing and reached the same conclusion, productivity is normally expressed as:

Productivity = Work Product / Product Cost

A ratio is used because you wish to compare what we get out to what we put in.

Generally speaking, productivity within software development is expressed as:

Productivity = Project Size / Project Effort

This is your basic productivity model and it is this that will be used to derive the composite and base metrics. Essentially, this means that we need to change the generalized model components, project size and effort, to specific, defined measures.

The obvious candidates for project size are lines of code or "Function Points," really the unit-less number that results from the application of Function Point Analysis to a requirement specification, high level design or produced system.

Both of these measures can be defined in such a way as to cater to enhancement projects. For Lines of Code you could consider the added, deleted and changed lines and the same principle can be applied to Function Point Analysis.

For effort we may choose engineering or person days, months or even years. My own recommendation for an effort measure would be to use person hours. This gets rid of many of the differences and debates about what comprises a person day. Assume that we decide to use Lines of Code and person hours as the components of our composite metric giving:

Productivity = Lines of Code / Person Hours

We are almost there now. The base metrics or items of raw data that need to be collected almost drop out from this composite. There is one very important step that needs to be addressed: we have to define our base metrics in such a way as to make them meaningful, and their collection feasible, within our organization. This is true of almost every metric that you will use within the program. Yet again you will need to talk to the people who are or who will be involved in the program to make sure that what you propose is practical, but once you have defined the base metrics you have completed your metric derivation.

Well, almost! You do need to ensure that what you have defined is practical and this is another area where pilot exercises can be extremely useful. You also need to consider the analysis and feedback of the data you have collected. Do not fall into the trap of many metrics initiatives that end up with masses of data that is not being used by the organization. I will have more to say about these subjects later. You also have to consider the implementation of the processes that will facilitate the collection, analysis and feedback of data. Again we will address this topic later.

Let us try another example of the derivation technique. This time I will cut down the discussion to the bare bones. Our requirement is to provide information to senior management about the field quality of software products. Discussion indicates that our customer is the System Development Director and he is interested in reliability as perceived by the customer. Reliability is seen as the key quality factor in this case. The requirement can be classified as a Business Entity Metric.

The attribute, reliability, can be defined as before, "the capability of a software component," in this case the delivered system within the population of products, "to perform its functions to a level specified in the requirement... within a given environment."

What are the characteristics that affect reliability? What is it about the product that we deliver that can affect reliability? Big systems tend to be less reliable than small ones so product size could be considered. The complexity of the product may be important and the degree of use of the product could also be a possible attribute. Other possibilities include the time pressure applied to the development project, the degree of testing, the extent to which other verification and validation techniques were used, etc.

We also need to consider the product characteristics that indicate the level of reliability. An obvious candidate includes the time between failures, and please note that the traditional "Mean Time Between Failures" may not be appropriate as the use of a mean average depends upon the frequency distribution of time between failures. Another possibility is the number of system crashes over a given period of time or the number of user raised faults. Notice that I am using faults here rather than defects. Bear in mind that the customer will raise defect reports but that some of those defects will be duplicated or result from a lack of understanding of, say the documentation.

This information itself can be important for other measures, for example for some usability measures, but I suggest that reliability is a function of the validated, non-duplicate defects, the faults detected by the user or customer.

Trying to combine all of these aspects would result in a very complex metric and, probably, a very frustrated metrics team member, so keep it simple. Talk to the managers and if possible to the users and pick on the most important aspects. I suggest that field reliability of a product can be modeled by:

*Product Reliability = User Detected Faults / (Product Size * Usage)*

What this model says is that quality or reliability is a function of the validated "pain" being suffered by the customer to the extent that he or she will complain about it; how big the product is, which I include so that I can make more meaningful comparisons between products; and, the degree to which that product is used. This may work for a single product but the requirement is for a business entity metric that will be used by a senior manager. To meet this requirement I suggest that an average Product Reliability be derived from a sample of Product Reliability figures taken over a period of months. The type of average depends on the frequency distribution. For a normal or Gaussian distribution the mean average is the most appropriate, but for skewed distributions median or mode averages are more appropriate. I strongly suggest that you talk to a statistician about this or at least consult statistical text books. Both sources of information can explain the reasons for this more ably than myself.

We now have our model and some components of our composite metric. User-detected faults I can live with in my composite; product size I can define as Lines of Code or, more preferably in my view Function Points; and, usage I can define as the number of sites on which we support the product.

So my composite metric becomes:

*Reliability is the average of the product reliabilities for a sample
at a given time where product reliability is defined as:*

Product Reliability = User Detected Faults / (Product Function Points * Sites Supported)

To get our base metrics we have to define the components of field reliability in more concrete terms. In this case I am tempted to simply amend the definitions to say that user detected faults are accumulated over a three month period while the other two components , i.e., product function points and sites supported, are a snapshot, most likely taken at the point of delivery or, maybe, at the end of the three-month period. .

And that is it! At this point I reach for my tin hat. Whenever you define a metric to meet a specific requirement you can guarantee that someone, somewhere will try to shoot it full of holes. There are various reasons for this, some valid, some not so valid. Nobody with any sense would claim that any of the metrics outlined above are perfect.

I claim that they satisfy the requirements in a pragmatic way but in all honesty I cannot say that the field reliability measure tells me everything I want to know about the attribute. It cannot, because I have identified many characteristics that contribute or effect field reliability and then I have ignored some! There may be good reasons for this. For example, I may feel that I have no way of assessing the complexity of the product at the full system level. What should I do? Should I devote possibly a great deal of time trying to solve the problem of system complexity before I provide a metric, or should I be satisfied with a coarser measure that gives me a reasonable indication of field reliability?

Look at who the customer is. Will a senior manager be interested in every nuance, every aspect of the attribute? I suggest not. A senior manager requires an indication of reliability levels so that trends can be identified and possibly so that meaningful targets can be set. Will they be meaningful? Well, remember that you have not done this in isolation. You have been talking to engineers and project managers while you have been deriving the measures so some degree of acceptance should be present. If you aim for perfection you will not hit the target for many years. Satisfying the requirement is what you should aim for and you should do this as quickly and simply as possible. Some claim that this is perfection anyway.

Now there may be valid reasons for people taking pot shots at the metrics. It may be that you have got it wrong or that you have, at least, not covered all the bases. In the case of field reliability we are talking about faults rather than defects but when a customer raises a defect you may not know if it is a duplicate or an invalid defect or an indication of a true fault. In some ways this is an implementation problem but it should be given some consideration now. If you define user detected faults to be the sum of all non-duplicated and validated defect reports raised and closed during a particular period of time together with all reports raised but still open, you will have some that should not have been included because they will turn out to be duplicates or invalid. You may feel that this is more acceptable than simply ignoring the open defects because you may have some clever individuals who realize that by never closing defect reports they improve reliability. This is not going to please the customer. So, if you go for the first option, try it out for a couple of months to see how many of the defects actually turn out to be "no fault" or duplicated reports. I suggest that the number will be insignificant especially as you may be able to spot the duplicates as they are raised.

Other criticisms may be more fundamental or important. Listen! If they are valid criticisms then change the model and the metrics but do watch out for the constant critics who you will never satisfy.

So, to summarize the steps in metric derivation as I have done it on many occasions and relating that to the *GQM* paradigm, Rombach (1), on which my approach is firmly based, the steps are as follows.

> **GOALS**: Identify the initial requirement and associated customers. Refine this to a specific requirement with an identified customer set. Classify the requirement within the high-level requirements of the metrics program.

> **QUESTIONS**: Identify the attribute that the requirement addresses. Define the attribute. Find out what others are doing. Identify characteristics of the product or process that contribute to or affect the attribute of interest. Derive a model by combining aspects or through the adoption of a technique.

> **METRICS**: From the model derive a composite metric by associating measurement units or scales with the aspects in that model. From these scales identify the base metrics that will need to be collected.

Then all you have to do is implement the metric. Now that is the hard part but we will talk about that later!

10.4   IDENTIFY EXTERNAL PRODUCTS

I have used a model or technique for deriving metrics but there is no point in reinventing the wheel. You will come across situations where there are already proprietary products available on the open market or techniques in the public domain that you can adopt, thus circumventing the derivation process. This means that you can move onto implementing the use of those products or techniques very quickly.

This does *not* mean that no work will be required. You will find that many of these products and techniques need to be adapted to your own environment but much of the hard work has been done for you. To illustrate the GQM approach I have discussed to the case where external products or metrics already exist externally to the organization, I will use the same metric derivation model as a framework.

By far, the biggest market offering, in terms of proprietary products, is in the area of cost estimation so I will use these to illustrate the mechanism. Elsewhere I have discussed various of these software tools and it is sufficient to say here that the list is large with new packages being added, it seems, every week. I have also discussed the value, in my view, that these products can offer so I will confine myself to talking about the process of satisfying requirements within your own metrics initiative.

Essentially, the goals step of the model needs to be addressed as before. You still need an identified requirement and an identified customer and you should classify the requirement within the high level metrics program requirements. You may also find constraints creeping into your requirements. For example, you may be constrained to using PC-based software.

It is in the "Questions" area that the most significant difference is seen. What is needed is for you to investigate the market place to see what is available. Only you will be able to decide which of the many tools is best suited to your needs given your requirements, any constraints and the persuasiveness of the salesman. One thing I would strongly recommend is that you get a feel for the product through hands-on experience. This is the only way that you can tell if the tool is easy to use and suitable. Ideally you should carry out a full evaluation using historical data and comparing the results with the predictions from the tool, but this can be difficult, not least because much of the information you need may not be available. If it was, you might not need a Software Metrics program!

The tools will tell you what information they require as input and these are obviously the base metrics you need to collect. Another word of warning: many of these tools ask for a great deal of information but supplying all of these inputs can sometimes distort the accuracy of the predictions. Look instead for the key "cost drivers" that affect the model by playing with the tool and also determine, again by talking to the people who know (the project managers and engineers), what are the important drivers.

Having made your selection all you need do is implement the tools. Yes, the hard part again!

You can also modify the derivation model to apply it to the selection of "public domain" metrics. These include most variants of Function Point Analysis, McCabe metrics and Information Flow metrics. Many of these come complete with analysis techniques or guidelines for use and some, such as the McCabe metrics, are also supported by proprietary products.

Again you need to go through the Goals step of the derivation model and you need to research the market to see what is on offer. A good way of doing this is to attend some of the training courses that cover the theory of metrics, and more and more of these are being staged. Or, even better, you can attend some of the metrics conferences that are now regular events.

Once you have gone through the Goals step and identified a market offering you are in the position of having brought in a model. Then you simply apply the derivation model in the same way as I have outlined above through to determining the base metrics you need to collect.

10.5 ADMINISTRATION DESIGN STREAM

Having defined a set of metrics, tools and metrics based techniques that you believe will satisfy the specific requirements placed on the metrics program you now have to consider the more mundane but very important areas of collection, storage, analysis and feedback.

10.6   MAP BASE METRICS TO AVAILABLE DATA

Defining the metrics and identifying the tools to support, say, cost estimation means that you have defined a set of base metrics and this raw data needs to be collected. Of course, you do not want to reinvent the wheel so it makes sense to use data that is already collected by the organization if possible.

This has two distinct benefits. First, it reduces the amount of work that you have to do as you do not need to design the collection system from the ground up and, second, it means that you reduce the amount of additional work that your data suppliers, often the engineers, have to do. This is always a good idea because any time spent filling in data sheets is time that could have been spent on system development.

There are some problems and disadvantages to using existing mechanisms and these should not be ignored. Very often the data supplied will not be exactly what you want. For example, if you have a defect reporting system it may not record the root cause of the defect. In this case you are going to need management commitment to enable you to change the existing system to record that data element but this is much less of a commitment, because of a lower cost, than that required for the development and implementation of a completely new system.

Another serious problem with existing systems is that they are often viewed as part of the unavoidable bureaucracy associated with, or perhaps more correctly hindering, "real" work. This often means that very little care is taken over filling in the "form" and that the data is then incorrect. The classic example of this is timesheets but you often see it in defect reporting systems. In this case, the system may record the root cause of the defect, perhaps in terms of the development lifecycle stage that injected the fault, but the field that records this may be filled in with the lifecycle stage where the fix was made. After all, why worry about it, nobody does anything with the data!

As mentioned earlier I have seen cases where defect reports have been re-analyzed, the percentage split between code defects and earlier lifecycle stages change dramatically. The problem was that engineers were fixing the fault by changing the code so that was what went into the "cause" field. Never mind that the design or the requirement specification was wrong.

If the problem with an existing system is that the specific data you require is not there then the obvious answer is to change the system so that it will supply the required item. This is often the best option. Another option is to change the requirement on the existing system. You will often find that there is another data item available that can almost give you what you want or alternatively that there is another system or method by which could provide the data. For example, in one case an organization I was involved with was looking for a way to measure software product size. The first choice was to use a tightly defined Line of Code count but we found that this data was generally unavailable, strange as that may sound. What was available was a measure of memory required by the system and investigation showed that there was a reasonable relationship between this and Line of Code size. Not a perfect solution by any means but a pragmatic one given the particular circumstances.

This idea of changing the requirement can be taken one step further. You are looking for base metric data because you have identified a model-based, composite metric that will give you useful information. You could always change the composite metric or the model if the raw data is not available. This does require that you be very objective about "your" measures but it is an option and should be considered. After all, these measures are not cast in stone.

If the data is being supplied but is inaccurate you have to deal with a more fundamental problem. You could just accept the data. From a theoretical point of view this is not a sound approach but it can be valid in some cases. If you consider the situation where an individual is booking time to two projects you may not get accurate data. He or she may book more time to one project during one week based on nothing more than a guess. Rather than spending time trying to impose accuracy you may just assume that if more time is booked to one project this week then the reverse will be true next week, or the week after, so things will even out. Not very accurate but it could be acceptable if coarse measures are required.

Of course, you will eventually have to bite the bullet and try to improve the accuracy of recorded data. I have more to say on this topic elsewhere.

10.7   ESTABLISH LINKS TO DATA ADMINISTRATORS

Once you know, in detail, the kind of information that is available you will need to form a link to the people who are responsible for administering the data collection systems that exist within the organization.

Obviously, you may already have been talking to these people as part of previous tasks but this now needs to be formalized. You should document your requirements on them and have them formally agree to those requirements. There seems to be two extreme reactions to such a request for data. On one hand, you may be seen as a major inconvenience: some data administrators do seem to take the view that life would be wonderful if only they did not have to put up with users. Remember, it is *their* system and you want something from them so be polite, be diplomatic but be prepared to use any clout you have if necessary! On the other hand, you may find that the administrator goes into paroxysms of joy at the thought of somebody actually using the data that they collect and analyze. If this does happen then build on it, do not destroy it with comments like, "well, you obviously need some help on this." You may laugh, and I have no wish to patronize, but I have seen potentially fruitful relationships destroyed by a single such comment.

Above all, be generous with acknowledgment and thanks. If someone helps you then say so, publicly and often.

10.8   DEFINE DATA COLLECTION MECHANISMS

Before you even think about going live with your program, try to have as many of the bases covered as possible. It is very tempting to instruct a project team to supply you with effort, defect and size data without telling them how to do it.

Remember, these people are software developers. That is what they are paid to do and that is what the organization wants them to do. If you want them to do something new, then help them to do it as much as you possibly can. You should define forms (with their input of course); you should tell them how often they should forward information; you should design the analysis techniques. At the very least this means that you get a measure of consistency. It can also mean the difference between a program that works and a program that fails.

This does not mean that you should do this definition task in isolation. On the contrary, you want them to be involved and to accept what is given to them but help them as much as you can.

10.9   DESIGN STORAGE, ANALYSIS AND FEEDBACK MECHANISMS

Having determined where and how you are going to get your raw data it does help if you have somewhere to put it.

Try not to fall into the trap of waiting until the data starts streaming in the hope that you will sort it out then. You have your high-level program requirements, you have your composite metrics and you have your base metrics definitions. These all act as inputs to the process of designing and implementing your metrics database.

Now the database may be something as simple as a spreadsheet or a PC database or it can be as complex as a corporate-wide Management Information System. It can be constrained by existing systems that are used by management or it may be an area that has never been addressed by your organization. There are strong arguments for, if circumstances allow, keeping the first implementation of your metrics database simple. For one thing, you will be feeling your way and, with the best will in world, you are unlikely to get it perfectly correct first time around.

My advice is to treat the first implementation of this database as a prototype and to use a simple spreadsheet or database application as the initial platform.

In one organization, a senior management decision has been taken to bring a large number of disparate internal MIS systems together under a single system. Tempting as it could be to consider this approach, it is educational to learn that the initiative is planned over twenty years and has an engineering head count that peaks in hundreds!

The system that you end up with will depend heavily on the scope of your own metrics initiative. My own preferred approach is to use a form of prototype. If you adopt a phased approach to the implementation of your metrics program you may well be able to build a metrics database within a PC quickly and easily using resources from within the metrics team. Operating that system gives you the opportunity to learn and then to modify the system with relatively little cost or public loss of face. As the metrics program expands you can migrate the database to a larger platform within the overall MIS strategy of your organization using the operational prototype as a major input to the development of the eventual system.

As far as analysis and feedback is concerned you may have a problem. The specifics of your analysis may depend upon the data that you get in. For example, whether you use means or medians as the "average" will depend upon the distribution of your observed values. While this kind of detailed question cannot be answered at this time, although you can make some educated guesses as data from software development of products is seldom "normally" distributed, you should consider the type of analysis you will be performing. Incidentally, if the data is normally distributed then the mean equals the median equals the mode anyway.

Within your program design you should consider the frequency of reports, the target audience and the style of the reports. You should also aim to store and analyze information that can be used to show the effectiveness of the program itself. For example, if one of the high-level program requirements is to improve the effectiveness of software estimation then it makes sense to record and store estimates within projects and the actuals against those projects. This enables you to demonstrate the effectiveness of the program over time.

This book is not about database design and a great deal has been written elsewhere about this subject. I suggest that information on that subject be obtained from a better source than myself and you should use expertise internal to your organization as a first port of call. Another subject that has had a great deal of attention over the years is the representation of information. Interestingly, most organizations totally ignore this advice.

Organizations seem to have a preferred style of graph with which they are comfortable. In some, you see histograms or bar charts everywhere; in others you hardly ever see a bar chart but there are pie charts in abundance. This is a great shame because the different styles of pictorial or graphical representation have different purposes and are suited to different requirements.

For example, if you want to show information changing over time you should not use a series of pie charts. It is much more effective to use a simple XY graph perhaps with an associated rolling average.

Another major mistake is to send a senior manager a matrix of raw data. I have seen so-called reports that consist of nothing more than page after page of figures. Managers do not have time to wade through all this information and if you want to get a point across then get the point across, not the data.

Of course, some people go to the other extreme. No raw data is presented but either lots of graphs suddenly land on the managers desk, or even worse, a couple of graphs covered in bars, lines and with small tables stuck in corners. The poor manager does not know what is being said and, if the choice has been to go for lots of graphs, cannot remember what was shown on the first page when he gets to page ten, or twenty or thirty. You may feel I am exaggerating but these are real examples of reports I have seen presented to managers.

Of course, at this stage of your project you cannot expect to design your feedback mechanisms in fine detail but you should determine the style of your reports and, based on the metrics you will be using, you will be able to plan the type of graphical representation best suited to your requirements for information. If in doubt ask an expert, a statistician.

My own choice for style of presentation is to mix words with simple graphs. This recognizes the fact that some people prefer to see pictures while others prefer text. It also means that you can forge links between different sections of a report perhaps linking productivity to your quality indicators.

You should also remember your engineers. They have supplied you with information. Can you give them anything back that they can make use of? If not then can you give them information so that they at least realize that the effort they put into giving you data is being utilized by the organization?

One way to do this is through a quarterly news sheet to all the teams contributing to the metrics program. It is amazing how well disposed towards a metrics initiative this can make people feel.

10.10 MARKETING AND BUSINESS PLANNING STREAM

These are key non-technical areas within a metrics program. Ignore them at your peril!

10.11 PREPARE A BUSINESS PLAN

Most organizations are large and complex beasts. Once you have gathered in the requirements for your program and designed specific components to satisfy those requirements (whether this involves deriving particular metrics or adopting techniques to help with, say, cost estimation), you will still have to implement the use of those components.

We have already looked at phasing within the metrics program and it is easy to understand how you may have to address certain requirements immediately while others are left on the shelf until phase two or three. We also briefly mentioned the other aspect of phasing, the phased implementation across the business. This is important because of the situation outlined below and the fact that we will probably be operating with limited resources.

It is very easy to fall into the trap of thinking that your work is complete with the issuing of instructions or standards. Please do not think that this is enough.

People need help to change. They may wish to adopt the ideas and concepts that you put forward but they will almost certainly run into problems trying to turn the concepts into a reality and they will need support to do this. I have come across examples of this in the areas of metrics, CASE technology and the introduction of Fagan inspections. All of these aim to improve the business efficiency of a software development organization and all of them have the real capability to achieve this goal but, so often they fail to deliver the goods because the support function is underfunded. For evidence of the importance of the support function I would suggest you read of the experiences of the Hughes Aircraft Software Engineering Division, Humphrey (1).

If you accept the necessity for support during implementation (and this can be as little as visiting a development team once a month to check on how things are going and to, let us say, keep the plate spinning), then I suggest you do a number of things.

First, build into your design the concept of support during the early stages of implementation. Based on experience, I believe it takes about thirty days of external support per development team to get a metrics program up and running within that team. This does assume that the team is adopting a number of components within the Software Metrics program. It is obviously less if you are simply, say, introducing productivity measurement.

If your organization agrees that a support team will exist for metrics implementation then a good way of building this support strategy into the design is to treat each development, or support, team as an account or client. Within the team you should identify a customer authority, preferably the team leader, and a facilitator. The facilitator acts as the local person on the ground who ensures that processes are put in place, data is collected and problems are identified.

The local customer authority manages the implementation of metrics within the team. It is also a good idea to draw up a contract or service level agreement between the metrics support group and the team. In this case, the metrics support group is servicing the team but there is also an element of service from the team to the support group. The contract or service level agreement should clearly state what will be provided by each party and when it will be provided. A real life example of such a document is given below although the names have been changed to protect the innocent. Note that the contract does not require a formal signature to work but it does no harm at all if you can get such a thing!

Service Level Agreement - Metrics Support Group and ALPHA Team.

As Agreed 20.11.20xx

1   Introduction

This document sets out the agreed level of support that will be provided to ALPHA Team by the Metrics Support Group relating to ALPHA Teams involvement in the Metrics program.

This Service Level Agreement, SLA, covers ALPHA Teams involvement in the four components of the Metrics program, Estimation, Applied Design Metrics, Local Project Control, and Management Information together with the Process Definition activities.

2   Staffing

Metrics Support Group facilitators: Paul Goodman.

ALPHA Team Customer Authority: A N Other.

ALPHA Team facilitator: J Doe, (up to 50% of his time will be allowed for metrics related activities over the next twelve months).

Viewpoint Authorities:

Estimation	A N Other
Applied Design Metrics	To be decided
Local Project Control	J Smith
Management Information	A N Other
Process Definition	J Smith

(Note that this is a large team so we have introduced the idea of local viewpoint authorities to spread the work, and the enthusiasm across the group. I also apologize to anyone with the surnames Other, Smith or Doe!)

3   Estimation

Metrics Support Group will provide:

A one-day training course on the 12th December 20xx.

Six days on-site support to assist in setting up Delphi sessions and the use of other estimation techniques. The dates of this support are to be agreed but will be provided during the period January - April 20xx.

Bureaux service providing off-site access to the CHECKMARK and GECOMO PLUS estimation tools.

ALPHA Team will provide:

General administration for the one-day training course including organizing attendance by ALPHA Team staff, provision of training room, overhead projector, white board and flip-chart.

4   Applied Design Metrics

To be decided.

5   Local Project Control

Metrics Support Group will provide:

A draft proposal document covering the recommended monitoring technique for submission to ALPHA Team management, after modification by ALPHA Team staff.

A half-day discussion session with J Smith and other interested parties to provide sufficient information for them to set up a project control system. This is scheduled for 20th November.

Two further half-day on-site sessions with ALPHA to address any problems that may arise. These will be provided during January - February 20xx depending on the current ALPHA Team workload.

ALPHA Team will provide:

Resources from J Smith's area to establish and administer the monitoring technique.

6   Management Information

Metrics Support Group will provide:

The Software Metrics Standards together with any updates.

One day of on-site support to discuss data collection, storage, analysis and feedback. This is scheduled for 8th January.

Further on-site support at one day per calendar month during February to June.

ALPHA Team will provide:

J Doe will act as the local metrics coordinator. His role will be to establish the mechanisms for collection, storage, analysis and feedback.

The metrics that have been targeted for initial use are:

Workarea Reliability Measure   Group Reliability Measure

> Local Correctness Measure   Maintainability Measure
>
> Development Productivity Measure
>
> **7   Process Definition**
>
> Metrics Support Group will provide:
>
> > Up to two days on-site assistance to derive a DFD representation of ALPHA Team's current development process. These days are scheduled for 14th and 22nd of January.
> >
> > A further one day is scheduled for 30th January when the derived model will be presented to various ALPHA Team staff. J Smith will carry out the actual presentation.
>
> ALPHA Team will provide:
>
> > The resources outlined above.
>
>

* Already provided to date.

>

Notice the way in which specific responsibilities are allocated to individuals, and the use of dates. As well as documenting what will be done when, this document is also a useful way of focusing the teams involvement in the program. Basically, they can see what they are getting into.

Notice also that one component of the program has been held back. In this case it was felt that we had enough to work with but as it turned out the development team did do a great deal of work on the Applied Design Metrics component before they formally adopted it.

It is good to build this concept of support into your program but you do need to be sure that you can supply that support, so you will need to do certain other things. Look at the resources you have available, then look at the number of teams within the organization that you have to support. At this point, you should realize that other functional groups not directly involved in development may also require support,.for example, your project control office, the marketing group and the testing teams. In fact, all of your customer groupings should be treated as potential accounts with their own contract covering implementation.

If my model is correct, one person working flat out can only support six startup accounts, allowing some time for holidays and for administration, during a full financial year. Such a situation will almost certainly force you to adopt a phased implementation and this should be reflected in your business plan. The plan should state how many teams will be addressed during each future financial year and should express the percentage impact of the metrics program across the organization year by year. Not only does this quantify how resources within the support group will be used but it also gives you clearly defined targets and shows that you are approaching the implementation in a businesslike manner.

Of course, your program may be structured in such a way as to work from the top down. It may be that you are introducing measurement initiatives across the whole organization and in this case your phases will concentrate more on the requirements that are being met rather than the penetration you are achieving year by year. This should also be expressed by your business plan which will form a cornerstone of your presentation to senior management when you seek approval to proceed.

10.12 PREPARE A MARKETING PLAN

We have already discussed the importance of publicity but, as you move rapidly towards implementation of the program, this becomes increasingly vital.

You have to consider two things. First you need to launch the implementation phase of the program. How will you do this in such a way as to achieve the necessary visibility and impetus? One possibility is to go "on the road." Perhaps a road-show approach will work in your organization. You may consider a senior management presentation, both to seek approval to proceed but also to act as the launch platform. The in-house magazines could be used especially if you have been using them as a vehicle for publicity during the metrics program development stages. Exactly how you launch the program will depend on the culture of your organization but please try to make it an event. Get people to notice it!

Second, you will need to consider ongoing publicity for the program targeted at both the organization in general and the participants. It is very easy to ignore this aspect of the program believing that you can sort it out at the time or that people "should" be aware of what you are doing. Think about it: do you know what is going on everywhere in the organization? I certainly have never managed that feat. Planning how you will publicize the program pays dividends in that you can plan the work involved and this is important if you are to keep control of the program. You can use all the vehicles we have talked about already but I would thoroughly recommend the use of a short, periodic news-sheet for participating teams which should also be circulated to senior managers. After all, you want them to get involved as well!

Interest and awareness needs to be turned into commitment and involvement. If you are taking a phased approach to implementation you will need to get teams to sign up to the program because, even with senior management commitment, you will not be able to force adoption of the initiative. As they say, a volunteer is worth ten pressed men.

There are, generally, four ways of getting groups to do what you want them to do. These four approaches are telling, selling, participating and delegating. Which approach you use depends upon the maturity of the group with which you have to interact. It would be nice to think that you could delegate the implementation of Software Metrics to the organization in general but this is unlikely to be effective. Most organizations and groups within them operate best in a selling or participating mode but you will often find that you first have to sell the initiative before you can be sure of participation.

So, how will you sell them on the idea of measurement? By this I do not mean the technicalities of the sales pitch but the approach you will use. I have found that the best way to deal with this is in three stages.

First you identify a potential client. This can be done through the Metrics Coordination Group. After all, you have been working with these people for a while now and you should be aware of who are the champions, the individuals who are more keen than others. Why not target their teams first? You may also have been involved with specific teams during pilots. Do they want to carry on their involvement?

Having identified the potential clients you need to use someone on the inside to get you in. Wherever possible, I use the manager who is keen to set up a meeting where I, as an external to the group (whether I am an internal or external consultant as far as the organization is concerned), come along and make a sales pitch to the management group of the team. To do this I would use a presentation that first explains what Software Metrics are and that provides examples of benefits realized by other organizations. As the program develops you can replace external examples with home-grown cases which carry much more weight.

Very often the management group will have questions and you need to be light on your feet to deal with these. It is very easy to get drawn into some of the office games people play in this situation. I tend to stress the fact that the program should be tailored to their own specific needs while still maintaining an overall conformity to the high-level requirements of the organization.

For example, I tend to go in with about twelve management metrics that the team could adopt but I only ever expect them to pick up four or five of these initially. Which four or five depends on them. Nor do I go through all of the metrics at this point. Usually, you find that about fifty percent of the audience is supportive, thirty percent ambivalent and about twenty percent are dismissive. On a bad day that twenty percent could be vocally hostile. Make sure you have an idea who are the likely champions and who are the stickers. I reckon that such a presentation has been successful if I can get the group to agree to a second, much less formal session a week or so later. If they agree to sign up right away then fine, but do not expect that to happen too often.

I tend to let them drive the second session, which is the final stage of sales pitch. I concentrate on answering questions in a way that makes them realize their ability to influence the program and I try not to dodge important issues or questions that I do not have answers for. Being honest pays dividends provided you also come across in a positive manner. At some point during this session I ask them if they want to sign up. Assuming the answer is yes I try to get them to appoint a local customer authority and, if things have gone well, a local facilitator with effort allocated at some ball park level. If things have gone really well we have changed the mode of operation from a sales pitch by me to joint participation in the program. Of course, each client is different but the use of a standardized approach means that you can concentrate on catering for those differences effectively.

All of this implies that you plan how you will sell your metrics initiative to your clients. This plan, together with plans covering ongoing publicity to the organization and feedback to participants, forms the marketing plan. Remember, if you fail to market you will fail to sell and you will need to sell unless you tell. Telling takes power and never really works for metrics programs anyway!

10.13 INFRASTRUCTURE DESIGN STREAM

10.13.1   Define the Infrastructure

Imagine the situation: the metrics team have spent months sorting out the requirements, they have derived metrics and evaluated products such as cost estimation tools and they have built up an awareness in the organization about Software Metrics. What happens next? Obviously, they will write a report and perhaps they will issue "standards" explaining their metrics and how they should be used. All they have to do now is sit back and wait for it to all happen. One year later they are still waiting!

I will say it again, people generally need help to change. Even with the best will in the world they will revert to their normal way of working unless there is someone around to facilitate and support change. This does not just apply to Software Metrics programs.

If you need convincing that standards are rarely used in the full sense then take a walk around your development area and ask to see the development process manual. Assuming the person you ask even knows where it is you may like to wonder why it is in such pristine condition. Do you really think that it is because everyone knows it inside out?

Once you accept that you need to support the process of change you have to consider how that support should be provided. There are a number of options and I will discuss some of these now.

An obvious choice is to retain the team that has developed your metrics program. They assume the responsibility for implementing the program.

The main advantage with this approach is that you do have, and can continue to develop, a center of expertise within the organization. A centralized group can also act as a focus for the initiative ensuring that there is a single point in the organization responsible for implementation and who can ensure coordination across different groups. After all, it makes little sense for one group to measure reliability by defects per thousand lines of code while another uses mean time to failure!

However, there are two major disadvantages with this scenario. First, the group may well be seen as being external to the software development process. Ownership of the metrics initiative by those responsible for software development is very important and this approach can generate a response along the lines of "not invented here so it's not for us." Secondly, if your organization is large in terms of the number of development teams a centralized group can find it difficult to provide adequate support to all those involved. Phasing obviously helps but this can slow down the implementation process to an unacceptable level.

A second option is to use a centralized group to quickly develop expertise within a small number of development teams and to then let these new experts spread the gospel to the others. This approach is very attractive to management as it costs very little. In fact, it would seem that you get the implementation for free. Believe me, there is no such thing as a free lunch.

This approach seldom works without the continued support of a central group and, unless the support is carefully planned it often becomes engaged in firefighting which demoralizes the central team because they know they should be out of it by now, and it demoralizes the development teams because they never get the level of support they believe they need.

The reasons why this approach has so many problems are complex. You must remember that any metrics initiative has many customer groups within the organization, not just the development teams. This means that a large number of groups and individuals with differing requirements need to be supported. This requires some form of central coordination or you get anarchy — or worse, apathy. Also, if one area does develop a level of expertise how can you ensure that expertise is made available to other areas? Remember, there will be a great deal of pressure on individuals with expertise to get on with their real work because metrics will almost certainly, in this scenario be seen as an extra, lower priority task.

So how can you put in an infrastructure that will *really* work? Let me outline an approach I believe will work for most large organizations, perhaps with some modification to suit your own specific structure. I will use the model organization described previously as the basis for this discussion.

Your starting position is this: you have a metrics program development team in place, even if this is only one person; you have a development customer authority; and hopefully you have a Metrics Coordination Group or the equivalent. I suggest that you should establish a centralized support group and the obvious choice for this is to staff it from within the development team. After all, these people have spent time developing exactly the kind of metrics-related technical knowledge that will be needed. How large a group will be needed depends on the size of the organization it will service, the scope of the program it will help implement and the speed at which the organization wishes to implement the program. This group can also take on responsibility for the ongoing development and extension of the metrics program. Remember that you may need to do some centralized analysis and feedback of results. More junior staff can be used for this provided they operate with guidance from the central group.

You will also need a customer authority for the implementation. This could be the same individual who has filled the role of development customer authority or it may make sense to target another person in the organization. The customer authority should be as senior a manager as possible provided that you can still ensure involvement. Remember you are only designing the infrastructure at this point so you need only target such an individual. Getting his or her commitment comes later.

The implementation customer authority should act as the chair for the Metrics Coordination Group and this group may well undergo some changes as you move towards implementation. These changes will relate to composition and terms of reference but I will discuss these specifically later.

In terms of our model organization, I see the support group reporting to either the Systems Development Director (the ideal case), or to the R&D manager. This may seem strange given what I have said about the "not-invented-here" syndrome but it does mean that the support group can be seen as impartial. We get over the NIH syndrome another way. If you are really lucky, the Systems Development Director will take on the role of implementation customer authority.

Within each functional grouping you should identify a local metrics coordinator. This person takes on the responsibility of implementing the metrics initiative for their group under the guidance and direction of the centralized group. The intention is to transfer expertise from the central group to these local coordinators as quickly as possible. In terms of our model organization I would expect to see local coordinators appointed to cover Support Development, possibly Operational Support, and Planning. You may choose to appoint a single coordinator for Product Development or you may appoint different individuals to cover Software Development and Test and Integration.

You have to decide whether or not to appoint these local coordinators on a full-time or part-time basis. Which option you choose depends very much on the size of the function they are going to support. If you have only a couple of Product Development teams it would be wasteful to appoint full-time staff but you do need to be realistic. Do not fall into the trap of expecting change to happen automatically. No one can argue, for example, against the proposition that quality is the responsibility of everyone within the organization, but to generate a quality culture does demand the dedicated resources of support staff; otherwise you end up paying lip service to the ideals of quality without seeing any visible improvements. The same is true of Software Metrics.

Of course, even with local coordinators appointed to support all of your major functional groups within the organization you are still failing to cover the needs of one very important group: senior management. Given the fact that this group is diverse in both its requirements and position within the organization, the central support group is ideally placed to supply the local coordination function for senior management. This is especially true when you realize that senior managers are the recipients rather than the suppliers of information.

Your local metrics coordinators form the foundation of the Metrics Coordination Group for the implementation stage of the program. During the implementation stage, the Metrics Coordination Group should also adopt a more proactive role than it has during development of the initiative. Its' terms of reference need to be very clear and should demonstrate that proactive role. A possible set of bullet points for a terms of reference is listed below.

The Metrics Coordination Group should:

> Own all metrics standards used within the organization
>
> Supply the requirements for additional work elements within the metrics program
>
> Prioritize those work elements
>
> Act as custodian of the metrics program plans
>
> Determine the strategy of the metrics program
>
> Act as a forum for the sharing of results
>
> Act as a liaison point with other organizational initiatives
>
> Champion the implementation of metrics.

This set of terms of reference implies that you may need a wider membership within the MCG. As well as the local metrics coordinators you may consider it worth having representatives of various customer groups.

Ownership of the Software Metrics program by the engineering function is vital to its success. To generate this ownership you may like to consider an additional level of implementation support within the metrics initiative. The concept of local facilitators is a very useful one in this context. Each development and support team will be expected to supply some information or data to the central support group, possibly through their local coordinators but to support and police this activity can become extremely onerous if you attempt to do it from the outside. Much better to have one individual within each team charged with this responsibility. This person can also act as a focal point for metrics within the team.

The role of local facilitator is, for all but the largest teams, a part-time one. Initially, the local facilitator will need to spend some time helping to set up the necessary collection procedures and can perhaps assist with local process definition but, as the program beds down, this role becomes less costly. You may well have realized that the local facilitators can also form a local Metrics Coordination Group within each functional area.

The infrastructure that supports the implementation of the Software Metrics program within the organization is shown in *Figure 10.2.*

There are two comments that need to be made regarding this infrastructure model. First, such a structure may not be possible during the early implementation stage. At this time it may be a target or ideal that you move towards. How you actually support the early implementation of a metrics initiative depends very much on how you phase that implementation. If your initial implementation is more akin to a pilot, say within two or three product development teams only, then centralized support may be sufficient. Alternatively, if you are only using a small set of management statistics based on raw data taken from existing systems within your first-phase implementation then a central support group working with local coordinators will probably be enough. However, if your program is wide-ranging both in terms of what it implements and who it affects, and many successful metrics initiatives are large in both these dimensions, then be sure that you address the question of support structure early.

The other point that needs to be borne in mind is that you should not expect your local coordinators and facilitators to spring fully armed from the organization on the day that implementation starts. They will need time to develop their roles and expertise. While this development continues they will need a relatively high degree of support from somewhere. A central support group staffed by individuals who have gained experience of Software Metrics theory and practice, even if only from pilot work, is ideally placed to provide this. This is shown by the dotted line in *Figure 10.2* and you, as the manager of the program should budget accordingly.

Figure 10.2   Example Organization of Staff Support Infrastructure

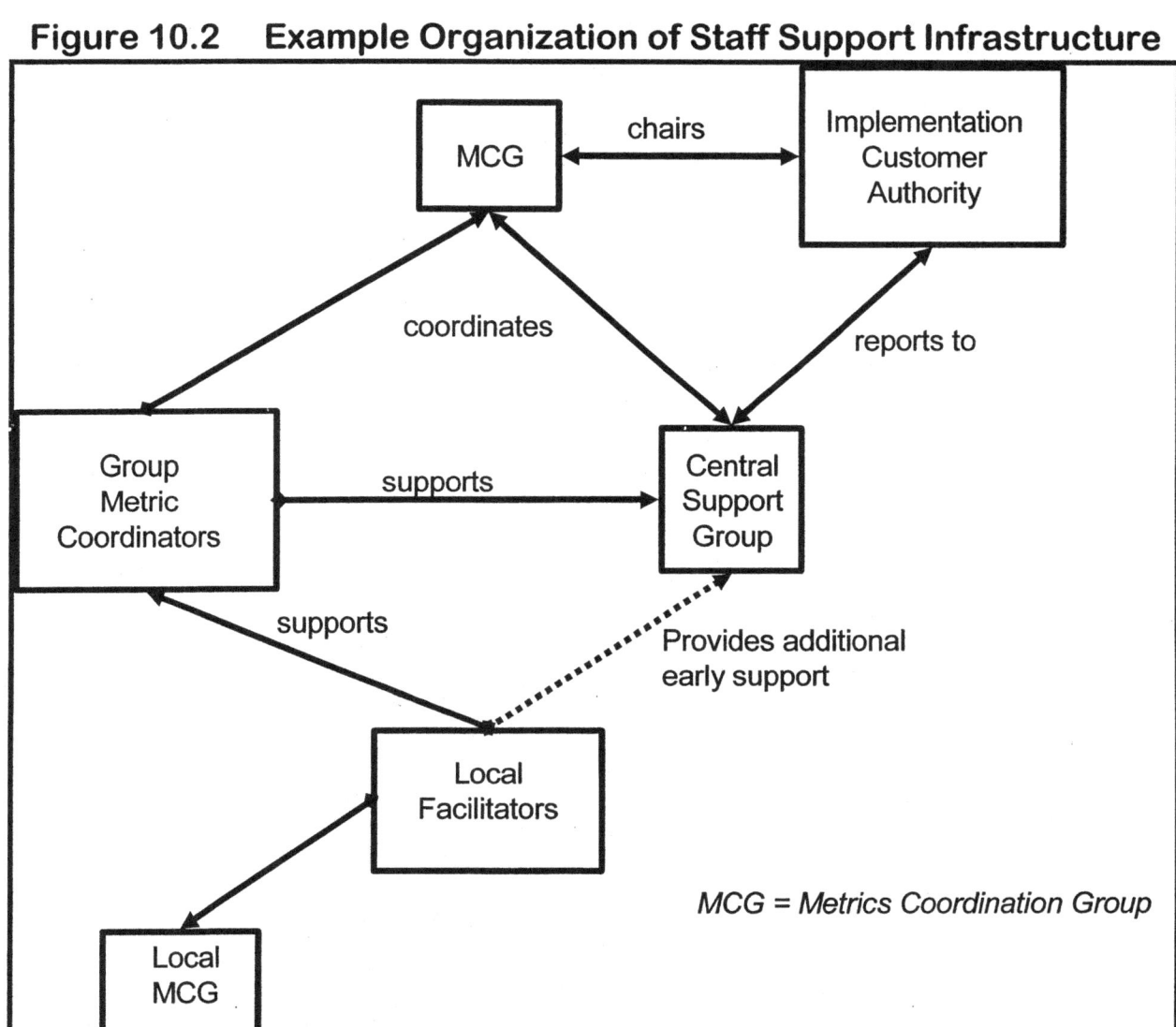

10.13.2   Define Support Training

Which brings us nicely to the initial training that should be given to the individuals that make up the support infrastructure for the metrics initiative.

If you decide to adopt the infrastructure model described above then you will have two specific training requirements that will need to be addressed.

The local coordinators require a significant amount of training if they are to fill their roles effectively. The best training that anyone can receive comes from experience, but these individuals will need something to quickly bring them up to a level where they can, at least, operate with support. Such training needs to address the following areas:

Motivation of the local coordinators

Background addressing the theory of those areas within the domain of Software Metrics that are included within your own initiative

General background covering other areas within Software Metrics. After all, your program, if successful, will grow and develop

Practical advice regarding the analysis and representation of data

Training in the procedures developed within your own metrics initiative and this can include training in the provision of training.

This is a tall order, made worse when you realize how little material there is around that you can make use of directly. There are some training courses available from external sources that you can use. These do, however, tend to address the theory of metrication. For example, you will find courses that teach the use of specific techniques such as Function Point Analysis or McCabe metrics. You will also find some courses that cover the majority of accepted metrics techniques as a single package. There are also some courses available that can help motivate individuals as to the benefits of using Software Metrics. These courses tend to be given by individuals with experience in the field and can be very useful in providing that initial practical view of the discipline but, being given by individuals, they tend to be biased towards that individuals' favored techniques.

Unless some other organization starts to offer training directly geared to the needs of those people responsible for the implementation of metrics initiatives, covering the areas outlined above, then you may well have to devise your own training program that blends external offerings with internal material. I believe that it takes at least six months to turn an individual into an effective metrics implementor just through on-the-job training and you need to reduce this once you start implementation.

A mix of external courses to teach specific techniques that form part of your own initiative, with reading material and a tailored course designed and built by yourselves, is probably the best option at this stage. The internal course will probably need a duration of about four days to adequately cover what needs to be addressed. If you have doubts about your ability to prepare and present such a course then you should consider making use of any internal training function that exists or you may wish to bring in some external consultancy. If starting from scratch, such a course will probably take you about five weeks to develop but it can be a worthwhile investment.

You also need to train the local facilitators. This is less of a problem because you will be supporting these individuals directly. In fact, the main aim of the initial training is to provide the necessary motivation. It is very possible that an external course will be sufficient.

10.13.3   Drawing the Streams Together, or Consolidation

Having designed the many facets of your Software Metrics program you now need to bring them together to form an integrated and complete picture. This will be taken forward to management for approval to proceed. It is possible that you already have authority to build the program or you may need full management approval for the next stage. If the former is the case, you still need to review your proposals with your customer authority. If the latter is the case, you will probably need to add in a cost/benefit analysis.

Bearing in mind that your requirements analysis will have probably identified a number of requirements now addressed through sub-projects or component designs within your overall metrics initiatives, two elements form the basis of your design. These are the sub-project or program component specific elements and the elements related to the overall initiative.

As far as the sub-projects are concerned I would suggest that you view the results of each of these as a "product." The reasoning behind this goes back to the idea of linking each requirement to a customer within the Software Metrics program. If you have an identified customer for each requirement then the way in which you satisfy each requirement can be viewed by the customer as a product that is being delivered to him or her. Of course, the product will not be traditional in the sense that it is a black box but, if you think about it, most products are not "traditional" in this sense anyway.

Assume that you have a requirement for a washing machine. More correctly, you have a requirement for some system that will clean your washable clothes. Traditionally you satisfy this requirement by going out and purchasing a washing machine, in this case a "white box." However, these days you are likely to purchase a white box with an associated service package. For example, the deal you negotiate may include delivery, installation, training through documentation together with a maintenance contract or service guarantee. The "product" is much more than just a white box.

In the same way, you can satisfy a requirement within a Software Metrics program with a package of deliverables which the customer can view as a product. For example, there may be a requirement within your initiative for some way to monitor, control and reduce the complexity of generic software systems, that is, systems that have existed for some time and undergo continual enhancement. An obvious way to satisfy this requirement is for the development team to purchase a static analysis tool that will, perhaps, reverse-engineer code to produce semiformal documentation such as structure charts, flowgraphs, etc. and that will perhaps analyze these in terms of specific metrics, McCabe Cyclomatic and Essential complexity metrics are obvious choices.

Fine — off you go and pay the money and you ship the tool out to your customers, the development teams. I believe that very little will happen as a result of this initiative. In this case, the tool is the white box but to get the most out of your solution you need to do more than just make this available to users. You will need to document how the output of the tools should be analyzed and used within your environment. You will also need to provide some background on the theory behind the metrics. This is especially true in a technical environment where people do not accept things just because someone "says" they work. You may also need to provide some training for the engineers to support your documentation. You will almost certainly have to provide some form of support or hand-holding to get development teams started in the use of these new techniques.

As you see, your solution now contains a number of distinct elements. You have documentation, perhaps in the form of in-house guidelines, training, on-going support and, lest we forget, you also have the tool. This will be true for most of your requirements and is certainly true for cost estimation, Applied Design Metrics, project control and management statistics. So, the design you take forward for review should include, against each requirement, information about the core solution, which may be a tool or a set of techniques or even a set of metrics, in-house documentation, the provision of training and on-going support.

These are the sub-project or program component-specific elements of your design.

You will also have prepared another set of proposals relating to the overall metrics program and how that will be implemented. These include your marketing plan and your business plan covering internal publicity together with high-level education and the implementation strategy respectively. You also have proposals for an infrastructure to be established to support the implementation strategy. You may also have some pilot results to add credence to your claims.

These elements of your design relate to the metrics program overall rather than to specific sub-projects within it, but please remember that they are a vital part of your proposals — at least as important as your specific "metrics" solutions.

How you actually present your design for approval will depend upon the culture of your own organization and its normal operating practices. You will almost certainly be expected to prepare your proposals as some form of document. Remember to link your solutions to requirements and business needs associated with specific customers or customer groupings within your organization. One approach that seems to be acceptable is to structure your design document as an interim report in the following way:

> **Introduction**: A high-level description of why the Software Metrics program was initiated. Keep it short!

> **Requirement Identification**: What specific requirements have been identified, which are addressed by this phase of the program; whose needs are addressed (the link to customers).

> **Product Description**: For each requirement, the core solution, in-house documentation, the provision of training and ongoing support along with the results of any pilot work that supports your solution. Remember that you are seeking approval to build so do not go into great detail about the pilots, simply use results to support your design solution.

> **Implementation Strategy**: Covering the marketing and business plan together with your proposals for the supporting infrastructure. Do not forget to describe the training requirements for individuals involved in this infrastructure.

If you have to seek senior management approval and your organizational culture requires it, you may have to carry out a cost/benefit analysis. This is very difficult to do for a Software Metrics program because there is very little material available from external sources that describes the costs and benefits of a wide-ranging metrics initiative. Why is this? I believe that there are a number of answers to this question.

One reason must be the difficulty in quantifying the benefits that accrue from some of the traditional areas of applied Software Metrics. For example, what is the financial benefit of supplying external customers with accurate cost and duration estimates for the development of software systems? You may be able to construct a model based on assumptions of lost business that results from over-optimistic estimates or you may operate under fixed-price contracts which certainly makes the cost of inaccurate estimates more accessible. Even in this case, you may also be operating under "lowest tender" conditions of bidding which can distort results. The reality is that we do not know the true benefits of accurate estimation in financial terms but we do know the cost of inaccuracy in qualitative terms. Basically, if we can demonstrate to end customers that our estimates are accurate, what we *say* it will cost is what it *will* cost, then that gives us a competitive edge over others in the industry. It makes us more professional, but this is difficult to model in terms of a cost/benefit analysis.

Another problem is the differences between metrics programs. It is very unlikely that your initiative will be sufficiently close to that of other organizations for you to be able to use their data. While you will almost certainly find similar elements between programs that can enable you to justify parts of your own program in terms of costs and benefits, you will find problems when you try to carry out a cost/benefit analysis for the whole thing.

Finally, we must realize that the use of Software Metrics within the industry is still in its infancy. Most organizations have only been using metrics as a practical solution to problems for a short period of time. Many of them are only beginning to realize the benefits now.

It may be that by looking at what organizations that are perceived to be successful are doing we can also get ahead of the game. These organizations are realizing benefits from the practical use of Software Metrics and they demonstrate this by their continued investment in metrics initiatives. Perhaps one of the most forceful arguments for the use of Software Metrics is not to answer the question "can we afford to do this?" but instead to ask the question "can we afford NOT to do this?"

In many cases your cost/benefit analysis can be replaced by ensuring that you have the commitment of the potential customers of metrics within your own organization. You get this by directing solutions towards their own specific requirements and by making sure that they are aware of this. You talk to them!

All of which is no help if your organization demands that you still supply a traditional cost/benefit analysis. If this is the case then the following may be of some help but I will be honest and say that this is not an easy problem to solve.

The budget necessary for the implementation of a Software Metrics program can be considered from a number of viewpoints. First, the work to define and build the program can be considered separately to the actual implementation.

Whether budgets are being considered for a particular stage or for the full program, the person preparing the budget should examine the likely staff and ancillary costs.

Within staff costs there will be two distinct elements. First, there will be the staff costs of those people directly involved in defining, building and implementing the program. We can call these people the metrics team. Second, there will be staff costs associated with the additional effort required from the software production function within the organization. These costs can be consumed by pilots, reviews of the program deliverables such as the design document, data collection and data analysis.

Ancillary costs cover many items including additional hardware such as PCs, software for data storage and analysis, proprietary packages such as cost estimation packages, consultancy for training and other purposes such as "buying in" statistical analysis skills and membership of external organizations such as metrics user groups.

Most organizations have standards covering the presentation of budgets for management approval and these should be used whenever they apply.

A checklist is provided below, *Table 10.1*, to assist with the identification of costs.

TABLE 10.1   COST ELEMENTS

Metrics team effort
Engineering effort
Hardware
Software
Proprietary packages
Training
Consultancy
Conferences
Special Interest Group membership
Travel

It is always advisable to build a contingency into budgets to cover additional work that may be identified as the program progresses.

Beware of giving "off-the-cuff" budget estimates. While it is not always possible to avoid this, it is common for such estimates to become the budget for the program. Generally, such figures are underestimates of the true cost and can quickly become a serious constraint on the work being done.

It is tempting to think that pilot activities will provide enough evidence of the benefits of Software Metrics to enable extrapolation to model the benefits of wider implementation. Unfortunately this is rarely the case. The reason for this is that many of the financial benefits depend on improved quality, and this may not be evident until a system has been in the field for six or even twelve months. Another reason is that pilot activities tend to address one aspect of Software Metrics and this may only show limited benefits.

Consider a development project that pilots the use of McCabe metrics to control quality. Assume that the project lasts six months from initiation to first live use. It may take a further six months to demonstrate a lower defect level than the norm for the organization, assuming that this norm is actually known. It may take twelve months of field use, and enhancement, to demonstrate financial benefits obtained from greater maintainability. This implies that it will take eighteen months to quantify the financial benefits arising from the use of McCabe metrics. It is almost certain that a cost/benefit analysis will have to be produced long before this point.

If we cannot use pilot results to build our cost/benefit analysis then the only route left open to us is the use of assumption.

It should be possible to estimate the cost of the program once the scope of the work has been defined. This is a good case for considering implementation separately as the earlier stages contribute to the scope definition for that stage.

When considering the benefit side it is now generally accepted, among metrics practitioners, that "the act of measurement will improve the process or product being measured." This is sometimes cited as the Hawthorn effect and this can be present. However, it is more often due to the results of the measurement activity being used to alter the process or product rather than any psychological phenomena. Beware that an alternative argument may be used against you, that "measurement itself has no intrinsic value" and be prepared to counter this.

If the basic assumption above is accepted it is possible to define financial benefits of a Software Metrics program as follows.

You should establish an average fault rate for the organization. You will also need to derive the average cost per fault perhaps by identifying the average effort involved to fix such a fault and the charge-out rate used by the organization's accountants. This type of information may well be available within the organization

Make an assumption that the implementation of Software Metrics will reduce the fault rate by some amount and calculate what this will save the organization based on the amount of software produced during a given period.

Because the Software Metrics program will probably require a relatively high investment during the first year or two, including the purchase of software packages and perhaps a higher level of consultancy support, you may find that the program "runs at a loss" for the first year or two. Because of this it is wise to supply a cumulative cost/benefit figure to show when returns can be expected. Senior managers tend not to query the detail of a cost/benefit analysis very closely provided any assumptions are made clear. They are much more interested in the bottom line that provides evidence that the investment is justified and has been considered in "business" terms. Be prepared to support your assumptions possibly using evidence from other organizations.

It is also worth describing the additional benefits of the program. The cost/benefit analysis as described above does not quantify the value of improved management information or more accurate cost estimates, other than to assume that these contribute to a reduced defect rate. These enabling aspects of a Software Metrics program often carry as much, if not more weight, than the cost/benefit analysis but, as discussed earlier, this can depend on the culture of the organization.

10.14 MOVING THE DESIGN FORWARD

Reports tend to be weighty things and are seldom read in detail by managers. Management summaries help but I believe that the best way to get your design proposals accepted is to make a presentation to the approvers. You can say so much more in a short space of time than you can possibly get across in a report or design document that you should grasp this opportunity with both hands. If the opportunity is not there then make it be there!

All the normal rules about presentations apply; keep it short, no more than thirty minutes with time for discussion afterwards; spend time planning the presentation and rehearse it earlier; be positive. If possible, go in with organizational backing and if you have set up a Metrics Coordination Group you have the perfect vehicle for this by getting their approval for the design proposals. You may also get organizational backing by getting prospective customers to approve your design solutions. You may even be able to get at least one senior manager so committed that he or she actually makes the presentation. This is ideal but try to make sure that you are there to provide technical support and to take the flak.

Once your design solutions have gone through the approval process you are ready to start the build stage of the program. Of course, operating in the real world you may have a number of sub-projects running in parallel. You may find it easier to take the design solution for each of these through review independently and, perhaps, at different times. If this happens, then take care to ensure that you do have designs for those parts of the program that affect the whole initiative, e.g., the business plan, ready for the first review.

10.15 SUMMARY

The Design stage of a Software Metrics program could be seen as the core of that programs development. Too often, there is a temptation to plunge into design without having done the necessary work of defining clear requirements; this is a temptation that should be avoided. Even with clear requirements it is very easy to concentrate upon the technical aspects of the program such as the metrics or measures at the expense of the equally important streams that deal with the marketing of the program and with its support structure. Avoid this trap as well if you wish your program to succeed.

11

Stage 4:

Component Build

Key Points:

Building the components should be mechanistic

Build the things you will need now rather than waiting until when they are needed

Having spent so much time and effort ensuring that you have requirements clearly specified and linked to business needs together with the work you have put in designing solutions to meet those requirements, this stage should be as easy as it seems in *Figure 11.1*:

Figure 11.1   Building the Components of
a Software Metrics Program

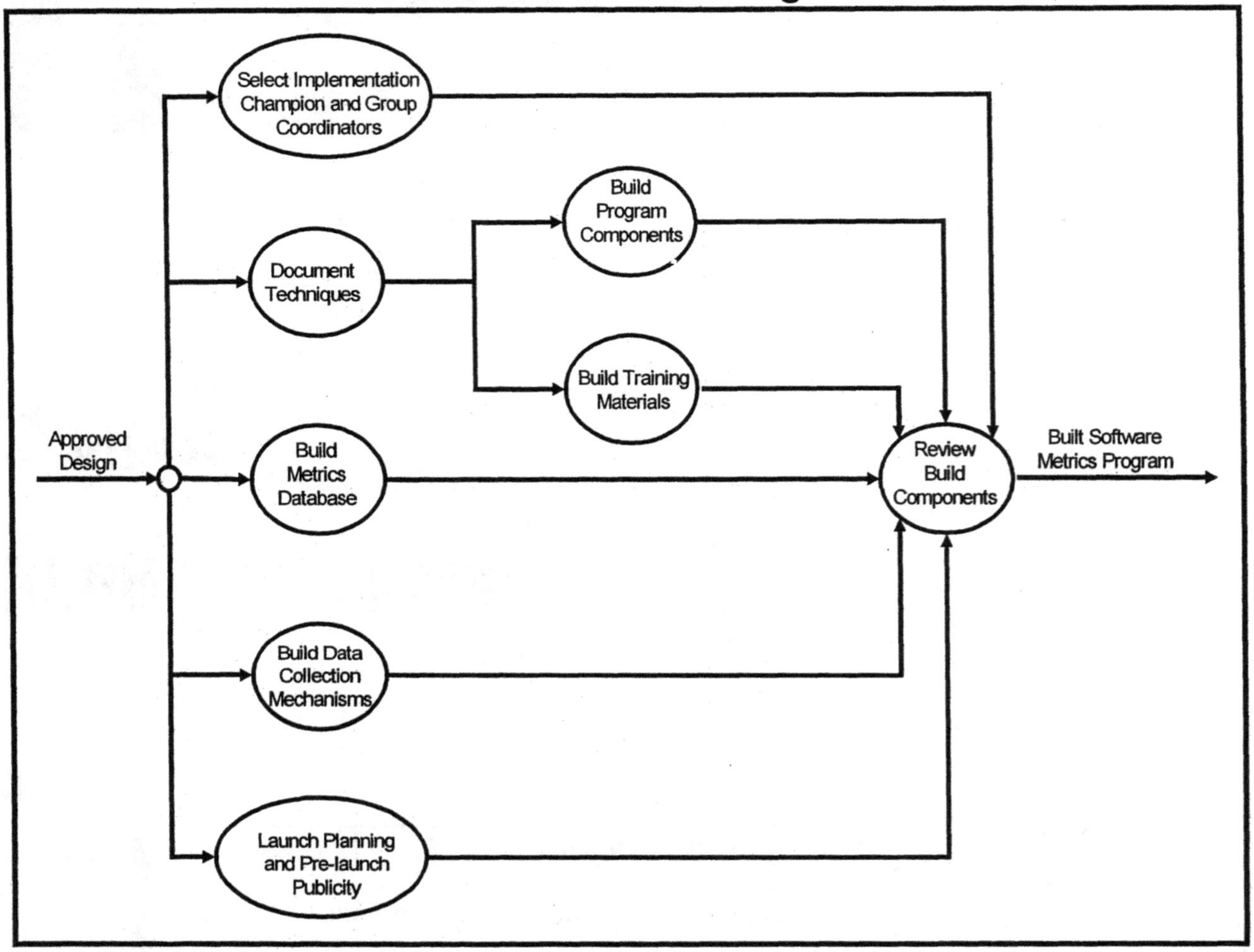

Of course, anyone who has worked on building systems of any kind knows that this is true in theory but that the build stage is, in fact, as difficult as any other stage, but in different ways. One thing that makes this stage difficult is simply the time it takes to change a design into something solid and working. Another problem is that you tend, during this stage, to be much more isolated from your customers. Breaking the stage into well-defined tasks is one way of dealing with the problems. Another is to ensure that you build reviews, perhaps by the Metrics Coordination Group, into your build stage.

You have two major work elements within this stage. First you have to set things up so that you are in good shape to start implementation; basically, to lay the foundations for that stage. Second, you have to physically build the components of your Software Metrics program so that you have something to implement!

11.1   LAYING THE FOUNDATIONS

11.1.1   Select the Implementation Champion and Group Coordinators

During the design stage you targeted a particular individual who will act as the champion, sponsor or even the customer authority for the implementation of Software Metrics within your organization. If you have not already done so, you should now obtain that individual's agreement to act in that role.

The more senior this person, the better — although you should realize that simply because a manager says something will be so does not necessarily mean that it will be. A high-ranking, involved champion makes life easier in that others in the organization perceive that the initiative has weight. However, attempting to implement a Software Metrics program through this kind of "authority by association" will not be enough. Successful metrics initiatives succeed because the customers of that initiative perceive benefits from involvement, not through begrudged compliance.

There is an interesting phenomena that comes into play when you start to implement initiatives that are intended to change the organization. Whatever rank the person is who supplies the VISIBLE authority for the initiative, the most active collaboration will likely come from individuals one rank lower. The degree of collaboration decreases the lower down the power pyramid you move and, more importantly, the degree of resistance increases dramatically the further up the pyramid you go.

In other words, if the Senior Executive Officer, SEO, or managing director champions the initiative, then board members will be, for the most part, cooperative. By the time you get to the project managers and engineers you start to run into cynicism, and arguments that this is yet more bureaucracy and simple inertia. You can overcome this problem by listening to what the more junior members of the organization have to say, by giving them solutions to their problems and, in a practical sense, ensuring that you have a good spread of seniority within your own development and implementation team. The spread of seniority within the MCG also becomes important.

This scenario is the easiest to work with because you, as the person responsible for making sure that the initiative happens and delivers results, will probably be quite senior within the organization anyway. After all, if the SEO is championing something he or she is unlikely to give that responsibility to a junior member of staff.

More difficult is the situation where the champion is somewhere in the middle of the pecking order. In this case, the person responsible for developing and implementing the initiative will probably be equivalent to a project manager. Because of some psychological effect that seems to come into play, that individual will operate effectively within their own peer group and will have little trouble convincing other project managers that, for example, metrics are a good thing.

The problem is that project managers seldom have the responsibility they should have when you think of the burden they may have to carry if things go wrong. For example, few project managers within the IT industry have true responsibility for their own project budget. Indeed, many do not even know what that budget is! Training is funded centrally as is capital investment. Staff head counts are allocated to the manager rather than being controlled by him. This means that, even when you have convinced the project manager that your proposals are sound, you have to spend time and effort convincing one, two or even more levels of higher management that even a small investment, perhaps in effort, is worthwhile. As you go up the tree, the amount of effort necessary to convince people grows. In simple terms, we seem to be suffering from a form of the "not-invented-here" syndrome again.

There is no easy way around this. You need to put the effort in but you should also start to play "personalities." Identify the senior managers who are willing to listen to you, who are more open to argument and who are at least willing to give your program a chance. Be prepared to tailor your program in the light of their comments and feelings while still retaining the integrity of your program. Do not waste time on the managers who are set totally against you. Finally, get yourself on an influencing skills training course and apply what you learn! After all, every little bit helps.

The worst case occurs when the champion of the initiative is a project manager with limited authority. The approach to metrication I have described so far will not work in this scenario. The organization lacks the necessary commitment. In this case I can only suggest that the project manager does things in a small way and attempts to build a center of excellence in the team. At the same time, he should try to identify and convince a more senior member of the organization to take up the banner and champion the cause. As King Robert the Bruce I realized after observing a spider spinning a web over and over, "If at first you don't succeed, try, try and try again!"

In some cases, you may be able to defer the formal selection of the implementation champion until the end of the build stage. If you have the commitment of the organization to the Software Metrics program then the actual champion becomes less important. In most cases you should still aim to have his or her commitment and involvement as early as possible.

Do not forget to select your local Coordinators as well as the champion. After all, the local Coordinators are going to be the people on the ground who will be making things happen. You need to be sure that they are the kind of people who can do this.

At the risk of sounding pretentious, there are different types of people in any organization. Some are talkers, others are doers.

Talkers come in many guises: some are traditional managers who pay lip service to change but are really too cynical to believe that an organization can change. Others are "technicians" who will appear to support change but whose stock phrase seems to be "yes, but!"

Doers also come in many forms. The obvious and visible doers are often senior managers who take a completely different view of the business than the view held by conventional managers. They are not willing to operate under the status quo but challenge conventional wisdom at every opportunity. Often they make enemies but are powerful enough to be able to afford to do this. An obvious example of such an individual was Margaret Thatcher: you may not agree with her but she certainly changed things, so many things that we tend to forget that she was the first female Prime Minister in the UK. Quite a change in itself!

Of course, you are unlikely to be able to get a gang of senior "doers" as your local Coordinators but you should aim to get the best people you can. In reality, you may have individuals nominated for you. This can cause problems as someone, somewhere will probably use this as an opportunity to get rid of some deadwood.

Try to retain some power of veto. If you have any doubts about your ability to select good staff, keep in mind that this is a skill that comes with experience and depends on the knack of reading people, so get the assistance of someone who demonstrates skills in this area.

The centralized support group, the involved commitment of an implementation customer authority or champion and the group coordinators form the core of your metrics initiative. The importance of these individuals cannot be overemphasized. Time spent making sure that you have the right people will pay dividends. Get this wrong and you will be storing up future problems.

11.1.2   Launch Planning and Pre-launch Publicity

Hopefully, you have been maintaining an awareness of the metrics initiative within the organization as you have gone through the previous development stages. Perhaps you have used in-house publications or staged presentations to interested groups. Regardless of what vehicle you have used for your publicity, you will need to ramp things up as you move towards implementation. This is especially true if your first phase includes something that affects the whole organization. For example, if your organization has never used a formal defect tracking system or fault database and if this is something you will be implementing then you should be telling the organization why, what and when this will be happening.

I saw a good example of this in a large telecommunications equipment supplier that decided to adopt the Xerox technique of "Competitive Benchmarking." One of the individuals involved in this wrote many articles for in house magazines and took every opportunity to talk to managers about this new idea. Indeed, at one point it seemed as if you could not pick up an in house journal without seeing something about Competitive Benchmarking in it. Also, it seemed as if everyone in the organization had heard of this individual's name and could link it to the technique. As a result, most everyone in the organization believed that it had adopted benchmarking, it was doing things with it, it was going to get results and it was ready to use those results. This was before the project had even gone beyond the pilot stage!

Of course, all this could have slid slowly to oblivion if there had been nothing more. Fortunately, the publicity was only a precursor to a full launch of Competitive Benchmarking and the same is true for the metrics initiative. You need some form of launch for your program and this should be an event.

It can be as simple as a statement by the Systems Development Director that Software Metrics is now an initiative supported by the organization, a part of the development strategy; or, it can be as complex as a road show. Whatever you choose as the launch vehicle you should aim for visibility within the organization.

An excellent method of getting this visibility is the Management Workshop or off-site meeting. We have discussed this earlier but now is the time it really comes into its own. Such a workshop takes a high-level of commitment by the organization but is very effective. To get this commitment you may have to take the plan for the launch forward as part of your program design. Essentially, you take as many senior managers as you can get off the battlefield and into a room for a day or two. Ideally, this room is off-site, possibly in a hotel or conference facility.

Once you have them, you take them through a guided tour of their problems and you present them with potential solutions to those problems. This only works when you get them involved in the proceedings so it must operate as a workshop, not simply as a series of presentations by the metrics team. In fact, the metrics team representatives will talk less and less as the event proceeds. The advantages of this approach are that it gets management involved, it confirms problems and it identifies the players who are ready to try solving those problems.

It also identifies the recalcitrant managers who may cause problems later but it also gives those individuals a chance to shift their stance in a face-saving manner as they are discussing things with their peers, not with some external expert who thinks he knows their job better than they do.

Try not to waste effort unless you are confident of a payback, and in some organizations it would take so much effort to organize a Management Workshop, or you may lack the leverage to make such an event a success, that it is simply not worth it. You must judge for yourself. The program launch can help you with implementation. It should be used to its greatest advantage but remember it is only one small step along the road to success. If the statement of intent is enough for you or all that you feel your organization is ready for then go for that.

After the launch you must make things work so target where you will do this first. This is important unless your first phase concerns the whole of the organization. In that case then your target is predefined, but in most cases the first phase of the metrics program is more akin to a large pilot exercise. By this I mean that you will be putting techniques and practices in place on a finite number of development, support or testing teams. Choose the first teams well!

Throughout development of the program you have been interacting with the organization. You will have identified groups and individuals who are keen to see the initiative succeed and you should use these as the foundation of your program. The chances are that your first phase will not affect such a large segment of the organization that you have to work with the less keen elements.

A model that I find quite useful is the 'rolling wave.' As shown in *Figure 11.2*, this highlights who should be targeted at any given time. As time goes on, the target changes.

Getting the right groups involved first means that you can use success there to convince the more skeptical groups within the organization to join you. Of course, if your initial groups are keen to see the metrics initiative succeed, then they are more likely to demonstrate that success.

A great deal can be said about the types of team you should select for the firsts phase. Should you go for teams working on small projects or large? Should you concentrate on high profile products, or the less important ones? Should you only look at teams who are already using new design techniques? If you go for small projects you have less communication overheads and probably a quicker payback; high-profile projects tend to give you more publicity but there is a risk that they could be cancelled as they could be considered speculative ventures; new design techniques tend to lend themselves to metrication, but how far have they penetrated the organization?

Figure 11.2   Targets

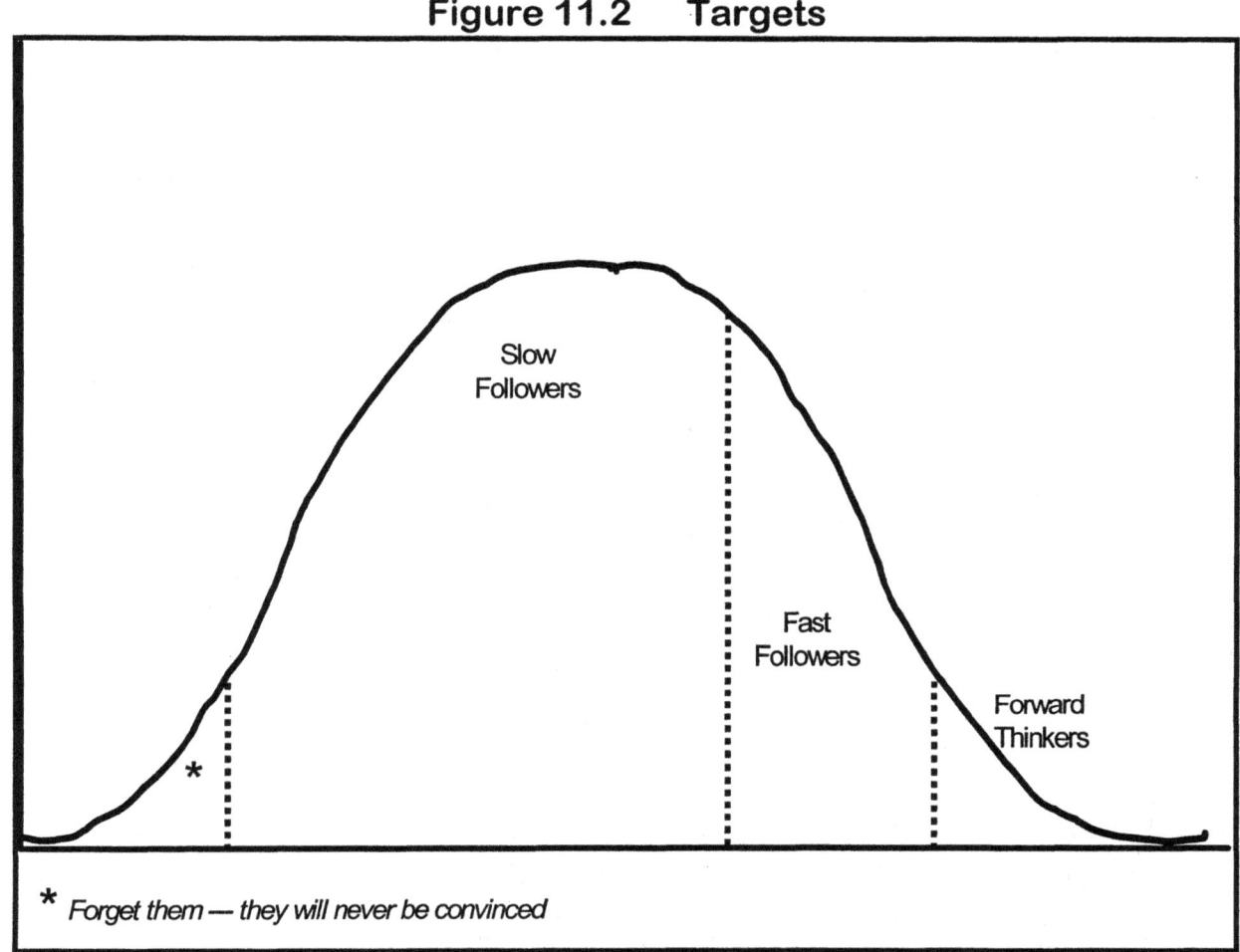

* Forget them — they will never be convinced

Basically it all depends. What it depends on most are the people involved. There will be problems associated with any project you target, but if the team members are keen to see metrics work they will overcome most of those problems.

Whatever criterion you use you should be very clear where your program is going before you start implementation. Target the teams you want to see on board but remember that you may not achieve 100% success. Target a few more than you want for your first phase so that you have a fallback position, then go for a 100% hit rate on your first choice.

11.1.3   Build the Program Components

What you have to do to build the components of your metrics program will obviously depend on the requirements that have been placed on that program.

For some the first phase will consist of nothing more than, say, productivity measurement being introduced to your software development function. This may sound simple but it can entail the introduction of a project sizing technique, maybe Lines of Code counters added to compilers or the use of Function Point Analysis, and a mechanism to capture project cost or effort.

For others the program may consist of a number of discrete components possibly covering cost estimation, project control, the use of Applied Design Metrics and a range of management statistics.

Whatever the program consists of there will be similarities in what has to be produced to enable the effective introduction of the various components.

11.1.4　　　Document Techniques

You will almost certainly have to document your design solutions for each high-level requirement in the form of a standard, a set of guidelines or a code of practice.

Such a document is a technical paper and producing these in a way that ensures that they are usable and workable, rather than producing something that sits on a shelf pristine and untouched by human hand, is a skill which takes time to acquire. Of course you may not have the time to acquire that skill so any assistance that is offered by technical writing functions in the organization should be used. Alternatively, rigorous review procedures can help to ensure readability.

Standards that are actually used tend to be concise, readable and coherent. In other words: keep it short, keep it simple or as simple as possible, and keep to the point.

It is a good idea to adopt a style for standards contained within the metrics program. You will find that spending time planning the general layout of standards will pay dividends in the future. Of course, there may be an in-house standard *for* standards that is already used within your organization and it would be foolish to make enemies by ignoring this. However, you will probably find that standing instructions like this concentrate more on detail than on basic structure. For example, your document standard may insist on a scope statement, an introduction, a document body with rules for numbering sections, sub-sections and paragraphs, and a summary. It is doubtful that such a standard will insist on a three-page scope statement followed by a five-page introduction. If you can get away with one line in each of these sections, then fine! After all, your potential readers are after the meat of what you have to say rather than the waffle one often finds in standards, be they internal or external.

Talk about the style of your documents with your customer authority and the Metrics Coordination Group. They should review any standards that you produce, so get them involved from the start. Using a general style means that your documents develop an identity. It also means that your potential readers get used to your style and can find their way around documents more easily.

When it comes to actually writing then all you can do is get your head down and get on with it, but there are some things to bear in mind. Most important is the 'KISS squared rule:' Keep it Simple, Stupid and Keep it Short, Stupid! I make no apologies for saying this yet again because it is so important that these rules are followed.

There are some traps that it is very easy to fall into when writing technical documents such as standards. I know because I have fallen into most of them at some point!

The first problem is akin to the personality change that comes over some people when they get behind the wheel of a car. Give someone a technical document to write and they seem to don a white coat, their hair becomes disheveled, a wild look comes into their eyes; the 'mad professor' in many of us takes over! The result is a document littered with big words, or even worse new words that only the author has ever heard of. Software Metrics papers are very prone to this and most of the words end with "-ity." We have seen maintainability, reliability, enhanceability and even diagnostability! Sometimes this is unavoidable but there is no excuse for much of the jargon that litters standards. If you do have to use unusual words or words that your audience may be unfamiliar with, then please make sure that you define what you mean, preferably both in the text and in a glossary.

Another problem with descriptive standards stems from the authors familiarity with the subject matter. When the first few chapters of this book went for review a comment that came back from more than one reviewer was that assumptions were being made about the readers familiarity with the subject of Software Metrics. These comments were valid and to counter this problem chapters were added to the book. This does illustrate that even the KISS squared rule needs to be applied with care. When we say Keep it Simple we actually mean 'Keep it as Short as Possible.'

A useful way of tackling this problem is to blend two styles in a single document. If you are describing a measure, say productivity, you can start with a brief, tight technical description of that measure. What is it intended to do? How is it defined? What raw data is required? How should results be presented? This can be followed by an elaboration of the main points that is more chatty, relaxed and that assumes no prior knowledge. If you are describing the presentation of productivity data you may concisely describe this by saying "productivity values will be plotted over time with an associated three-point rolling average." There is no harm in describing what is meant by a "three-point rolling average" as part of the elaboration.

Supplying too much information can also be a problem. Assume that you are writing a standard to describe how your organization will use Function Point Analysis. Does your reader really need to know that they were devised by Alan Albrecht a good many years ago, that there are some nineteen variations available and do they really need even a brief description of all nineteen variants? This is a very easy trap to fall into. After all, you have spent time and a considerable amount of effort digging up all this information. You needed it to be able to make a reasoned set of recommendations to your organization. You want the organization to be aware of all your good work. Believe me, your organization will be much more appreciative if you get in something that works and if you are able to make it work inside your organization than if you continually blow your own trumpet by telling them things they do not need to know.

Also remember the old saw about pictures: a picture is worth a thousand words. In reality some people prefer text but others prefer pictures. You do not know the leaning of a particular reader so whenever possible use both. KISS certainly applies to pictures. There is little merit in producing one complex picture when two, or even three, would do the same job. In fact two or three may work where one fails due to over-complication.

One final piece of advice: most organizations or sites have someone on staff who is a good technical writer. You can find such people by asking around. Who has written decent standards? Have any of your colleagues written articles on effective writing? If you can find such a person, try getting their comments on your first attempts. Then listen to what they have to say and act on their comments.

The standards that you produce are the public face of your program. Personally, I believe that even the best standards in the world are liable to be underutilized unless they are actively supported. People work best when they have a good relationship with other people and you must be prepared to support your customers when they first start to apply the techniques you recommend. It is very tempting to believe that you will be able to do this on the hoof, that is, to make it up as you go along. Forget it! If you are to offer a professional support service to your potential metrics users than you need to think about how you will do that.

This support can take many forms but one example is outlined below. If you are introducing a set of management statistics to a development team then you may feel it necessary to model their development process first. This would seem to be a sensible approach. How will you do this? Perhaps you will apply some basic systems analysis skills to the problem, gathering information through interviews with individuals involved in the process. You need to plan those interviews. How will you start things off? How will you get your colleague talking about their work honestly and openly? Plan your strategy, be prepared, be flexible but use your plan to get what you need from the interview. Document your approach so that more junior team members can benefit from your experience and as you learn from experience update your strategy.

This approach of planning before the event should be used whenever you interact with other people within the metrics initiative. Of course you will suffer relapses. You will go in unprepared to a meeting or you will keep your plans to yourself, but aim to document your plans and you will start to build a permanent foundation for the future and you will develop a professional public image. Eventually it will become part of your makeup: you will be increasingly professional. Then you should take time out, every now and then, to examine the way you are interacting with people to see if you can make it even better. You are going to be preaching continuous improvement. "Practice what you preach" is always good advice!

11.1.5   Prepare Training Material

You are introducing new concepts and techniques to the business. You will have to provide training in both the concepts and the techniques.

Many of the rules that apply to the production of standards also apply to the production of training courses. Tell your audience what they need to know, sell them the ideas, involve them in the course through the use of worked examples and exercises and, finally, delegate the responsibility for action to them. A good training course does all of these things and depends so much on the skill of the presenter that it is sometimes frightening to think about the responsibility that you take on when you first stand up to welcome the group of attendees — frightening until you realize that most people are there because they want to learn, they are open-minded, they want to enjoy themselves and are willing to get involved, they want to leave the course and apply what they have learned to make things better.

Of course there is often one bad apple. Mind you, I usually find that if you give such a person enough rope the other participants will generally hang him.

As always, planning is what makes a course work well. Plan the content, plan the timings, plan the exercises — especially plan the exercises! These are by far the most difficult part of any course to get right. If you make them too simplistic they will be seen as such and be devalued. If you make them realistic they will often be too complex too manage in a course environment. I try to be honest about exercises in courses. Tell the participants that exercises are there to make a particular point more solid, to help understanding and to give them a chance to try things out. Seek their cooperation and you will often find that it is given freely and unstintingly.

Generally, I allow five days' effort to develop one day of training material. For a course on a new subject that I am less familiar with this can double. Budget accordingly.

Do not fall into the trap of thinking that a training course is a concrete entity cast in stone. Training is a two-way exercise and I have never yet presented a course without making changes to it after the event. Some of the best parts of courses I now use have come from ideas given to me by people who have attended previous presentations.

Good training courses are well-planned but they also tend to be given by people who know their subject well. As far as Software Metrics are concerned it is unlikely that a training department will have people who are experienced in the use of measurement techniques within software development. I have always sought to have metrics training presented by members of the metrics team. This approach has worked and I recommend it. Once measurement-based techniques become established within the organization, the responsibility for ongoing training can be passed to the relevant support function. By this time there will be more people available who have experience in using such techniques and who can then present effective training courses.

11.1.6   Build the Metrics Database

You are developing a Software Metrics Program. You will be collecting information, data. It would be a good idea to have somewhere to store this data, facilities to analyze the information, mechanisms to feed back the results of this analysis. You need a metrics database, and preferably a simple one!

Unfortunately you have two problems, well, two major problems anyway. If you look around the marketplace you are unlikely to find a metrics database package that is perfectly suited to your needs although a few vendors do market offerings in this area. You could investigate these offerings and you may well decide that they are suitable for your requirements or that you could tailor them to your needs. The other problem, the more serious, is that you do not know your requirements at this stage.

But, hold on! You have spent a considerable amount of time gathering the requirements for your program, you have designed your program and, surely, the results of these activities give you the requirements for your metrics database. If only it were so.

In an ideal world this would be the case, but you have yet to implement even the first stage of your metrics program. It would be foolish to think that you are not going to gain experience and knowledge from that implementation that could impact upon the structure of your program. The reality is that you have developed a prototype metrics program that you are about to try out for real. It would make sense to adopt a similar strategy for your metrics database.

Of course you can use external offerings as the basis of your prototype database or you may decide to develop it internally. There are many database packages around that are well suited to this approach.

Whichever road you decide to travel, you should treat the development of your metrics database as a sub-project in its own right. What are your requirements as you see them now? Use these to drive your design solution and then implement that solution on your chosen platform.

Be prepared to adapt your database as your program develops. Do not fall into the trap that one organization did: they did sterling work in developing their program right through to implementation and then found that some of their measures were not giving them the information they required. They sought help through a public conference asking the question "what should we do?" The answer was simple but surprised them: "change your measures!" Yes, this implies that they would have to change their database. Is it really worth investing vast sums of money in an all-singing, all-dancing metrics database when fundamental changes may be necessary? Personally, I prefer a cheaper prototype that I can even throw away if necessary.

In the same vein, you may be pressured to build your database within an overall management information system. Perhaps you should tie into existing systems? In theory this makes sense. In fact it makes sense in practice as well, but only as a long-term objective.

At this stage the risk of change is too high unless you have very flexible MIS with a tremendously efficient support team who can respond to very volatile requirements. Management Information technology is still such a young area within software development that most MIS support teams are already completing the equivalent of the labors of Hercules just to satisfy basic requirements. They will not thank you if you hit them with more technical problems where even the problems change radically over time. In this case, time is on your side, so use it.

So, for the first phase I suggest you aim for a prototype metrics database, possibly even on a spreadsheet if your first implementation has a small scope. Build it so that it is of reasonable quality and such that it can be changed as you gain experience and knowledge from your implementation. If you need a politically acceptable face on this approach you can always say that the full database implementation tied to existing systems is planned for phase two, or phase three if you can get away with it.

11.1.7   Build the Data Collection Mechanisms

This is an area worth some discussion in its own right. The way in which you collect this data is important to your program and also depends on the components of your first phase. Data collection is fraught with difficulties but many of these can be overcome by setting reasonable expectations and applying a degree of pragmatic management. Sometimes this is known as using common sense!

Your engineers are employed to develop software, and anything else that they do is considered overhead. These overheads may be very important to the business or to the development of your staff but they all reduce the time that is available for the work that earns the organization revenue, or to carry out the organization's core business. It is sometimes instructive to add up all the time you spend during one week on activities that are not directly related to your primary work objectives. For example, filling in expense claims, non-vocational training, team meetings or briefings, dealing with unsolicited mail from both internal and external sources. All of these things eat into your work week.

Now imagine that you have a metrics program running. Perhaps you ask your engineers to fill in time sheets, to complete defect reports, to fill in project history files. It all takes time!

There is bound to be a reluctance on the part of project managers and others to sanction the imposition of yet more bureaucracy on their staff. You have to accept this and overcome it. Now obviously, you should never suggest that this data be collected just for the sake of it. Data collection should always be associated with benefits even if these are only assumed at this stage. If you have applied the principles outlined in this book so far you will only be suggesting the collection of data to satisfy the requirements of managers for information so they should be less concerned than if you arbitrarily suggest that engineers supply you with elements of information for which there is no clear need.

The guiding principle behind data collection is that it should be nonintrusive. I guarantee that if you investigate the situation you will be amazed at what information is already collected by the organization. Examples of this data can include problem reports, time or effort data, staffing information and financial data including IT spend and, in some cases, return. Of course, this valuable data often disappears into a black hole and is never seen again. Whenever possible you should use these existing mechanisms as the supply source for your data requirements by breaking out of the black-hole syndrome.

There are problems with this approach. Because the data is so seldom used for any obvious purpose the people who have to supply it usually take very little care to supply accurate information. How honest are your timesheets, for example?

You have to be very clear about the validity of your currently corrected data and you need to take steps to reeducate people about the need for accuracy. Often this involves a program of education and close cooperation with the custodians of existing data collection systems. One thing that works in your favor is that these maligned individuals are often only too glad to have someone take an interest in what they are doing and they will move heaven and earth to help you help them.

The other thing that helps you is that engineers would also like to see their efforts being used to benefit the business. If you can convince them that there is a need for timesheets they will often take the necessary care to ensure that you get reasonably accurate information. The thing that has convinced me of this is the number of project teams that I have come across who have additional data collection systems running in parallel with organizational systems. I have lost count of the number of project teams who run a local time recording systems if there is no corporate system. Sometimes they run the local system alongside the company system because the corporate version does not give them what they need.

Why do they do it? Quite simply they see that their own team leader is making use of the information he gets from this extra piece of bureaucracy. A feedback loop is in operation that says, "look, I know it's a pain but the boss is doing something worthwhile with this stuff. Decisions are made based on this information that affect me. I had better make sure that the information is correct or I could get even less time for design, (or coding or testing or training), next time." Self-interest is a great motivator.

Something else that typifies these shadow collection systems is their targeted simplicity. Very often, time recording systems, a convenient whipping horse for this type of discussion, are specified by accountants and have little relevance to the project teams. The shadow systems are designed by the people who need to use the information and this makes them "fit for purpose." They are also invariably simpler than the company system. Simple systems work!

You also need to be very careful about the level of accuracy that you ascribe to even simple systems. Do you measure effort in engineer hours? Do your engineers work a nominal 7.5 hour day? If so you may feel that the timesheet for any day should add up to 7.5 hours. This implies that you expect your engineers to be able to record time to at least half hour precision.

As with many areas, time recording generates jargon and different people use different terms for the same thing. Basically, what you need to do is put a structure on the "stuff" your people do in work, effectively arriving at a *Work Breakdown Structure* (WBS). I will suggest a WBS that would be suitable for a generic IT department. First, divide the stuff people do into divisions of Work Classes. Suitable Work Classes would be:

> *Project Work* to cover software or system development. Remember that if you are working across numerous projects your people should be able to record the Project Identifier within the time recording system.

A second class would be *System Support* to capture the work done in this area. The Project Code would be replaced by a System Identifier. I find it sensible to manage this type of work on an annual basis. Significant enhancements to supported systems or new releases, I recommend managing under the Project Work Class. System Support can also encompass Help Desk Operation.

Finally, I would suggest an *Administration Class* to cover staff management, non-project-specific meetings and all the other "stuff" that organizations need to enable them to work in their core business area. I suggest including a "Leave" Activity to cover absences.

Within Work Classes, work can be broken down into Activities. The Project Class could include Requirements Definition, Design, Build, Test, Implementation and Hand-over. Do not forget the Project Management Activity. If System Support is managed on an annual basis you may simply wish to record effort against Initiation, Execution and Review, and Close-down Activities.

Each Activity can consist of Tasks and it is at this level that staff would record effort against blocks of time. Remember that the KISS rule applies here as everywhere. If you find yourself defining more than about seven Tasks within an Activity you are almost certainly going to too great a level of detail. Of vital importance is to remember two things: you will probably be asking engineers to complete timesheets, albeit electronically, and you do not want this to be overly intrusive or time consuming. Second, if you collect data make sure it is analyzed and fed back to the providers as well as to managers. Even if staff cannot make direct use of the data they can at least see that it is being used constructively.

This approach to time recording is simple, but unless your organization is very mature in the operation of its business (and this has little to do with the age of the company), it is as much as you can reasonably expect.

The one thing about simple solutions is that they generally work, and as soon as people see something that works they tend to try to make it work better. This is perhaps one reason why human beings have developed as we have but the thing about tinkering is that you may end up with things that do *not* work. This is where a second tier comes in.

On your timesheets you should allow for user-defined fields. This can be as simple as a two digit or character sub-booking code. Of course you need to ensure that your database can sort and total on the sub-booking code.

Some project teams will completely ignore the sub-booking code, which is fine, but others will start to use them for all sorts of interesting purposes.

After a while you can survey the project teams to find out what they are doing, what benefits they are getting and then you adopt the best and start to apply it to the whole organization. The end result is a time recording system that is simple, effective, non-intrusive and one that has been developed by its users.

I have illustrated some of the principles of data collection using the time recording system as an example but the same principles apply to most if not all such systems.

11.2   REVIEW BUILT COMPONENTS

Within this stage of the development of your Software Metrics program you will have numerous items to review. There are standards or guideline documents, training material and process designs among other things.

Do not skimp these reviews as they cover items that form the public face of your metrics program. The Metrics Coordination Group or a subset of it can usefully form your review group. You may decide to go for walkthroughs or you may decide to use full, formal Fagan Inspections against the design and requirements documents. In any case it is the act of reviewing that is more important rather than the method that is used.

11.3   THE FINAL COUNTDOWN

You are almost ready to go. You have built the components of your metrics program, the database is waiting to take data from these components and to analyze it, and your feedback mechanisms are in place. You have set up the support infrastructure for your program.

If you have decided to use local metrics coordinators or facilitators within the engineering groups and you have selected these, then you are ready to train them. In most situations there is only one thing left to do: management must now be committed to the implementation of the program.

If you have consulted with your potential users through the development of the program, remembering that senior management is a very important customer of your program, then this vital step will be much easier. If you have sat in an ivory tower, building your program in isolation, shut of from the development and management functions of the organization then you will probably get no further.

As always, how you gain management commitment for implementation will depend upon the culture of your organization but I would suggest that a presentation supported by endorsements from the Metrics Coordination Group and a detailed report is probably your best option. You will almost certainly have to present some form of cost/benefit analysis at this point.

Unless you are extremely lucky, the best you will be able to do is prepare this using sensible assumptions as to the benefits. Be realistic but also challenging. Use your business plan to present a simple cash flow analysis over, say, five years. If you can get help from the financial people then do so. It all helps.

In the end, commitment to implementing a Software Metrics program depends on two things. You have to present a proposal to the business that is coherent, complete and that offers the business the opportunity to realize real benefits. Also, the business has to be ready for it! It is no good offering software development the capability to predict field reliability based on obscure statistical techniques if they have never even bothered to collect defect data before. Equally the business must be mature enough to realize that there are serious problems in trying to develop software without management control, without a sensible degree of discipline and without clear goals.

Finally, the business must realize that there is no such thing as a free lunch and that the only certainty is uncertainty. These may be cliches but they are true. A metrics program costs money to operate but it can be money well spent. Organizations that use Software Metrics effectively also realize that there are few off-the-shelf solutions. Some of what they do will not pay off but if they follow the common-sense approach of gathering clear requirements for metrics techniques, and if they take care to design adopt or adapt solutions, their chances of success are much higher.

Once you have everything ready, once you have management commitment then all you have to do is implement the program. Wave the wand and watch it all happen.

If only it were so!

11.4   SUMMARY

Building the components of your Software Metrics program should be straightforward if you have invested effort in defining clear requirements and in designing those components. Despite this, a considerable amount of effort may be required to turn clear designs into solutions that are ready to implement. This effort is necessary and the expenditure cannot be avoided.

As always, it is important to devote effort during the build stage to every component of your program. That includes the nontechnical aspects such as training material and documentation.

12

Stage 5:

Implementation

Key Points

Making a success of implementation means making a success of working with people

The best plans, requirements and design still need work to make them a success

---

12.1 A PEOPLE-ORIENTED ISSUE

The problem with implementation is that it involves other people.

This is a key point to remember because a Software Metrics program is more to do with people than about the metrics and the techniques normally associated with such initiatives.

People are awkward. They come in many shapes and sizes but more importantly they all have personalities that must be catered for and egos that must be stroked. To successfully implement a metrics program you must develop and apply interpersonal skills like you may never have before.

Imagine that you have senior management commitment to take your program forward and that this involves introducing something new to a project team. We could be talking about different ways of deriving cost estimates, we may be talking about using Applied Design Metrics to get designs better. If you look at any project team I can guarantee that you will find a broad range of personalities with which you have to interact. You have no choice about this if you are to succeed.

During the industrial revolution in England a group of workers went around the country smashing the new machines because they feared they would put them out of a job. These people became known as Luddites and their genes are still with us today. Of course you would not expect today's Luddites to attack your proposals with crowbars and hammers although you never know. Today's Luddite uses more subtle but equally effective techniques of destruction.

The situation is made worse because individuals who appear to us to be Luddites are often sincere in their criticism. Put forward any new idea in any field and there will be those who balk at its introduction, people who wish to preserve the status quo or those who have heard all the hype before and who genuinely believe that software development, for example, can never be managed and controlled through the use of quantified information.

As you start to work with the project team you will see these attitudes manifest themselves in "office games." An individual may continually seem to agree with you and then throw in the dreaded word, "*but*." "Yes, *but* we work in a different way;" "Yes, *but* we do not have the resources to devote to this kind of initiative;" "Yes, *but* this is just common sense."

Of course you can counter most of these arguments. If you look at how the team develop software you will probably see some differences in detail or terminology but I guarantee that software development does not differ much between teams or even organizations. Requirements, Design, Build, Implementation and Testing; these basic components will be there in some form or another.

How much is being wasted within the team through delivered defects that need to be fixed or through poor maintainability. Only a small proportion of this will pay for the metrics initiative. If you never invest in the future you will have no future.

And of course it is common sense! If we only applied common sense in what we did then our problems would disappear overnight. Unfortunately common sense is like expert estimators: both are rare commodities especially within software development. Common sense says you try out high-risk, new systems on low-key, unimportant projects.

How much has your organization invested in CASE technology over the years based on a gut feel that it will pay benefits? Incidentally, Software Metrics is a low-risk proposal compared to most initiatives that occur within software development. To support this statement I would ask you to compare the cost of implementing a new design tool, project planning techniques or a new development environment to the cost of a Software Metrics program. I believe that you will find the cost of the measurement initiative significantly lower than the others.

My favorite "*yes, but...*" is the one that goes, "*yes, but* we need the tools." By tools what is meant is "where are the whiz-bang computer systems to support these metrics, where are the expert systems, where are the relational databases?" These questions fascinate me for two reasons. First, we have managed to develop large, complex systems in both the IT world and the non-IT world with little more than pencil and paper so why do people believe that the "tools" are a prerequisite to improvement? Second and more importantly, "tools" can only be introduced when a process is understood to the degree that it can be de-skilled and if the environment is amenable to the application of "tools." For instance, you cannot automatically collect design metric data unless your designs are held in an electronic media.

This does not mean that I am in any way "anti-tool." Indeed I long for the day when every stage of software system development is supported by an effective tool-set. When that day comes, Software Metrics will be part and parcel of development — always assuming, ,of course, that we can get the people issues right!

The "yes, but..." game is just one of many that you may come across but, if you will excuse the pun, it is especially difficult to counteract. If you continually try to defend the program in the face of a continued onslaught you will eventually run out of ammunition. A question will be asked for which you do not have an effective defense. The only way to counter this ploy is to meet it head-on but to use the age-old principle of turning an opponent's energy back on themselves. "Yes, but given the current state of software development we have to do something positive to make things better. We have to make this program work for us. Unless you have an alternative, of course?"

This approach takes confidence but then if you do not believe in what you are proposing you cannot expect others to!

Office games apart, resources can be the biggest problem with the implementation stage. Implementing a Software Metrics program within a team does mean that the team itself must put some "cash" up front. This is usually in the form of resources or effort. The problem is that the amount of resources needed is very difficult to quantify until you have some experience of doing it within your environment. Here honesty really is the best policy. You should be able to give some broad brush estimates for the amount of effort involved and you should do so, but do tell the team manager that these are estimates. Setting yourself a limit, basically using a banded estimate is often worthwhile. After all, software development team leaders are well used to working with rough estimates, they do it every day or they would not need Software Metrics to help improve estimation!

If you do make the mistake of dodging the effort issue you will be storing up trouble for yourself in the future.

All of this sounds rather negative but remember that most individuals involved in software development are only too aware that they need to improve the way in which they work, manage and control software development. Most are also very willing to try pragmatic approaches to get that improvement.

In any team there will be the natural Luddites. There will also be natural champions. Concentrate your efforts on the champions and accept that there will always be some people you will not convince.

The whole point of the implementation stage is to turn potential customers of the metrics initiative into participants in the program. If you succeed in this they will quickly become the owners of the program and you will have delegated its operation and continued enhancement to them.

Remember what you have to achieve; you will do some selling and telling to achieve participation. You and your customer will work closely together until you can pull back, having delegated the program to them. One trick is knowing when to let go; learn it.

The time to let go is when they are doing more of the positive talking and technical innovation than you are, then you have succeeded.

12.2   THE LAUNCH

Implementation truly starts with the launch of the program. This is the point when you use the commitment from the management for implementation and you demonstrate to the organization that you are in a position to carry out that implementation.

You need publicity for the program if you are to attract customers, so you should make the launch an event in some way. We have already discussed this when talking about planning the launch so all I will say at this point is that you should now put those plans into effect.

We may be talking about nothing more than a memo to department heads or we may be talking about a road show. Whatever, make sure it happens.

The one other thing that you may need to consider relates to your Metrics Coordination Group. So far this group has acted as the steering committee for the development of the initiative, a sounding board for possible solutions. Effectively, they have been the recipients of information and they have provided feedback on that information. They have also, hopefully, provided requirements data but this has been prompted and driven by the metrics team. As you enter the implementation stage this group should become much more proactive.

The Metrics Coordination Group now needs to own the program: it is the custodian and should be the focal point for metrics in the organization. This is a different situation to that which has existed during the development of the program when you and the other members of the metrics team will have provided that focus and the drive that fuels the program.

As part of your launch event you may like to hold a "final" meeting of the Metrics Coordination Group and during that meeting target individuals within the organization that will form a new group. You can also draft new terms of reference for the group which will need to be ratified by it. If you have chaired the Metrics Coordination Group during program development then it is now time to hand that role over to someone within the software development function. If you are very lucky, the Systems Development Director will take on that responsibility.

12.3   IMPLEMENTATION

Even if you have a clear mandate for the implementation of your metrics initiative you still depend upon cooperation from your customers. You must communicate with your customers and communication, along with all other aspects of implementation, takes effort. That is the key point that you must drive home to your organization: implementation is not free even though most of the creative work has, or at least should have been done beforehand.

Implementation is the most deceptive and risky stage of this whole lifecycle. Look, for instance, at this chapter. It is a very short chapter and the activities it identifies are few. The reason for this is that the planning, the designing and the constructing of the metrics program has been done during earlier stages and this, the implementation stage, is simply a question of transferring technology from a few areas to every area. This need not be difficult or complex but it does cost!

Now imagine the following situation. You have 20 product groups within which you wish to implement Software Metrics. Even with a mandate to implement from on high you will still need to sell metrics to those product groups and their managers. I say again, you can tell teams to measure until you are blue in the face. You have to sell them on the idea!

Having sold the concept you have to train people, you have to support them and you have to help people make the concepts of the program work. It all takes time. If you were to allow thirty days of internal consultancy effort per product team just to sell them the concepts and get them over the first hump of the learning curve that would not be excessive.

That means that we are talking about 600 person-days of effort across the twenty teams for initial support. You will also have to maintain contact with those teams, albeit at a much reduced rate, for some considerable time. If you do not keep this contact up, and I would recommend at least one day per month for twelve months, then the team could backslide and you may as well not have bothered.

Of course these figures are generalizations but you may be surprised at how close they are to your own particular support costs.

One final point regarding implementation. The biggest problem that you may face may be with your facilitators or support staff. Do not expect them to be able to make the transition to their new role overnight because for most of them this will be a complete change. We must accept that we work in a technical industry. Good support staff have experience of that technical side of our work, are possibly very good at it because they should really have a deeper understanding of it than the average engineer.

However, far beyond that in terms of importance is an ability to operate in what is basically a sales environment. Many IT people find this very difficult.

There is a very interesting book called "The Strategy of the Dolphin," Lynch (1). This book has a model for classifying people as carps, sharks or dolphins. I find this a very pleasing model and will simply say that what you want as supporters or facilitators are dolphins.

12.4 SUMMARY: CLOSING THE CIRCLE

I truly hope that you as the reader do not feel shortchanged by this chapter. Implementation really is easy — costly, but easy — provided that you have laid the foundations properly during the earlier stages. Of course, no matter how good your preparation is, there will be problems that will have to be overcome, but if you have come this far they should not be unsurmountable and remember that the most difficult problems to overcome will be associated with people rather than with the technological aspects of your program.

The circle is closed by going right back to the very beginning: by taking up some of those items that for one reason or another could not be addressed by the first implementation of your initiative or program; by starting the second phase of your initiative even while you are implementing the first.

In other words — we do it all again!

13

Section 2:

A Summary

As you will have gathered by now, the development and implementation of a Software Metrics program is not something that should be undertaken lightly. Section 2 of this book has attempted to provide a guide through the complexities of such an undertaking but it may be worth summarizing the key messages of *Section 2*. I will endeavor to do that now.

So the aim of this chapter is to summarize the messages of the preceding chapters as succinctly as possible. The question is, how can I do this? What I would like to do is present to you a set of slides (figures) that summarize the overall approach to Software Metrics programs contained within this book. These slides have been used on real, live audiences and seem to go down quite well. In fact, they have formed the backbone of this book as I have been writing it and are as much the foundation as the summary. As to what use you make of these figures in the future, that is entirely up to you. If any of them could be used to get your message across, then please feel free to reproduce them as required.

Figure 13.1   A Project-Based Approach

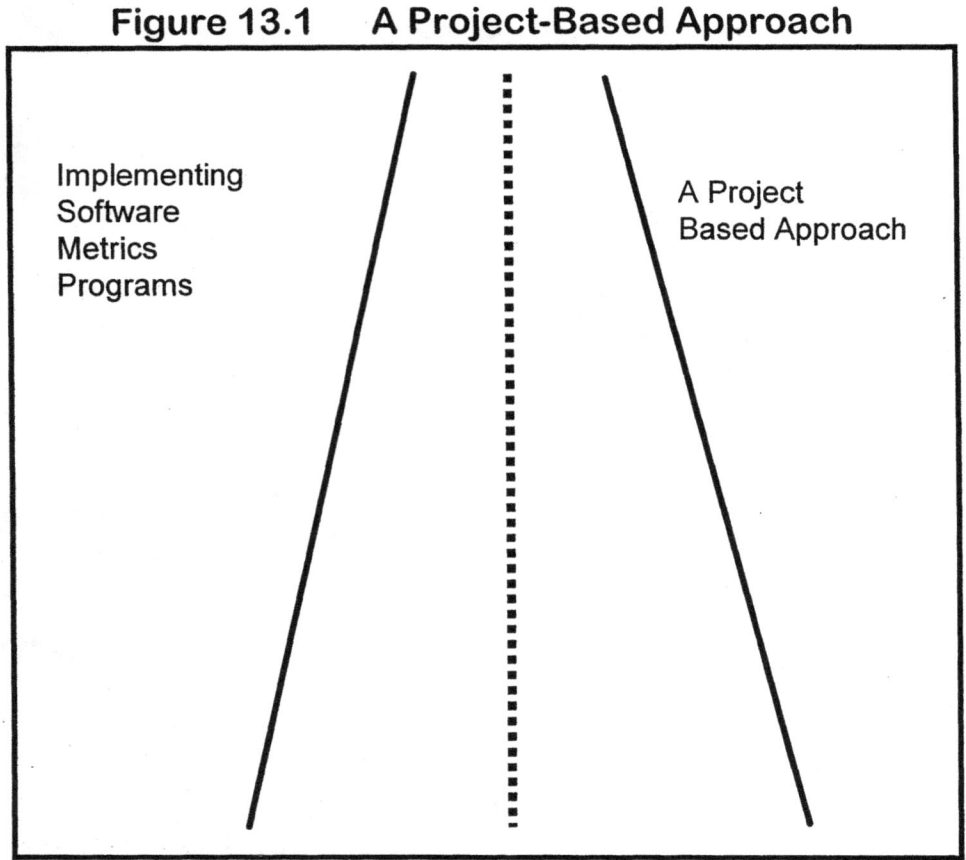

We start with what this book is about. *Figure 13.1* is the title slide of this show and it says quite clearly that the Implementation of Software Metrics programs, in my opinion, relies on the use of a project based approach. Having read section two you are well aware of that already. Let us move on.

Figure 13.2   Topic Scope

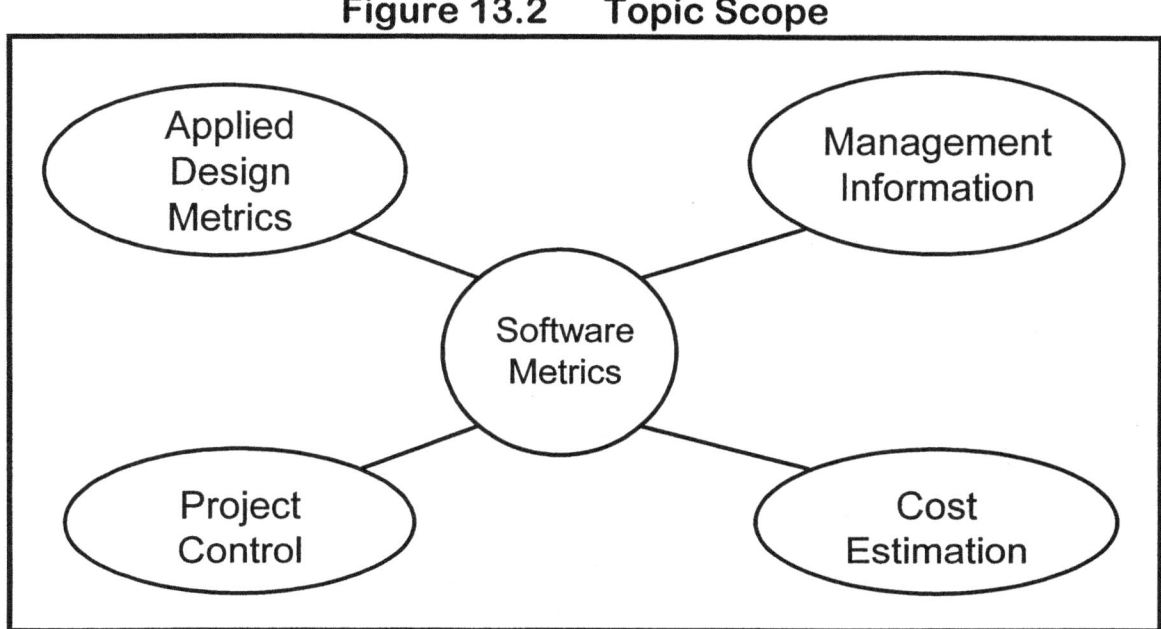

Looking at *Figure 13.2* we consider the scope of Software Metrics as a topic. As the slide shows, I consider the application of Software Metrics to fall under four main categories.

Management Information is the classic approach to Software Metrics in that it gives managers the information they need to do their job. Without management information they are flying by the seat of their pants and probably do not even know in which direction they are heading. Management Information itself is a very large topic and can typically include the management of procurement as well as more commonly recognized elements such as project productivity measurement or the prediction of quality levels for a product.

Cost Estimation is an area of Software Metrics application that has been widely discussed within our industry. In fact, some people would see cost estimation as "Software Metrics." Cost estimation is important because it is the results that come out of this exercise which drive project planning, bidding for work and probably the whole environment in which our staff work for many months. Poor estimation of project cost can actually drive an organization out of existence.

Having estimated the cost of a project and used this to drive the planning of that project, it is sensible to keep track of progress against that plan. It is here that project control techniques come in. "Will I be on time and within budget?" are simply two of the questions for which this area of Software Metrics seeks to supply answers.

Finally, we can consider Applied Design Metrics. These are measurement-based techniques that can be used to improve the quality of intermediate deliverables produced during the development or maintenance lifecycle. Included in the Applied Design Metrics topic are Information Flow and McCabe metrics.

Figure 13.3   Basic Strategy

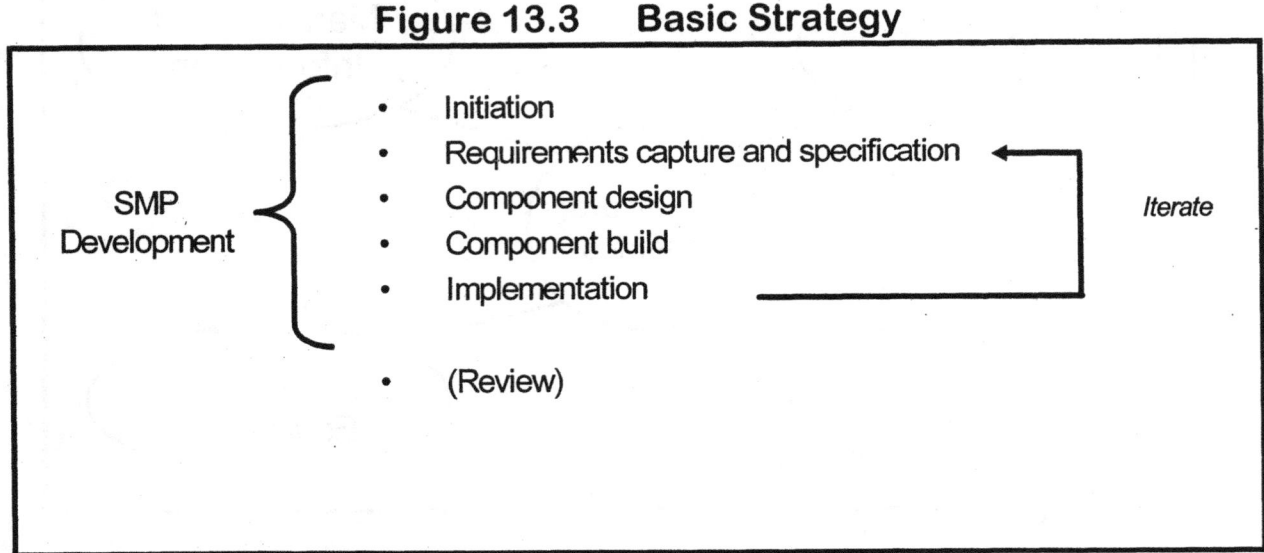

Given the wide scope of the topic we call Software Metrics and the fact that most organizations are large and complex I suggest that you apply a phasing principle to your program. Target specific topics and specific areas of the organization at a particular time.

I also suggest that the development of a Software Metrics initiative consists of the following stages, as shown in slide *Figure 13.3*. Adopting a project-based approach to a measurement initiative implies that certain things are considered. For example, plans for the project should exist, reviews should be recognized as necessary, resources should be allocated and management and control mechanisms should be in place.

13.1 INITIATION

Looking at the Initiation Stage, *Figure 13.4*, there are many triggers that can start a Software Metrics initiative and there are many individuals within an organization who can recognize such a trigger. As this is often beyond the control of the person who will be responsible for implementing the program we will not dwell on this. However, it is worth remembering that the more senior an initiator is, the more vague the requirements are likely to be. Vague requirements are not good news for a Software metrics program.

Figure 13.4   Initiation Stage

Triggers

      Productivity/quality concerns

      Management/customer demands for information

      Fear

      Control = competitive edge

Initiators

      IT management

      Senior management (non IT)

      Quality, Process Improvement or R&D function

      A 'technocrat'

13.2 REQUIREMENTS SPECIFICATION

Once you get past the Initiation stage you can adopt a formal project lifecycle, *Figure 13.5.* First, find out what is required. If at all possible, obtain a customer authority, that is someone to whom you will deliver and who will decide what is to be delivered.

Look to your customers — these are usually internal to the organization, rarely external, although it is the business needs of the end customers that provides the context of the metrics program.

Figure 13.5   Requirements Specification

- Obtain Customer Authority

- Identify customers and customer groupings

- Set up liaison mechanisms- e.g. MCG

- Obtain requirements - standard systems/business analysis

- Group requirements - identify subproject streams

- Prepare and review requirements specification

- Specify TOR

13.3   COMPONENT DESIGN

Remember that your Metrics Program, this thing that seemed so simple and clear such a short time ago, may well consist of many sub-projects as a result of your requirements gathering work, *Figure 13.6.*

Figure 13.6   Component Design 1

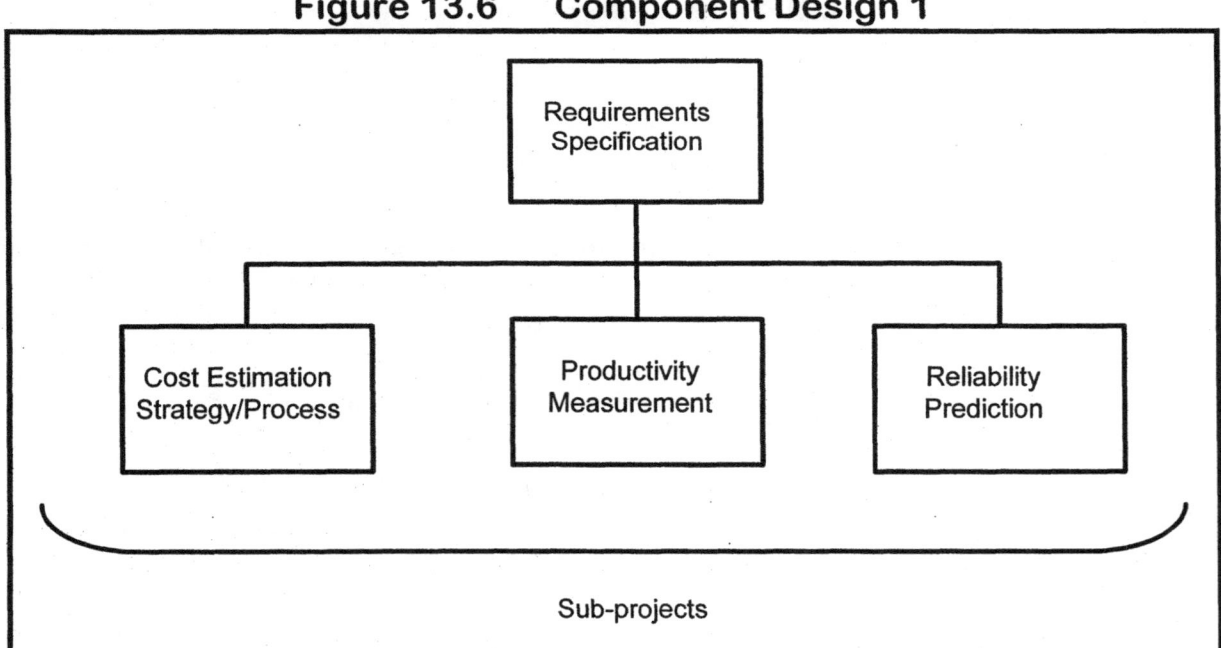

Having sorted out what your program is expected to deliver, you now have to build the components of the system that will meet those requirements! The key thing to remember during this stage is that you cannot ignore any one of three major streams, *Figure 13.7*; the measures and measurement based techniques, the marketing strategy that you will use to implement those measures and the infrastructure that you will use to support that implementation.

Figure 13.7   Component Design 2

Three major streams
     Metrics and Metrics Based Techniques
     Marketing and Business Planning
     Infrastructure Design

Do not ignore any element!

Notice that it is only now that you start to consider the metrics. Remember the heresy contained within this book. It is not difficult to measure — it is only difficult to convince people of the need to measure and to then get them to do something about it.

The Design stage is where you start to look in more detail. As far as marketing and the business planning side of things is concerned you need think about education, publicity, sales strategies and rollout plans. You look at the infrastructure and you have to consider centralized versus distributed metrics functions or follow my advice which is a compromise as shown on *Figure 13.8.*

Figure 13.8   Component Design 3

Ignore the staffing infrastructure at your peril
Central support versus distributed functions

A large organization compromise (tailor and scale to suit your environment)

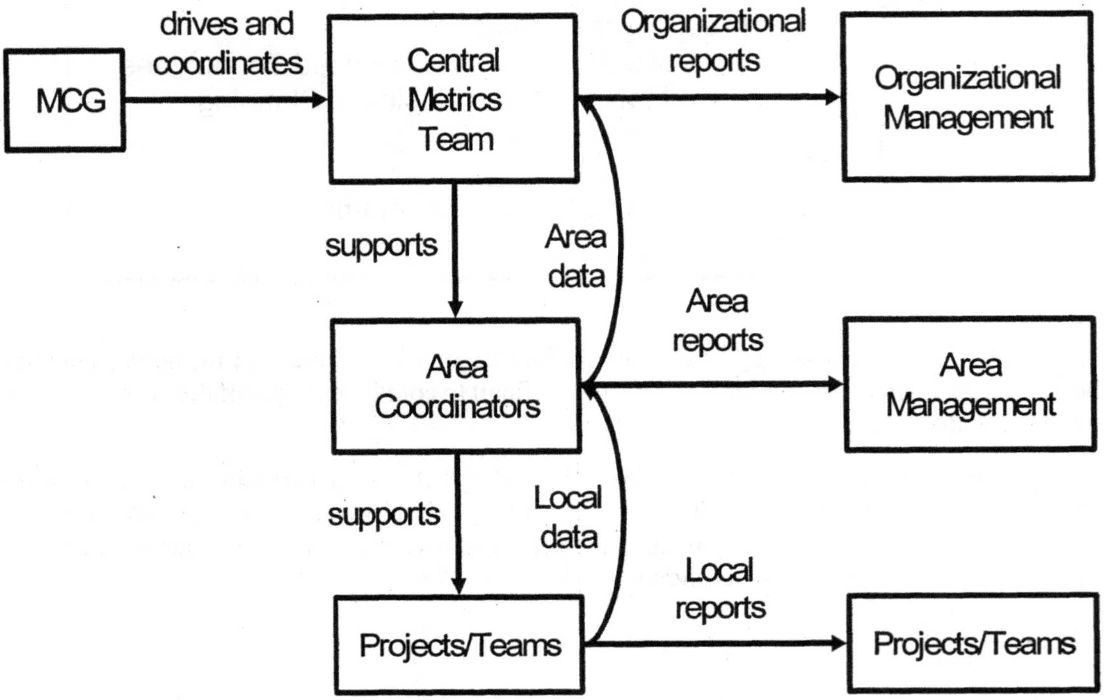

```
            drives and                    Organizational
            coordinates                   reports
  ┌─────┐              ┌──────────┐                  ┌──────────────┐
  │ MCG │─────────────▶│ Central  │─────────────────▶│Organizational│
  └─────┘              │ Metrics  │                  │ Management   │
                       │  Team    │                  └──────────────┘
                       └──────────┘
                            │        Area
                        supports     data
                            │                Area
                            ▼                reports
                       ┌──────────┐                  ┌──────────────┐
                       │  Area    │─────────────────▶│    Area      │
                       │Coordinators│                │ Management   │
                       └──────────┘                  └──────────────┘
                            │        Local
                        supports     data
                            │                Local
                            ▼                reports
                       ┌──────────┐                  ┌──────────────┐
                       │Projects/Teams│──────────────▶│Projects/Teams│
                       └──────────┘                  └──────────────┘
```

13.4   COMPONENT BUILD

Building the components of your measurement program should be mechanistic, *Figure 13.9*. This does *not* mean that the build process will not consume significant resources or take a considerable elapsed time to complete: it simply recognizes that most of the work should have been done during the requirements specification and the design stages.

Remember that what you should aim to deliver are complete solutions. That means training, procedures support services, etc. Having these things ready makes the next stage possible.

Figure 13.9   Component Build

Write procedures and standards - never enough on its own
Prepare training material
Build prototype database
Obtain software packages if necessary
Train Coordinators, i.e. 'build' the staffing infrastructure

13.5   IMPLEMENTATION

Implementation is all about people and this brings its own class of problems. The rules for mitigating the effects of these problems are simple and are often seen as common sense. Common sense is not easy to acquire at the start of a project but these guidelines or rules may help, *Figure 13.10.*

Figure 13.10   Implementation

Sell the program to the projects
Train the staff
Provide the processes and procedures
Tailor to local conditions

You will need to sell the metrics program to your customers, that is to your colleagues and associates. To help these people to implement the components that form your measurement initiative you will have to provide training and procedures or, if you prefer, written guidance addressing the application of measurement. You may well have to make changes to your generic solutions to make them valid for a specific environment. You can view this as tailoring a basic pattern to provide a bespoke service to your customers.

Figure 13.11   Implementation 2

Hold their hand
Visit teams regularly
Listen to concerns
Beware of 'other priorities'
If you take data away - PROVIDE FEEDBACK!

Having done all of this you still cannot walk away. You must help your customers to use, on a day to day basis, the strategies you have provided. This means holding their hands, it means visiting them regularly, listening to concerns and, above all else, helping them to feedback the results of their efforts to their local managers and to the organization in a way that facilitates process improvement, *Figure 13.11*.

Having got a part of your measurement program running you do it all again!

13.6   A RECIPE FOR SUCCESS

What do I see as the important, pervasive and fundamental points that need to guide any measurement initiative? The easy answer is to point you towards the whole of Section Two but if I have to identify a small set of key points, bearing in mind that for particular circumstances others may join the list, I would choose the following:

Avoid ivory towers, which means that you must know your internal market, identify your customers and listen to what they say so that you can identify their requirements together with the business benefits that they wish to realize.

Software Metrics is a large topic and organizations are generally both large and complex. You cannot do everything at once so chunk it down into phases of activity.

Provide solution packages, that is, procedures, training and support. All three are vital.

Do not ignore the infrastructure. This does *not* just mean the fancy metrics database with all the bells and whistles which may be unnecessary at the beginning anyway. It *does* mean the organizational support mechanisms that facilitate or ease the use of metrics.

Finally and very simply, treat the measurement initiative as a project in its own right.

14

Alternative Approaches

to Metrication

Key Points:

There are no shortcuts, but we can always look at reducing scope

This chapter does not offer any shortcuts in terms of avoiding the development and implementation lifecycle for a metrics initiative described in this book. To do that would give the impression that it is possible to succeed without, in some way, addressing the questions of requirements, component design, building and implementation. I firmly believe that this is not a feasible option for a successful, and I stress the word *successful*, measurement initiative.

However, I also recognize that the program described, or implied, in the other chapters of this section is what could be called a total metrics initiative. In other words, it recognizes that Software Metrics is a topic covering considerable scope and it implies that the whole of that scope be addressed. Although phasing has been mentioned it may be worth discussing this concept in a little more detail. Correctly handled, phasing can help deliver results to the organization relatively quickly thus overcoming one of the problems with metrics initiatives, the long lead time.

14.1 PHASING OR SCOPE VARIATION

Software Metrics is a wide-ranging specialty covering the whole of the software development and support lifecycle. It is likely that your organization is also large with many functional groups making it complex in structure. An obvious way to reduce costs, duration and up front commitment is to reduce the scope of your initial program in one or both dimensions.

Targeting one development team, for instance, can enable you to develop a Center of Excellence within your organization and you can use this to demonstrate the beneficial effects of what you wish to implement across the whole organization. Working with one team that is not too large should mean that you can get a program running within six months. Of course you will depend upon the willing cooperation of the development team and you will still have to go through the various metrics program development and implementation lifecycle stages. You benefit from having a very limited marketplace for this first phase of the program.

Of course, there are a number of problems with this approach to metrication. If there were not then all organizations would do it this way. One problem is that really being able to demonstrate benefits will take much longer than six months. You may be able to get your program running in six months but to genuinely show benefits you may have to wait for perhaps another twelve months before hard data becomes available that you can use to convince others in the organization. This is especially true if you are concentrating on things like the measurement of field reliability.

Another problem is to do with the "not-invented-here" syndrome. Even if you have hard data available you may find that other teams take the attitude that just because it worked for one group does not mean that it will work for them. This is always a danger with pilots, and really we are talking about a form of pilot here. The reverse can also happen where you find it difficult to promote the use of something tried in the pilot group because that group is seen as a center of excellence. The feeling you then encounter is one of resistance because the pilot group are seen as being favored in numerous ways.

The last major problem with this approach is that you can suffer from a lack of visibility. Especially in large organizations, working with only one team may mean that your metrics initiative is unnoticed by those in the organization with real power. You need that notice if you are to effect real change.

Despite all of these problems, tackling the first phase of your initiative in this way can pay off, especially if you take care to abate the risks outlined above.

And then there is the second dimension: Software Metrics is a big topic — what if we make it smaller?

This approach can work very effectively and has been the seed from which some of the best regarded measurement initiatives, certainly in Europe, have grown. I include in these a leading UK Bank, a large government department and a leading European industrial organization. All of these organizations now have established, and it would seem effective, measurement programs and all of them started by concentrating on specific areas within the Software Metrics domain.

The technique is to identify a key trigger that is very important to your organization or to a specific customer. Whoever the customer, senior management must be aware of the area of concern.

Concentrating on a very specific area of Software Metrics means that you can reduce the learning time for the individuals involved by a great deal. If you then drive things forward such that you essentially pilot a technique or approach, possibly under the guise of an evaluation, you can get results quite quickly, certainly within nine months providing your topic is amenable to that time scale. Do bear in mind that you can not expect to show benefits from the use of, for instance, design metrics in that timescale if it takes nine months for your project to simply move from design through to coding.

Provided that you are sensible in choosing a topic that can give results within a reasonable time and that you then push those results up to senior management you could quickly end up with a full-scale metrics initiative to manage.

As always, there are no perfect answers to life's problems and there are some problems with this approach. Addressing one area of Software Metrics may mean that you pick the wrong one for your organization or that, for whatever reason, you do not get good or helpful results on your first attempt. Another danger is that the focus of the organization shifts so that what was a vitally important problem yesterday is suddenly less important. In wider ranging initiatives the occasional failure can be hidden behind successes. Of course, one way to reduce the risk is to go for two topics at a time if you have the resources.

14.2   IN BY THE BACK DOOR

If you have authority or responsibility for a metrics initiative and you sit within some functional group removed from mainstream development, perhaps as part of an R&D group, then reducing the scope of your metrics initiative may well appeal. What do you do if you do not really have management's eye or the explicit responsibility for process improvement within the organization, through metrics or through any other means?

It is possible to slide metrics into an organization through the back door but it can take a long time and it can be quite frustrating in the short term. Let us set up a scenario and then look at a particular solution that may work.

You are a manager. You do not report directly to the Systems Development Director, in fact there are numerous levels of management between him or her and your lowly self. You are responsible for a particular software product and you know that you and your team are struggling with problems. You believe that there are better ways of doing things and you have perhaps come across the idea of management through measurement at a seminar. Such a concept appeals to you but you know that you do not have enough clout to drive such an initiative through the organization. Anyway, apart from anything else most of your time is spent managing your own team.

Try this approach. Get your first-line reports and any other team members whose opinion you especially respect into a room for a few hours. The agenda is "process improvement." Ask your colleagues what the major problems are today. From what they say and subsequent discussion you should be able to arrive at a small set of key requirements that need to be addressed to improve things for your group. Obviously you need to concentrate on items that you can affect.

Assign one individual the task of designing a solution that will satisfy the requirement. Give them visible support; help but do not overshadow, and aim to get a revised process in place within two months.

Run it for six months and at the same time target the next major problem area. Do not go for sledgehammer solutions. You are looking for levers to move things to a higher level of effectiveness. This means that you cannot put in fantastic, whizbang, automated solutions and that all you may end up with, apart from a better process, is a paper and pencil system supported, possibly, by a spreadsheet.

Within nine months you should be able to identify a significant improvement in the way your group operates. Of course, you will not be the only one to notice this. Management will also become aware of improvements and so will other teams. You may well find that you start to get inquiries from these other groups and from management. The problem with this is that you may end up managing the metrics initiative for the whole organization.

An excellent example of metrication came from a large European organization. One divisional manager got fed up with not being able to control software development projects, and to counter this put in place a process based on simple and regular information-gathering from project managers using straightforward metrics about progress against plans. Things improved quickly and dramatically. The end result was the extension of the project control process to all software development divisions. The fundamental key to this approach is that, as an individual, you can accept responsibility for improving things. The question is, will you accept that responsibility? Measurement is only one aspect of this work ethic. Measurement gives solid information on which to base management decisions and, furthermore, can demonstrate unequivocally that improvement has occurred.

14.3   HITCHING A RIDE

Many organizations have introduced the concept of process improvement under some guise or other. Over the years the names and the emphasis of the basic models may have changed, although it is interesting to note, as someone who has been involved with such initiatives for many years, that the underlying concepts are still the same. Such programs invariably require a high degree of senior management commitment and oblige an organization to change its existing culture.

Measurement is a fundamental part of process improvement in any guise and such a program offers an ideal opportunity for the introduction of Software Metrics.

The key to using this approach successfully would seem to be the identification of short-term objectives that are achievable, and to then use the momentum generated during one phase to fuel the next. One of the big advantages of this linking strategy is that you can use the senior management commitment to the larger program to give authority by association to the metrics initiative, thus reducing the amount of effort needed to sell metrics. Do note that this effort requirement is *never* reduced to zero!

14.4   HARD AND FAST

This final alternative is one that demands a high degree of senior management commitment because it involves money.

One of the biggest problems with any Software Metrics program can be the lack of in-house experience, either in terms of technical knowledge or in terms of experience relating to the management of cultural change. This means that individuals who are responsible for doing the work have to spend time learning the subject. They will also spend time investigating specific techniques that turn out to be unsuitable for their particular environment. They may try things out within pilots and evaluation exercises where somebody with experience of such techniques would have been able to say, with confidence, "this will work if we do it this way because, in a similar environment, it worked last time."

Of course, just because something worked before somewhere else does not guarantee that it will work in your environment, but there are some requirements and, more importantly, some solutions to these requirements that are common to most organizations. An expert should be aware of these and will also be able to identify what needs to be changed to tailor a generic solution to a specific environment or organization.

For example, most organizations would benefit from being able to record information about defects in their software systems as delivered to the customer. One question that must be asked is "what information should be recorded and to what level should those records be kept?"

An in house team could spend a considerable amount of time researching this concept by reading technical papers and talking to other organizations; discussing in committee what would be the best data and finally drawing up the proposals for a defect recording system. Experience shows that the eventual system may well be difficult to operate and to use to get meaningful results because the first attempt is often too detailed.

Any expert should also talk to potential users and operators of the system to ensure that he or she does not try to make a solution fit where it really does not. However, an expert should be able to help an organization establish a workable and useful defect recording system very quickly.

In this case, the solution may be as simple as agreeing to a high-level lifecycle for software development and putting in mechanisms, often no more than simple forms and a database, to record point of injection and point of discovery of the defect together with some additional information such as system name, date of discovery and date of closure. This limited amount of information can be used to provide data which, in turn, can be used to assess the effectiveness of the development process. An expert should also be able to determine quickly, whether defects should be recorded at the system, program or program component level so that the needs of the organization are met.

The obvious question is, from where do we get this expertise? If expertise does not exist within the organization the only solutions are to recruit it or to buy it in. In other words we are talking about the use of external hires or consultants. To get external hires may not be acceptable if it increases the permanent headcount of the organization and even if you get the go-ahead there are not many experienced metrics practitioners in the marketplace. This is slowly changing but it will take some time before the demand for such experience is less than the supply. You could also be very unfortunate if you recruit the services of a consultant only to find that they have a large learning curve to climb. This may sound like a contradiction but most organizations have experience of a consultant arriving to carry out a piece of work only to find that very large briefcase you hoped contained the fruits of past experience actually contains lots of books about the topic in question. Not exactly a good way to build confidence in the eventual solution.

Now the big problem with consultancy, even assuming you can get the right people, is that it costs money! For this reason you can only use the strategy of a consultancy driven program if you have senior management commitment to spend the necessary money.

You also need to have clear objectives that you expect the consultant or consultancy team to achieve. This can be more difficult than you may think and it often pays to set things up in three distinct stages. The first stage is simply to identify suitable consultants. If you are already involved with a consultancy organization and you feel comfortable with them then you have a good starting point but do remember that Software Metrics is a young discipline and that, even among consultants, practical experience of the topic is scarce. How you identify suitable consultants is something that only you can determine, but the one suggestion I would make is that you do look for evidence of previous experience, preferably in the area you are interested in. For example, someone with experience of Applied Design Metrics, say the use of McCabe metrics or Information Flow Metrics may or may not be knowledgeable about cost estimation models.

The second phase is all about scoping and planning. Many organizations are reluctant to pay consultancy rates simply so that the consultant can prepare a proposal and plans for the real work. The advantage that you get from this approach is that you can get to know the consultants and you get some indication of their effectiveness without contracting large sums of money. The consultants get the opportunity to get close to your organization and the time to properly plan the work ahead. This increases the likelihood of success so everyone wins.

Of course, you must make it clear to the consultants that the proposals and plans produced must be for your organization. You do not want to pay for generic solutions lifted from textbooks, even this one! You can do that yourself.

Once you have an agreed proposal you can start the third phase, the real work. You will need to consider the management of this strategy. Someone from your organization must have responsibility for the project because, at some time in the future, the consultant will walk away and you will be left to carry on. A clear customer authority and resources to review deliverable are vital components of a consultancy driven program.

The transfer of knowledge from the consultant to the organization is also a deliverable of the project. This strategy only works when the consultants and the organization's own staff work together. Consultancy-driven with organizational ownership and involvement are what you aim for. To help achieve this, do not lock your consultant away in an ivory tower; instead, have regular project meetings to discuss the approaches being used, progress, plans and deliverables. This may add slightly to the cost as it all takes time but it is money well spent. As has been said many times by many people who have suffered the pain, "we never have the time (or budget) to do it right, but we always have the time to do it wrong."

The consultancy-driven approach to metrication depends upon senior management commitment because it costs money, cooperation and, most importantly, trust between the consultants and the organization and vice versa.

The disadvantage of the consultancy-driven approach is that it costs. Its advantage is that you can have a working software measurement program in place much more quickly than if you try to do it solely with internal resources.

These alternatives can all help with the metrication process but underlying them all is a project-based approach that uses a lifecycle of the kind described in this book. Do not be tempted to cut corners on that or you will increase your probability of failure significantly.

SECTION 3

GENERAL DISCUSSION

In this section we look at and discuss some general topics related to Software Metrics

15

The Home Stretch

In this chapter I want to take a personal view of where we are with Software Metrics and where we might be going. Obviously, this is influenced by the time of writing.

The first edition of this book was originally published in 1993. Since then I have worked in the fields of Software Metrics and process improvement, generally within the IT industry, and during that time I have carried out many assignments for a diverse range of organizations. Sometimes I have acted as a consultant advising internal resources; sometimes I have been "in the line" as a manager, albeit on fixed-term contracts. This has all been valuable experience for me and, I believe, of value to my clients. I have learned much more than I knew when I originally wrote the first edition of this book, but everything that I have learned has reinforced for me the value of measurement within IT organizations.

As I approached the formal research for this second edition, I believed that those lessons and the work carried out by the many individuals, both within the industry and within academia, would mean that much would change. I genuinely felt that there would be many new things to say and that the older references would need to be updated with more recent material. All of us internalize the lessons we learn from life and we apply those to the way we act, we may modify our behaviors or adopt slightly different ways in our approaches to work. As anyone who has ever taught, presented or written a report or a book knows, a key stage is the formalization of those experiences and lessons such that they can be expressed and communicated to others.

While I still believe that I have learned many, many things over the intervening years I also now believe that most of those lessons have been to do with the psychology of the interaction between people and functions within organizations. I have to be honest and say that, at a technical level, what was true in Software Metrics then, and the techniques that worked, is still true Consequently, not many changes were necessary to the contents of Section 1 of this book. Of course there has been progress. Function Point Analysis has been refined but primarily this refinement has been to clarify meanings. There is now an international standard for Functional Sizing Metrics. But it has been the further institutionalization of metrics within the IT industry where progress has been most evident, rather than in radical changes to the techniques that we, as professional IT managers and consultants, use.

I was extremely fortunate to enter the field in which I work at a time of "newness" and, to some extent dynamism. When I started working in Software Metrics, what we were doing was not even generally recognized under that title, which incidentally I did not coin. As my brother once said to me "does that mean you measure how many centimeters of software there are?" At that time, within the IT industry, management was often "by the seat of your pants." Even if experience showed otherwise for a few metrics, many of the measurement techniques developed in the eighties and early nineties are as relevant today as they were then.

But our industry that was large and important back then has also experienced incredible growth. New applications for software are increasingly being explored and, of course, the Internet opens up a completely new world. Although I would prefer that it were otherwise, the number of organizations that have well-established measurement programs in place that are being used on a daily basis to inform management decisions are still few.

As an industry we face a similar problem to a ship's captain of an oil tanker. You cannot stop such a ship or change direction quickly. It takes time. This is one reason why the old joke about power always giving way to sail is inaccurate. Ask any small boat skipper if he expects that oil tanker to avoid him or if he has to avoid it — the answer will be unequivocal. As an industry, our situation with respect to management based on quantitative information is not that different to what it was when I first put pen to paper for the earlier edition of this work over a decade ago. Depressing isn't it?

So, one lesson that I have, I hope, learned is that the process of change is slow. Not only does our industry equate to the oil tanker but it is an oil tanker that is growing longer and more massive even as we progress through the water. And we have no captain! This is fundamental to change. Someone, or some group, has to be responsible for the change if it is to occur. It is perhaps no coincidence that India, the country currently with the highest proportion of high-maturity-level organizations as assessed by one particular approach, is also one of the countries whose government has made a firm commitment, and devoted resources, to developing their IT industry through the production of high-quality software. Of course, lower labor costs are always quoted as a contributing factor but no organization would sacrifice the quality of its second-most important resource (their people being the first) on the basis of cost alone.

If we are to accelerate the rate of change, governments and significant government organizations must take some responsibility to ensure professional management in our IT industries. The good news is that more of them are doing so.

There are also other factors that give rise to the hope that the rate of change may increase. Although the proportion of organizations with established measurement programs may not be much greater than it was years ago, in terms of absolute numbers there are many more. This means more experience within the industry and less opportunity for other organizations, and individual managers within those organizations, to deny the benefits of measurement to support management.

In this section I would like to move away from the problem of developing and implementing a metrics initiative or program and close the book by discussing various topics that fall within the area of interest of anyone involved in Software Metrics. I hope to do this not from the implementation standpoint of the previous sections but more by introducing and discussing certain areas that you may find of interest.

This material comes from many sources in both the academic and industrial environments so specific credits will not be given unless I believe it necessary for someone who wishes to follow up the ideas presented here.

I intend to start by looking at two areas that originated in the United States but are also being implemented in organizations all over the world. These are the Goal, Question, Metric (GQM) paradigm from Basili and Rombach when they were at the Software Engineering Laboratory or SEL and the Process Maturity Model from the Software Engineering Institute and fully described in Watts Humphries' book, "Managing the Software Process."

I have already discussed the Goal, Question, Metric paradigm in other parts of this book but I have included it here to emphasize the fact that it is a technique that is extremely robust and, in my view, should be included as a tool within any serious measurement initiative. A great deal of credit must go to Vic Basili and Dieter Rombach for expressing, so elegantly, a process-based solution to an issue that has caused many individuals a great deal of pain.

I would also like to stress that there is a great deal more to this paradigm than is often presented at conferences and seminars. It is certainly more than setting a goal, asking a few questions and, hey look, we got ourselves a metric. The model is rich and before you think you understand it I suggest you read material such as Rombach (1).

I believe that you will hear more and more about the GQM approach to metrication over the next few years. You will also hear more and more about the Software Engineering Institute's (SEI, www.sei.cmu.edu) Process Maturity Model. Like GQM, you should also realize that the Process Maturity Model has more to it than may first be obvious.

This model forms part of a technique that can be used to assess the effectiveness of a process for software development. Immediately you can think of two applications for such a technique. If I own such a process, perhaps as the manager of an IT function, then I would like to assess that process. Such information can perhaps help me to decide the best management initiatives; if the scoring mechanism is widely accepted then a good score will do me no harm at all and could do me a great deal of good; even a bad score is not a disaster if I can show improvement over time.

The other application has a very different emphasis. If such a technique gives me an objective mechanism by which I can assess a software development process then I, as a purchaser of software systems, can use that process to assess potential suppliers.

These two applications have been recognized by the SEI who have established two processes, the *SEI Assessment* and the closely related *Software Capability Evaluation*. The main differences are that an organization carries out an SEI assessment for its own benefit, that same organization may have a Software Capability Evaluation carried out on it, especially if it is your intention to supply a U.S. government department or agency.

15.1   SEI ASSESSMENT

We should realize that both these techniques are essentially the same, only the emphasis being different, so I will briefly describe the process behind an SEI Assessment.

The first step is a management commitment to the assessment and, most importantly, to the improvement plan that results from the assessment. Next, a small team from the organization is trained by the SEI or one of its accredited trainers. Notice that we are essentially talking about a self-assessment here, but one done to a recognized and accepted formula.

Next, plans are prepared to ensure the assessment can be rapidly completed, typically within one or two weeks, and then projects or areas are selected for that assessment. The selected project or area teams then fill out a questionnaire of, currently 101 yes/no questions.

The assessment team then corroborate the questionnaire data and delve much deeper through a series of intensive interviews and group discussions. Note that the questionnaire is not the whole assessment. These interviews actually form the key to the SEI assessment technique. Penultimately, results are presented to management together with a set of recommendations for improvement.

The last step is for the organization to prepare and implement action plans to realize those recommendations and that is seen as part of the assessment process, not separate from it. Now this is the key. The main deliverable of the assessment is the improvement plan. The great value of the model is that, once you have evaluated where you are within the parameters of the model, the model itself indicates those areas or key processes that you should next address.

But what about the Maturity Model? This usually forms part of the management sign up discussions and a score against it also results from the assessment. It is simply a five-level representation of the maturity of a process where these levels range from initial or ad hoc, through repeatable, defined, managed and optimizing. See *Figure 15.1*.

Figure 15.1   The CMM Process Maturity Framework

LEVEL	PROCESS CHARACTERISTICS
Optimizing	Process improvement is institutionalized
Managed	Product and Process are quantitatively controlled
Defined	Software engineering and management processes defined and integrated
Repeatable	Project management system in place, performance is repeatable
Initial	Process is informal and unpredictable

It is this Maturity Model that most people have picked up on although some have also latched on to the questionnaire. Most do not go for a full understanding of the SEI assessment technique which, to judge by the experiences of part of the Hughes Aircraft organization, is a shame. Having bought into the SEI assessment mechanism and followed through on recommendations this group moved from level 2 to 3. It took them 2 years to do it and cost about $450 000. Why bother?

Well, they estimated savings of $2 million PER ANNUM! Even if they have overestimated I do not believe that they have done so by much.

How they did it is described in the IEEE Software Engineering Transactions issued July 1991, Humphrey (1). This paper, together with some of the discussion papers that follow it both supporting and criticizing the assessment process make interesting reading.

We all know that there are few perfect solutions so what are the problems with the SEI assessment process and the associated Software Capability Evaluation? We should also ask why the Maturity Model has generated so much interest and how it can be used.

The first problem is an interesting one. How would you feel if your customers insisted on your development process being assessed? Obviously there has been, and continues to be, some resistance to the idea of having to suffer a Software Capability Evaluation. However, when the organization insisting on that evaluation is the US Department of Defense and you want a piece of their expenditure to come in your direction you may well feel it judicious to swallow your pride. I feel that the reality is that the industry is moving more to a situation where customers will demand that the capability of their suppliers be expressed in recognizable forms, and the SEI approach is certainly a step in this direction. What we need to be very careful about is that we do not allow ill-conceived and possibly harmful initiatives to be foisted on the industry. This is more probable if suppliers of software seek to resist these initiatives. We stand a much greater chance of getting workable and helpful assessment mechanisms if suppliers and customers, professional developers and academics cooperate.

It must also be said that the SEI two-pronged approach that, essentially, offers the same techniques for supplier evaluation and self assessment, encourages such cooperation and has contributed to the adoption of their mechanisms.

A more fundamental concern, and it is no more than a concern on my part, lies with the *success* of the SEI approach and the maturity model, not with the approach and the model themselves. The reason for this concern is that more and more publicity is being given to the maturity model and its five levels but little understanding exists of the SEI assessment technique as a whole, and that whole is important if the maturity model is to be understood in context.

We have had this problem with the Goal, Question, Metric paradigm and I must admit I do not see an easy solution. The fundamental problem is that the maturity model is a very convenient mechanism that can be used to describe the capability of an organization. Like all models you lose a massive amount of detail when you do this but people can relate to that model, especially more senior managers.

Things that work, and in this context the maturity model does work, tend to get used. We, as professionals, must remember that much more lies behind the maturity model and we must use it correctly. The SEI have attempted to address this by accrediting assessors but this is a difficult process to complete, especially for non-US based professionals. Hopefully, we will see a wider form of accreditation in the future.

The SEI have also developed additional, supporting models for other aspects of IT management including the *People-CMM* focused on human resource management and development, the *Personal Software Process* focused on the development of individual software engineers and still more.

The SEI have now drawn together and updated a number of the models they have developed and have released the *Capability Maturity Model Integrated* for Systems Engineering, Software Engineering, and Integrated Product and Process Development or *CMMI-SE/SW/IPPD* for short, (which we will call the CMM-I). Measurement is a Key Process Area within the CMM-I, progress indeed.

Other topics that seem to be generating interest today in the area of metrication are measures for enhanceability and user satisfaction. Almost all of us are living with systems that we expected to replace years ago, but still they go on. Not only do they still exist but they are also continually enhanced. I do not believe that anyone has got to a system in the same state as the axe that had three new heads and four new shafts and was still as good as the day it was bought, but who knows? If as we now realize is possible, systems can have vastly extended lifespans, then being able to control and manage the enhanceability of that system is important. Elsewhere in this book a simple model of an enhanceability measure is proposed but this topic is one that merits more discussion within our community.

As far as user satisfaction is concerned it should come as no surprise that this is seen as important. Satisfied users provide repeat business, they tell other potential customers and can generate new business, and a satisfied customer is much less likely to cause us pain on a daily basis. But how do you know if your customer is satisfied? The obvious answer is to ask them, but ask them in a way that enables an objective answer to be obtained rather than by means of a quick phone call.

There are two points to bear in mind about user satisfaction assessment. First, your business environment will impact heavily on how you address this problem. For instance, if you are cooperating closely with a client on a large project you can build user satisfaction evaluations into your project control mechanisms so that the user has a chance to express any concerns they have. Remember you must drive this because many problem are not large enough to make the user or customer actively complain, but it only takes a few of these 'little' problems to leave a nasty taste for the user. Alternatively, you may be maintaining a system for a user. In this case an annual meeting with a structured format can work in assessing user/customer satisfaction. Finally, you may be selling a product to many customers. In this situation you may not be able to ask all your customers how they feel, but you can sample.

The second point to remember is that user satisfaction does not depend solely on satisfying their expressed requirements. A classic example of this could be the organization that has a service level agreement (SLA) with a client that requires an engineers on site within one hour of a problem being reported and that 99% of all problems be resolved within one day. If a supplier organization achieved this tight constraint they would be surprised if the customer cancelled the contract. What if the engineers always arrived within an hour but were surly and condescending when on the client site? What if the client had trouble reporting faults because the idiots on the switchboard always routed the call to the wrong department? What if every time a fault was fixed it seemed to trigger ten more? The only way you will become aware of these problems is when the client walks away from you, unless you regularly make sure that the client is satisfied.

The most interesting trend from my point of view is a move away from measurement per se. This, I feel, is a real indication that we are maturing as an industry. More and more organizations are realizing that measurement for its own sake will do little to solve their problems. Only a quality management, and notice I say *management,* not *improvement*, approach towards process optimization will do this. Of course, measurement is a cornerstone of this approach. This shift of emphasis opens up a whole new topic and this,

I believe, will be one of the most interesting areas to be involved in over the next few years. The leaders, of course, will be the ones who get on and do it. They will reap the benefits.

Even with this trend towards the implementation of true process improvement there will still be areas of particular interest to the Software Metrics community and I would like to consider some of those now. We can take this opportunity to look at some techniques that are perhaps less well known than they should be and to consider their possible impact on the area we call Software Metrics.

The first area I would like to consider is that of formalization within Software Metrics. I remember teaching an evening class of students some years ago, the idea being to introduce this group of students, that ranged from storemen to army officers, to the intricacies of computers. My starting point was to explain that most individuals are, in effect, lazy and that the use of the term computer was actually incorrect. What we should talk about is the computer system. This gave me a good lead in to an explanation of operating systems, programs, hardware and how these various elements hang together to make up something that can do useful work.

The point of this example is to illustrate our misuse of words. This misuse continues with the use of the term "Software Metrics." Technically speaking a metric is a unit of measure such as the amp, a nautical mile or a parsec. In software terms an example of a metric would be a line of code, provided it were clearly defined, or the McCabe metric known as *cyclomatic complexity*. And that is it: a metric is no more and no less than that unit of measure and there is a discipline concerned with the definition and use of such things. That discipline is *not* what we know today as Software Metrics.

Now you may ask what is in a name? I must admit that I have some sympathy for this view believing that if you want to call our area of interest Software Metrics then, provided it is seeking to promote best practice, you call it Software Metrics. You can call it statistics if you want! However, I do recognize that laziness in the use of terms can be symptomatic of a deeper malaise. There is a tendency within Software Metrics, and I will continue to use that term for this book to avoid any more confusion, to tend too heavily towards pragmatism.

Now bearing in mind one of the main themes of this book, that pragmatic solutions are often perfectly acceptable, that last statement may come as a surprise. Pragmatism is all very well but we must always remember that there are certain rules that you do not buck. For example, there is a great tendency to add simple measures together to produce a more "complete" indicator of some characteristic. For example, let us say that we recognize that the simple line-of-code measure does not totally reflect the effort needed to make an enhancement to a section of code. Furthermore, assume that we consider the McCabe Cyclomatic complexity measure a valid measure of complexity. So the model says that by combining LOC with Cyclomatic complexity we will have a better measure of enhancement effort, so add them.

The two basic measures use different scales and cannot be added in this way; it is simply against the rules of mathematics.

I once had the great pleasure of attending a "mathematical nightclub." This was an event staged by a group of tutors for the benefit of newcomers to the world of mathematics. It was here that I saw it "proved" that 2 equals 3. I also learned how to make a reasonable amount of money at any party but that's another story. 2 equals 3 if you miss the sleight of hand that makes you skim over the line in the proof that says divide by zero! Equally, excuse the pun, if you 'add' LOC and Cyclomatic complexity, then you are performing a sleight of hand because you cannot add quantities of different units together. The reason I have taken so long over this story is that this addition of Cyclomatic complexity and LOC is one that I come across about every twelve months! The point is that you can only get away with this type of thing if you do not apply any formalism in your definition and use of Software Metrics.

The challenge facing the software engineering sector of industry is to adapt to this greater degree of formality in a positive way. One concern that is sometimes expressed is that standards, such as those defined by the International Standards Organization (ISO, www.iso.org) may not be workable within particular organizations or areas but it should be noted that the current trend, at least as far as Software Metrics is concerned, is towards guideline standards rather than prescriptive mechanisms. Having said that, the realities of business and particularly the demands of customers may force us to accept standardization more readily than we might otherwise.

15.2 OTHER MEASUREMENT-BASED TECHNIQUES

Having looked at some relatively large-scale trends I now intend to shift the focus to look at some specific techniques that have not yet caught the attention of the metrics community in general but which, in my view, have considerable potential for the future. Within this chapter it will not be practical to describe these measurement-based techniques in full and I see these descriptions as more of a taster. If further information is required, references are provided within the bibliography.

I would first like to look at a technique known as *Data Envelopment Analysis* (DEA), an extremely intimidating name for something that is inherently elegant and practical. DEA is a development of the mathematical technique known as Linear Programming and it is used in the following way.

Imagine the situation where you have identified two characteristics of your process or products that are common across the organization, for example you may consider productivity and reliability. Further imagine that you have measures associated with these characteristics and you have collected data from a number of projects. Now, what many managers want to know is how these different projects have performed in terms of these two characteristics.

One thing that you may consider doing is to present a graph with productivity as the *x* axis and reliability as the *y* axis. So, the performance of each project can be described in terms of two-dimensional vector coordinates. This is all very well, but managers often want information in non-graphical form. They also like comparisons against "best in class." Within the DEA technique these requirements are met by identifying the boundary cases and using these to describe an envelope around the set of observations. For any particular project, its performance can then be represented by drawing a vector from the origin, through the project point to the boundary.

Performance is then expressed as a ratio of the distance from the origin to the project point compared to the total length of the vector to the boundary. This is shown in *Figure 15.2:*

Figure 15.2   Performance

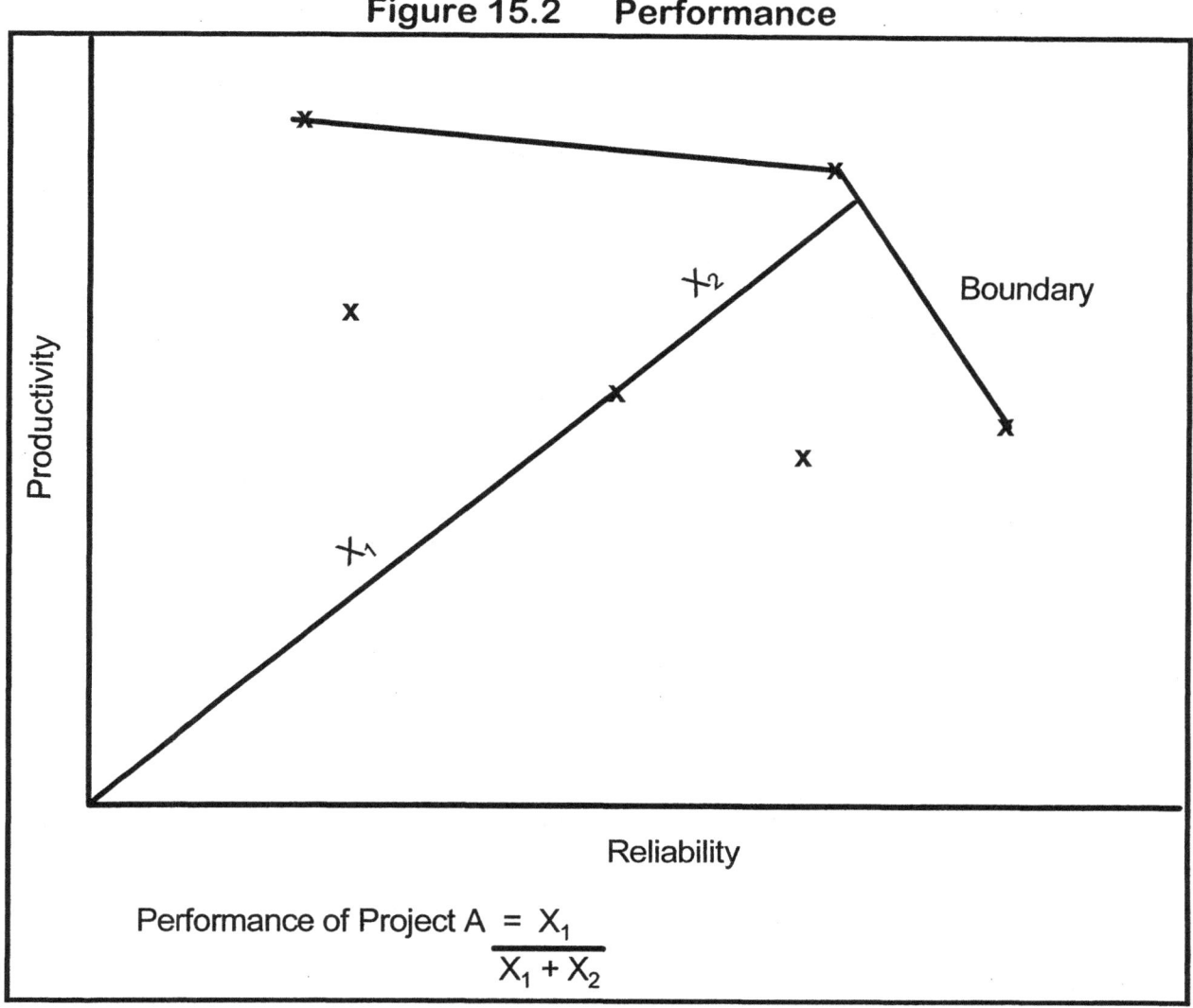

Performance of Project A $= \dfrac{X_1}{X_1 + X_2}$

The great beauty of DEA is that the technique can be applied to more dimensions than two; in fact, to any number subject to the computational capabilities available to you. DEA has been used in the United States to compare educational establishments and is also being used now within the IT industry. Tool support is also available.

For more information about DEA please see Elam (1) and Charnes (1).

I would like to close this chapter by considering an aspect of Software Metrics that is often considered but seldom actioned, which is a great pity because its impact could be huge. The area I refer to is that known as the soft, or environmental, factors.

Soft Factors are all to do with the people aspects of software engineering; in fact another way of referring to this topic is "peopleware" and there is an excellent book by Tom DeMarco and Tim Lister that bears this title, DeMarco (1). One reason that this topic gets such little attention is because of managers' reaction to it. So often you find that managers see any initiative in this area as one that will lead to demands for more money, bigger offices, more desk space, etc., yet soft factors go much further than this.

There is, of course, another point to consider. If you were a manager and it was proved, beyond reasonable doubt, that giving your staff more of something would increase quality and productivity to such an extent that the cost of giving would be more than outweighed by the return, what would you do?

The sad situation in the vast majority of organizations today is that the information to assess the payback from improved environments is not even collected. Even worse, we know that some teams perform well in adverse conditions while others cannot perform adequately even when everything is going right. Why is this? What, for example, is the effect of team composition in terms of experience, age, even gender?. What size of team is the optimum within your environment? When did you last attempt to discover the morale level of your team other than by listening in on the grapevine?

Yet there are organizations that do apply management principles to the soft factors, although they are few and far between, and who seem to be getting good results. IBM did invest heavily in one installation specifically designing it to provide an office environment that was wanted by the workforce. One reference at the time claimed a 30% higher productivity rate than that found in other sites doing similar work, McCue (1).

A problem with Soft Factors is the question of data collection so I would like to describe one experiment that I was involved in that gave limited but promising results in that area.

The purpose of our experiment was really to see if data could be collected rather than to try to assess specific soft-factor impact but we did get some interesting results as you will see.

Our first problem, of course, was what to actually collect. There are very many potential soft factors about which data could be collected but this leads to a classic "data hunter" scenario and we felt that should be avoided. The approach adopted was quite simplistic but seemed to work. A colleague and I sat down together and, over the course of a day, brainstormed out a whole raft of potential factors. All the classics were in there such as experience of team, availability of terminals and compiler speeds. There were a few others that crept in from the dark, for example the gender mix of the team. Is this a valid soft factor, in other words could the gender mix within a team affect performance in any way? When venturing into this area one can only depend upon personnel experience, so I can only talk for all male teams and the mixed variety. What I have found is that mixed-gender teams tend to work better than single-gender teams, although I freely admit that this is a subjective opinion. However, why might that be the case.

First, I believe that the broader range of interests commonly found in mixed gender teams acts to increase team cohesion. An all-male team can easily get caught up in, say, the world cup to the extent that work suffers. Second, and perhaps this is the real reason such teams work, I find that people in mixed gender teams are more polite to each other than in all-male teams. This is merely an observation but I will also state that politeness is, in my opinion, the oil that lubricates the social machine. Perhaps such lubrication helps to improve performance in teams as well as in engines.

I include the discussion on mixed gender teams to show that we did give some thought to the various factors that we were considering at that point. Some we really had some fun with!

But we then had a problem in that we were suffering from an plenitude of riches! We had some sixty or seventy soft factors identified and we knew that we could not collect, or use, data on so many. To reduce the set we ran a limited survey. We circulated our list of soft factors to a number of experienced software engineers and managers and we asked them to score the factors in terms of impact on performance. This was a subjective assessment based on their experience. This was where we had our first interesting result. Because of the way the organization was structured at the time we were able to include representatives from an American plant in the survey as well as individuals from the United Kingdom.

Not only did the two groups identify the same set of factors as most important, the importance given to each critical factor (judged by the percentage ranking it as critical rather than merely important), were also almost identical. This went against the perceived wisdom that said there were significant differences between the U.S. and UK environment and came as a surprise to us. Basically it seemed to suggest that we were operating with the same value system. This was an interesting result, but not one that would "stand up in court." Our sample size was too small, our analysis fairly simplistic. We got what we wanted from the exercise but we did not believe that it could go any further at that time. The gender mix in teams did not survive, either!

By means of this survey we were able to reduce our initial set of factors down to about thirty. The next step was to come up with some way to measure those factors. Now, I wish that I could tell you that we came up with some wonderful new measurement technique but the reality is that we gathered data on almost all of those factors by means of a good old-fashioned questionnaire. There were only two factors about which we could collect data from some other source: the experience in the industry and the experience within the organization of team members. This data was available from the personnel department, but in the end we asked the pilot group directly anyway.

Which brings us to the next part of the exercise, the pilot. We were lucky enough to have the cooperation of a very helpful group within the organization and they had a six month enhancement project starting at just about the right time. We spent some time with this team explaining what we were after and why. We identified a specific individual to coordinate things within that team and off we went!

The approach was relatively straightforward. Some of the factors we had identified as potentially critical to performance lay within the domain of the project manager, for example information regarding promotions was most easily obtained from the project manager, while some factors concerned the whole team. A third subset of factors also lay with the project manager and were unlikely to change much over short periods of time. To cover these three areas we set up the following mechanisms. First, the project manager completed a questionnaire at the end of each month. Second, all team members completed a different questionnaire monthly. These were anonymous. Third, the project manager was interviewed at the beginning, the midpoint and the end of the project.

We completed the experiment by reporting to our own management, by analyzing the collected data and by feeding back to the pilot group. What did we find out?

Remember that the purpose of the experiment was to test the feasibility of such a data collection exercise and we were pleased to learn that nobody in the pilot group felt that it was intrusive. The actual cost for the team questionnaires was about ten minutes per person per month. An extremely satisfying result was that the project team response to the exercise was very positive.

They felt that such a mechanism gave them a chance to influence their own environment, which does not simply mean bigger desks, and also gave them a chance to report things that were good as well as drawing attention to things that were bad. Certain changes were needed to the questionnaires and we realized that the administration of the exercise would need to be improved, but overall the results were positive. We could collect that kind of data.

We also got a couple more interesting results. One of the soft factors identified was awareness of the local development process so we asked our team members whether or not they felt familiar with that process. Almost invariably the answer was 'yes.' At the end of the pilot we introduced the team to process modeling notations such as those used elsewhere in this book and asked them to draw out their own view of the development process. The results were interesting, and varied! Even allowing for the fact that different team members were involved with different viewpoints, different processes were described there. So much for common understanding of the process being used.

The other interesting result was that during the course of our pilot a number of individuals were made redundant in a completely different part of the organization. While this did not directly affect our group you would expect morale to be affected. Not surprisingly, our morale indicators did register a significant drop for that month. The surprising thing, if our indicators could be believed and we would not claim that they were anything but coarse, was that morale returned to its normal level by the end of the next month.

We found the results of this experiment very encouraging. What was not so encouraging was the brick wall we then ran into. It was obvious to us and to our immediate management team that there was merit in establishing mechanisms to collect this type of data across a large part of the organization but it was also a political bombshell and would have to be handled with great care. While we did map out a strategy for achieving implementation of our proposals, the politicking, marketing and effort involved would have cost multiples of the original experiment. Sadly we had other priorities.

This is typical of many areas in Software Metrics, and for process improvement in general, that simple techniques that could genuinely be used to make things better for all concerned, including managers, become political footballs within the organization. Fortunately, there are some individuals working within these organizations that can and do play the political game and who also recognize the worth of techniques such as those mentioned in this chapter. Very occasionally such individuals reach the upper echelons of power. When that happens the impact is large and far reaching.

15.3   SUMMARY

I hope that this chapter has introduced some different ideas that you may not have come across before. Of course it is a very personal view of which topics are receiving attention in terms of applied research today and which may be important in the near future. There are many things happening today in the broad spectrum of activity covered by the term Software Metrics and even if only some of them impact on our engineering discipline then the face of that discipline will undergo major change over the next few years.

16

Closing Thoughts

This book has dealt with the development and implementation of a Software Metrics program. Hopefully it has done so in a practical way and you will have gained some appreciation of the work involved and the type of tasks that need to be addressed. Perhaps you have been surprised by the relatively small part that "metrics" have to play in this work and how much the involvement of people can affect the success or failure of such a program.

If you follow the lifecycle laid out in Section Two of this book you will stand a relatively good chance of implementing your program but, in the end, it all comes down to you.

There is one final point that I would like to make. Software Metrics are a very "hot topic" in our industry today. Every conference and seminar that you attend will have some mention of metrics and you see it more and more as a topic in the trade press. People are even writing books about metrics! My point is that Software Metrics in isolation are useless.

Only when they form part of the enabling function within an organization's will to improve its process and its products can Software Metrics deliver their full potential.

Measurement simply puts you in a position where you have the chance to solve problems. Let's face it, before you started measuring you probably did not know what your problems were, you just knew they existed. As for solving them without any form of measurement, forget it. If you do not measure, how will you know when the problem has been solved?

Do not fall into the trap of thinking that measurement will solve all your problems; it will not. Only you can solve your problems. Measurement does help, though. The other thing that helps is to share your problems and concerns with others who face similar circumstances. By far the best advice I can give to close this book is that you take the trouble to attend conferences and seminars that address the problem of measurement in a software engineering environment. Talk to people who have faced or who are facing the same situation you face and you will be happy to find that many people have found solutions.

Appendix A

Useful Organizations

In this appendix I have listed examples of organizations that I or my associates have found to be useful during our work in the area of Software Metrics.

The International Function Point User Group (IFPUG)
191 Clarksville Road
Princeton Junction, New Jersey 08550 USA
Telephone: +01 609 799 4900
www.ifpug.org

United Kingdom Software Metrics Association (UKSMA)
admin@uksma.co.uk
www.uksma.co.uk

Netherlands Software Metrics Association (NESMA)
(Formally NEFPUG)
www.nesma.nl/english/index.htm

International Standards Organization (ISO)
www.iso.ch

References

Ahlgren
Lead Times and Soft Factors,
M Ahlgren & C Wohlin,
Proceedings Eurometrics '92, April 1992

Albrecht (1)
Measuring Application Development Productivity,
A J Albrecht,
Proceedings Joint SHARE GUIDE Symposium 1979

Boehm (1)
Software Engineering Economics,
B Boehm,
PrenticeHall

Boehm et al (1)
Software Cost Estimation with COCOMO II
B Boehm et al
Prentice Hall

Bollinger (1)
A Critical Look at Software Capability Evaluation,
T B Bollinger & C McGowan,
IEEE Transactions on Software Engineering July 1991

Charnes (1)
Measuring the Efficiency of Decision Making Units,
A Charnes & W Cooper,
European Journal of Operational Research, volume #2 , No 6 November 1978

Crosby (1)
Quality Improvement through Defect Prevention,
Phillip Crosby Associates Inc
Training Materials

DeMarco (1)
Peopleware
T DeMarco & T Lister
Dorset House 1987

Deming (1)
Out of the Crisis,
W E Deming,
MIT Center for Advanced Engineering Study 1986

Dolle (1)
Experiences of Software Quality Management in Software Maintenance - A Case Study,
P Dolle & K Jackson,
UK Computer Measurement Group Conference Sesasion 145, May 1992

Elam (1)
Evaluating Productivity of Information Systems Organizations in State Government,
J J Elam & J B Thomas
Public Productivity Review, (USA), volume 12 Number 3, Spring 1989

Fenton (1)
Software Metrics - A Rigorous Approach
N E Fenton

Chapman & Hall 1991

Henry (1)
Software Structure Metrics Based on Information Flow,
IEEE Transactions on Software Engineering Volume 7, Number 5 ,1981

Humphrey (1)   Software Process Improvement at Hughes Aircraft,
W S Humphrey & T R Snyder & R R Willis,
IEEE Transactions on Software Engineering, July 1991

Humphrey (2)
Managing the Software Process,
W S Humphrey,
Addison Wesley 1989

Humphrey (3)
A Discipline for Software Engineers
W S Humphrey
Addison Wesley 1995

IFPUG (1)
J C Penney Inc. Presentation,
IFPUG Conference Proceedings Autumn 1990

Ince (1)
An Empiracal and Theoretical Analysis of an Information Flow Based System Design Metric,
D Ince & M Shepperd,
ESPRIT Project 1 MUSE Report Paper

Irvine (1)
Implementing a Software Metrics Program,
G Irvine et al,
QA Forum, (UK), Working Party Report

IS9126
Software Product Evaluation, Quality Characteristics and Guidelines for Their Use
International Standard 9126,
International Standards Organization

Kitchenham (1)
Empirical Studies of the Assumptions Underlying Software Cost Estimation Models,
B Kitchenham,
Proceedings of European COCOMO User Group 1991

Kitchenham (2)
An Evaluation of Some Design Metrics
B Kitchenham & L Pickard & S J Linkman
Software Engineering Journal Jan 1990

Lehman (1)
Program Evolution and its Impact on Software Engineering,
M M Lehman & F N Parr,
Proceedings 2nd International Conference on Software Engineering 1976

Littlewood (1)   Software Reliability Measurement,
B Littlewood,
Proceedings IEE Colloquium on Software Metrics 1990

Lynch (1)
Strategy of the Dolphin,
D Lynch & P L Kordis,
Arrow Business Books

Matsubara (1)
Ten Myths of Japanese Software Development
Matsubara
Proceedings Joint EOQ/Software Management Circle Meeting

Mermaid (1)
The Mermaid Project - A Status Report,
Issued at ESPRIT Technical Week November 1989

McCabe (1)
Reverse Engineering, Reusability, Redundancy The Connection,
T J McCabe,
American Programmer October 1990

236

McCue (1)
Architectural Design for Program Development
IBM Systems Journal
Volume 17 Number 1 1978

Putnam (1)
Software Costing and Lifecycle Control,
L H Putnam,
Proceedings IEEE Workshop on Software
Quantitative Models 1979

Rodgers (1)
Customer Satisfaction Metrics
P Rodgers
Leeds Polytechnic
QA Forum Presentation, January 1990

Rombach (1)
Benefits of Goal Orientated Measurement
D Rombach & V Basili,
Tutorial CSR 7th Annual Conference on Software
Reliability and Metrics September 1990

Rook (1)
Software Reliability Handbook,
ed. P Rook,
Elsevier

Rubin (1)
Keynote Presentation,
H Rubin,
Proceedings EFPUG Conference 1990

Swanson (1)
The Dimensions of Maintenance
E B Swanson
Proceedings IEE/ACM 2nd International
Conference on Software Engineering, 1976

Symons (1)
Software Sizing and Estimating, MkII FPA,
C R Symons
John Wiley and Sons, 1991

INDEX

Administration Class 192

Ahlgren 7

Allan Albrecht 16

AMI 30

Andrew Hiles vi

application or product boundary 18

Applied Design Metrics 63, 64, 165,
. . . . 174, 186, 204, 216

Association of Project Managers v

Barbara Kitchenham 74

Barry Boehm 7, 52

Base Metrics 131

Basili, Vic 8, 30, 147, 221

Boehm 38, 44, 45, 46, 112

"bottom up" estimating 55

Bozoki's Ranking Technique 53

British Computer Society v

British Telecomm 86

Business Entity Metric 132

Business Entity Metric 132, 151

Business Excellence Model 123

Cap Gemini Ernst & Young v

Capability Maturity Model 123

Capability Maturity Model Integrated 224

Capers Jones 45

CASE 196

CASE technology 162

Caswell 127

Caswell 127

Center of Excellence 212

Charnes 227

CHECKMARK 45

CHECKPOINT 45

CMMI SE/SW/IPPD 224

CMM I 224

COCOMO 7, 38, 44

COCOMO 45

Cohesion 73

commonality 110

Competitive Benchmarking 183

Complexity 64

Component 73

Component Build Stage 93

Component Design 93

Composite Metric 131

COnstructive COst MOdel 7

COSMIC 15

COSMIC 21

Coupling 73

Cranfield School of Management v

Crosby 28, 51

Crosby 123

Customer Relationship Management v

cyclomatic complexity 225

Cyclomatic Complexity 65, 68, 71

Darrell Ince 74

Data Envelopment Analysis 226

data flow diagram 90

Data Flow Diagrams 75

data hunter 228

data hunting 28

DEA 226

DEA 227

defect 137

defect 138

defect density 10

Defect Reports 138

Definition of Software Metrics 6

Delphi 56, 61

DeMarco, Tom 26, 227

Deming 28, 123

Department of Defense 7

Design Stage 93

DFD 90

Dieter Rombach 26

Du Pont de Nemours 8

Elam 227

Embedded Environment 45

enhanceability 149

enhancement project boundary 18

Enterprise Resource Planning v

ESPRIT MERMAID project 46

Essential Complexity 65, 68, 173

Estimation by analogy 56

Eurometrics '91 conference 26

European Economic Community 1, 7

extendability 149

Fagan inspections 162, 193

Fan in 74, 76, 77

Fan out 74, 76, 77

fault 137

feasibility checking 80, 81

feasibility study 100

flowgraphs 65

FPA 15, 16, 18

Function Point 17

Function Point Analysis 2, 8, 15, 16, 18

. . . . 30, 42, 49, 58, 153, 172, 187, 220

Function Point scores 45

Function Points 132, 153

Function Points 30

functional decomposition 55

functional entities 53

Functional Sizing Metric 21

Functional Sizing Metrics 220

Gartner v

Goal, Question, Metric 221, 223

Goal, Question, Metric paradigm 147

Goal/Question/Metric 130

Goal/Question/Metric paradigm 30

FPA 15, 16, 18

Function Point 17

Function Point Analysis 16, 187

Function Point Analysis 42, 49, 58, 153, 172, 220

Function Point scores 45

Function Points 132, 153

Function Points 30

functional decomposition 55

functional entities 53

Functional Sizing Metric 21

Functional Sizing Metrics 220

Gartner v

Goal, Question, Metric 221, 223

Goal, Question, Metric paradigm 147

Goal/Question/Metric 130

Goal/Question/Metric paradigm 30

GOALS 156

GQM 130, 221

GQM 156, 221

Grady 127

Henry 77

Hewlett Packard 8

Howard Rubin 26

Hughes Aircraft Software Engineering Division 62

Humphrey 80, 162, 223

IEC 32

IEEE Software Engineering Transactions . . 223

IFPUG 21, 48

IFPUG 49

Implementing a Software Metrics Programme 109

Ince 77

Information Flow 204

INFORMATION FLOW index 75

Information Flow metrics 73, 216

initial development project boundary 18

Initiation Stage 92

initiator 97

Inland Revenue 32

Institute of Management v

Integrated Project Support Environment . . . 119

Inter measures 64

International Electrotechnical Commission . . 32

International Function Point User Group . . . 21

International Standards 123

International Standards Organization 32

International Standards Organization 226

intra measures 64

Irvine 109

ISO 32

ISO 9000 iv

ISO/IEC standard IS9126 138

JC Penney 48

Jones 45

Kafura 74, 77

KDSI 45

Kitchenham 46, 77

Larry Putnam 44

Lifecycle Model 90

Line of Code 30

Line of Code 158

McCabe Metrics 65, 72, 120, 172, 176, 204, 216

McCue 7, 228

Mean Time Between Failure 33

mean time to failure 10

Meredith 80

META Group v

Metrics 156

Metrics Coordination Group 127-129, 136,
139, 142, 144, 166, 168, 169, 178, 180, 193, 198

Metrics Council 127

Model Based 44

Modified Delphi Technique 52

MTBF 33

Murphy's law 29

Organic Environment 45

organizational trigger 97

Outlook Journal iv

People CMM 224

Peppers & Rogers v

performance 151

Personal Software Process 224

PERT 53

phasing 109

Pilot projects 146

PMI Fact Book iv

PriceWaterhouseCoopers v

Process Maturity Model 221

Product Reliability 154

Product size 138

Productivity 152, 153

progress checking 80

Progress Monitors 84

project 137

Project Management, a Managerial Approach 80

Project size 138

Project Work 191

Publicity Campaign 118, 119

Putnam 38, 45

Putnam's Program Estimating and Reporting Tool,
PERT 53

quality 138

Quality Managers 31

Questions 156

RAG Technique 84

reference entities 53

Reliability 150

requirement classification 148

Requirements Definition 92

reverse synergy 127

Risk Management 80, 82, 83

Rombach, Dieter 8, 30, 130, 147, 156, 221

Rook 49, 112

Rubin, Howard 26

SDL Block diagrams 75

SEI 223

SEI Assessment 221, 222

SEL 221

Semi-Detached Environment 46

service level agreement 224

Service Level Agreements iv

Martin Shepperd 74, 77

Size 137

SLIM 38

SMP Repository 103

Soft Factors 228

Software Capability Evaluation 221, 223

Software Engineering Economics 52

Software Engineering Institute 221

Software Engineering Laboratory . 26, 130, 221

Software Metrics: Establishing a Company Wide
Program 127

Software Reliability Handbook 49

Specification Review 142

Spiral 112

Standish Group International v

Statistical Process Control 35

Symons, Charles 16

system boundary 18

System Support 192

Technique Based 44, 48

thousands of delivered source instructions . . 45

UKSMA 17, 21

United Kingdom Software Metrics Association
. . . . 17, 21

Usability 33

Voyager satellite 32

Waterfall 112

Watts Humphries 221

WBS 191

Wideband Delphi Technique 52

Work Breakdown Structure 191

Work Classes 191

Xerox 183

ABOUT THE AUTHOR

PAUL GOODMAN has more than nineteen years experience of the industry and particular expertise in the support of Software Measurement and Software Process Improvement (SPI) programs for clients.

He first became involved with Software Metrics while working at a major UK Government department. The measurement program that was initiated by Paul and his colleagues is still running today and that department is recognized as one of the leading UK institutions in the field of Software Metrics.

Paul firmly believes that using data to enable better management is vital within IT. If you have data you gain deeper understanding, and with understanding comes a greater chance of improving the situation; that is solving the problems. On the other hand, if you don't have data you don't have facts, all you do have is opinion.

The other main area within Software Metrics that Paul focuses on is implementation. Still today, too many measurement initiatives within IT organizations fail the implementation hurdle. There are many reasons for these failures but Paul does believe that some, indeed many of them are avoidable.

Since leaving the Civil Service, Paul worked to implement a Software Metrics program within a major telecommunications company in the UK and the United States. Since then, Paul has worked as a consultant supporting many clients from all sectors of the IT industry. Today he works out of the UK office of Meta Group Incorporated, an international IT consultancy and research organization.

Paul is a past Chairman of the UK Software Metrics Association (UKSMA, previously the UK Function Point User Group), and was a founder member of the ISO WG12, the international working party for Functional Sizing Metrics. Paul was also a member of the "Extended" international IDEAL Enhancement Project team which looked at improving the IDEAL Software Process Improvement Implementation Model developed by the Software Engineering Institute of Carnegie Melon University.

He has served on a number of international metrics committees and was also a founder member of the European Software Process Improvement (ESPI) Foundation.

Paul is a regular presenter at international conferences.

ABOUT THE PUBLISHER

THE ROTHSTEIN CATALOG ON
SERVICE LEVEL MANAGEMENT

www.ServiceLevelBooks.com

and

THE ROTHSTEIN CATALOG ON
DISASTER RECOVERY

www.DisasterRecoveryBooks.com

THE ROTHSTEIN CATALOGS ON SERVICE LEVEL MANAGEMENT and DISASTER RECOVERY have served as these industries' principal resource for 1,000+ books, software tools, videos and research reports, since 1989.

They are divisions of **Rothstein Associates Inc.**, an international Management Consultancy and Publisher focused on service level management, business continuity, crisis management, risk mitigation and disaster recovery, since 1985.

A complimentary CD-ROM containing our catalogs will be sent upon request to: **info@rothstein.com**

OTHER BOOKS AND RESOURCES FROM

ROTHSTEIN ASSOCIATES INC.

www.rothstein.com
info@rothstein.com

SERVICE LEVEL AGREEMENTS:
A FRAMEWORK ON CD-ROM FOR IT AND TECHNOLOGY

10th Edition, by Andrew Hiles

Now every IT services professional can have effective SLAs! SERVICE LEVEL AGREEMENTS: A FRAMEWORK ON CD-ROM FOR IT AND TECHNOLOGY brings together all of the critical elements needed to build a Service Level Agreement, with extensive templates, examples and tools. It reflects the combined expertise and SLA development experience from over 50 man-years of consulting effort.

THE COMPLETE GUIDE TO IT SERVICE LEVEL AGREEMENTS:
MATCHING SERVICE QUALITY TO BUSINESS NEEDS

3rd Edition, by Andrew Hiles

Covering all aspects of Information Technology Service Level Agreements (SLAs), this essential manual is a step-by-step guide to designing, negotiating and implementing SLAs into your organization. It reviews the disadvantages and advantages, gives clear guidance on what types are appropriate, how to set up SLAs and to control them. An invaluable aid to IT managers, data center managers, computer services, systems and operations managers.

CREATING A CUSTOMER-FOCUSED HELP DESK:
HOW TO WIN AND KEEP YOUR CUSTOMERS

by Andrew Hiles & Dr. Yvonne Gunn

This volume and the companion product, **Help Desk Framework CD-ROM** came about as a result of the authors' own practical experience in Help Desk operation and management and of hundreds of workshops the authors have conducted world-wide over the last fifteen years. It is intended to be a practical reference guide, but the suggestions, checklists and templates all need to be interpreted and amended in the light of the culture, technology, service maturity and constraints of each individual organization.

SERVICE LEVEL AGREEMENTS:
A FRAMEWORK ON CD-ROM FOR SERVICE BUSINESSES

by Andrew Hiles

SERVICE LEVEL AGREEMENTS: A FRAMEWORK ON CD-ROM FOR SERVICE BUSINESSES brings together the critical elements needed to build a Service Level Agreement for service or supply businesses (non-technology focused), with extensive templates, examples and tools.

MORE BOOKS AND RESOURCES FROM ROTHSTEIN ASSOCIATES INC.
www.rothstein.com
info@rothstein.com

SERVICE LEVEL AGREEMENTS:
WINNING A COMPETITIVE EDGE FOR SUPPORT & SUPPLY SERVICES
by Andrew Hiles

This book holds the key to creating enduring, satisfying and profitable relationships between customer and supplier. It shows how both internal and external services and supply can be aligned to meet business vision, mission, goals, critical success factors and key performance indicators. The techniques described will help you balance service cost against quality, leading to competitive advantage and business success. They can be applied to any industry, to any supply or support service. They have been used by leading companies internationally — and they work!

BCM FRAMEWORK™ CD-ROM
by Andrew Hiles

BCM Framework consists of a number of easily tailored modules that are selected from our database of client work from a combined total of over one hundred years of consultancy experience - modules that are hand picked as the most relevant to your own situation, culture, organization, equipment platform and infrastructure. It contains documents, examples, checklists and templates covering each of the DRII / BCI's ten disciplines, model project plans, questionnaires and Business Recovery Action Plans for with Organization Schematics and role descriptions, with some vital - and often forgotten - actions included. These are in MS Word®, MS Excel® and MS Project® formats designed to be easily tailored to your organization's needs.

ENTERPRISE RISK ASSESSMENT AND BUSINESS IMPACT ANALYSIS:
BEST PRACTICES
by Andrew Hiles

This book de-mystifies risk assessment. In a practical and pragmatic way, it covers many techniques and methods of risk and impact assessment with detailed, practical examples and checklists. It explains, in plain language, risk assessment methodologies used by a wide variety of industries and provides a comprehensive toolkit for risk assessment and business impact analysis.

AUDITING BUSINESS CONTINUITY:
GLOBAL BEST PRACTICES
by Rolf von Roessing

"The work not only provides a general outline of how to conduct different types of audits but also reinforces their application by providing practical examples and advice to illustrate the step-by-step methodology, including contracts, reports and techniques. The practical application of the methodology enables the professional auditor and BCM practitioner to identify and illustrate the use of good BCM practice whilst demonstrating added value and business resilience." — Dr. David J. Smith, MBA LL.B(Hons), Chairman of the Business Continuity Institute, Education Committee

---

MORE BOOKS AND RESOURCES FROM ROTHSTEIN ASSOCIATES INC.

www.rothstein.com

info@rothstein.com

BUSINESS CONTINUITY PLANNING:
A STEP-BY-STEP GUIDE WITH PLANNING FORMS ON CD-ROM

by Kenneth L. Fulmer, CDRP

This popular book for those new to business continuity gives a step-by-step outline filled with precise instructions, risk and business impact analysis guidelines and forms for creating your basic business continuity blueprint. It serves as a workbook for those organizing a plan and as a guidebook for those responsible for implementation. Clear and complete, Business Continuity Planning will prove an invaluable resource and guide for managers, owners and planning coordinators.

DISASTER RECOVERY TESTING:
EXERCISING YOUR CONTINGENCY PLAN

Philip Jan Rothstein, Editor

From this book, the contingency planner can understand more than just how to test: why to test, when to test (and not test) and the necessary participants and resources. Further, this book addresses some often-ignored, real-world considerations: the justification, politics and budgeting affecting recovery testing. By having multiple authors share their respective areas of expertise, it is hoped that this book will provide the reader with a comprehensive resource addressing the significant aspects of recovery testing.

BUSINESS CONTINUITY PROGRAM SELF-ASSESSMENT CHECKLIST WITH CD-ROM

by Edmond D. Jones

This book and companion CD-ROM contains a comprehensive set of questions assess the status of an organization's business continuity program. The questions may be used by a new or experienced business continuity planner to assess the overall program to determine those areas needing work. The same checklists can be used by internal or external audit or by others having a responsibility for evaluating an organization's business continuity program.

BUSINESS THREAT AND RISK ASSESSMENT CHECKLIST WITH CD-ROM

by Edmond D. Jones

This manual contains checklists that an individual or group may use to evaluate the threats and risks which may impact an organization's campus, facility or even specific departments within the organization. Each of the checklists shown in this manual and a cover page that may be used to assemble your own checklists are contained on the CD that accompanies this manual.

BUSINESS CONTINUITY AND HIPAA:
BUSINESS CONTINUITY MANAGEMENT IN THE HEALTH CARE ENVIRONMENT

By James C. Barnes

This book examines business continuity planning as adapted to encompass the requirements of The Health Care Portability and Accountability Act of 1996, or HIPAA. We will examine the typical business continuity planning model and highlight how the special requirements of HIPAA have shifted the emphasis. The layout of this book was designed to afford assistance, hints, and templates to the person charged with the task of implementing business continuity planning into a healthcare organization.

SOFTWARE METRICS
BEST PRACTICES FOR SUCCESSFUL IT MANAGEMENT
by Paul Goodman
ISBN 1-931332-26-6

REGISTRATION AND *FREE* CD-ROM

If you purchased this book *other than* directly from Rothstein Associates, please fill out and return this form to register for future updates, and for your complimentary CD-ROM containing **The Rothstein Catalogs on Service Level Management** and **Disaster Recovery**. (*If you purchased this book directly from Rothstein Associates – you are automatically registered; be sure to let us know if your address changes*).

To qualify for future updates and receive your complimentary CD, please fill out this form <u>completely</u> and return it by fax to 203.740.7401, email to <u>info@rothstein.com,</u> or mail to the address below.

PRODUCT: **Software Metrics** ISBN 1-931332-26-6

First Name _____ Last Name _____

Company/Organization _____

Department/Mail Station _____ Title _____

Street Address _____

City _____ State/Province _____

Zip/Postal Code _____ Country _____

email address _____ Phone _____

Where Purchased _____ Purchase Date _____

Check here if you would you like to receive a complimentary subscription to our email newsletter, **BUSINESS SURVIVAL™: BUSINESS CONTINUITY AND SERVICE LEVEL MANAGEMENT FOR KEY DECISION-MAKERS** (*be sure to include your email address above!*) ☐

Check here if you would like to receive a complimentary CD-ROM containing the latest version of **THE ROTHSTEIN CATALOGS on DISASTER RECOVERY and SERVICE LEVEL MANAGEMENT**, these industries' principal resource for hundreds of books, software tools, videos and research reports since 1989. ☐

THE ROTHSTEIN CATALOGS ON SERVICE LEVEL MANAGEMENT and DISASTER RECOVERY ROTHSTEIN ASSOCIATES INC.
4 Arapaho Rd.
Brookfield, Connecticut 06804-3104 USA
203.740.7444   Fax 203.740.7401

Rothstein Catalog On Service Level Books